She Persisted

By Kathy Crabb Hannah

This book is dedicated to my *STRONGER SISTERS*. Your stories changed me. They increased my heart to the point I thought it would explode. You are my constant prayer and my occasional cake buddy. You gave me a new season, a new passion, and a front row seat to watch GOD fix it. Sometimes HE chose to "do it" with a miracle, other times with a gentle pat on the back as HE helped *YOU,* fix *YOU.* The journey has been one of the greatest honors of my life. I thank God for trusting me. I pray I never disappoint you.

Table of Contents

Acknowledgements

Thank You:

To God: You blow my mind. After all this time I'm still shocked when I see You do the impossible. Thanks for always loving me. I know it's tough at times.

To my amazing children and grandchildren: You amaze me on a daily basis. Your commitment to the gospel of Jesus has been the most blessed part of my life. You are truly the best people I know.

To my Steve: Your loyalty is unmatched and your love undeserved. Nevertheless, I gladly accept both. The Lord surely loved me, He sent me you.

To my forever friend Linda: You patiently walked this road with me. I know you are tired and you're ready to be out of manuscript-reading hell. I'm blessed to have a friend like you, and I know it.

Credits:

Hair and Make-up: Eden Nicole Boomer
Photography: Micah Schweinsburg
Graphic Design: Micah Shcweinsburg
Editing Service: Kevin Anderson and Associates

Foreword

Thoughts from "the sisters"

We are all so quick to put platform ministries on pedestals. The book, *Stronger*, helped me realize that there is purpose in pain. It showed me that going through the things we do gives us an opportunity to shine brighter than we have before as ministers of His Gospel. Mrs. Kathy's event, Stronger, has impacted hundreds of women. I, myself, struggled with fear and all of the torment associated with it. 1John 4:18. "God met me at that retreat and chains broke." I've been a pastor's wife for almost 20 years and never have had God heal my heart the way He did that night. I'm forever grateful. Kathy's heart is bigger than this world and she will do anything at any cost for someone to get their miracle. Proud to call her my friend! ~ Laura

I had followed and loved the Crabb Family for years, but met Kathy on a personal level following my life changing tragedy: The suicide of my husband. My life was in shambles—I had 4 kids, little income, bills piling up, chaos, and stress unimaginable. But God... God knew I needed to be

Stronger, and He made a way. I was empowered by the book that was written from the heart of this angelic woman to the heart of the reader. I somehow snuck in the time to binge read page after page, cover to cover in a matter of days. On days I'm feeling low, I OFTEN go back and read the passage about the closet. It gives me hope that through our struggles, our faith in God, and His mighty promises, He will see us through. *Stronger* didn't take my problems away, but it did show me that through brokenness, there can still be beauty, prosperity, faith and strength. A new wholeness. ~ Angelina

Kathy Crabb and *Stronger* have changed my life. I was spiritually dying and mentally breaking down. I had gone through breast cancer, my husband left me in the midst of chemo, and my son was on drugs. I had lost my home and everything that I had. No money. I had lost all hope. Someone gave me a copy of *Stronger* and it gave me so much hope. And I started praying harder than I have prayed my whole life. I knew that if God could bring Kathy out of what she went through that He would me too. I just had to pray and trust harder. My first encounter was at Stronger 2017. I had to meet this woman that gave me so much hope. ~Tammy

I met Kathy at the first Stronger retreat in July 2015. I was going through a divorce after 30 years of marriage. The sisterhood formed with other ladies have brought me closer to the Lord and brought me through a lot of tough times and healing. Words cannot describe what Stronger has meant to me. ~ Lynn

Since the day I was born, the devil has tried to get me in every way he can think of. I've dealt with a mother who is a prescription pill addict and was once an alcoholic. It has been a tough life. I've known of Kathy since I was a little baby but really got to start knowing her in my teen years. Her words of wisdom always inspire me and she never fails to remind me that God loves me and He will get me through those tough times! I'm thankful for Kathy's love to love on people and for her raw and real personality! She is truly a gem and has a soul like no other! ~ Autumn

Preface

In 2014 I went to the Smoky Mountains and wrote my first book, *Stronger* in a matter of days. All 93,045 words were written outdoors on a balcony that had a full-on view of Mount Le Conte. I wrote the book in the middle of the winter while wearing scarves, a couple of fuzzy leopard robes, and Ugg boots. It was cold at times, but I persevered. I was on a mission. I wrote *Stronger* for me. I had never written anything more detailed than a Facebook post. Yet I had to do it. MY soul screamed to be heard; I had no choice but write it. I doubted my ability, but I never doubted my perseverance, and I finished in record time.

This time, I wrote for you. It was tough at times, truly daunting would be a better description. There's so much to say! You have lots of struggles, granted. But I pray that you will read, and realize that you too can make it. You are only bound by your choices. NO ONE can destroy your future but you. And you're ABSOLUTELY not going to. You're going to throw that head back, maybe wear a small tiara, and march proudly to the throne room and tell HIM exactly what you need. He's not going to ignore you. You're going to become serious about answers; you will say, "God, I'm not leaving until you bless me," Boom! For those of you that will actually DO this? It's a life changer, a complete game changer. WOW!

Come. Let's walk. Put your shoes on, let's go.

The Walk

I rubbed my eyes and looked around and realized I had been asleep, finally—well, at least for a minute or two, or twenty. I was a disheveled mess, lying piled up in the middle of Mom and Dad's bed, still in my jeans and shirt. That bed was situated in a catty-cornered position in that master bedroom that had been my parent's room for the past eight or so years. Mom insisted on catty-cornering her furniture. I hated it! To this day I won't participate in catty-cornered furniture arrangements unless it's a sofa. Sofas get a pass.

The master bedroom was filled with the morning sunlight, and the white lace curtains looked especially stiff. Mom starched them back in those days. I've never quite understood the purpose of starch. It seems to be a thing of the past and I for one am glad. Dad built that house for Mom the year I was five; we moved in when I was six. It was her dream house, and it was a stunner. The all-brick colonial ranch was in the nicest neighborhood in town at that time. Indian Hills was a destination neighborhood for my parents.

My dad had worked night and day since he was very young. By 1961, the year he built this house, he was a forty-three-year-old self-made man who could write a check for most things he wanted, and he had enough credit to buy anything his heart could desire. He had a couple of airplanes in a hangar at the airport, three boats at Rough River in a slip, a hundred or more pieces of heavy equipment, a nice home, nice cars, and several properties. He had furnished my maternal grandparents with a house to live in, as well as a few others.

But oddly enough, we never took a vacation. There are no "happy" photos of a family standing on a beach, at a picnic, or even on those boats. The family was very fragmented. We gravitated to the most normal thing we could find. For me? That was financial security and the Jesus stories. Financial security, courtesy of Dad; Jesus stories, courtesy of Mom.

Dad was a very generous man. He understood the principals of sowing and reaping. He never professed Christ to me, not once. But he walked out a very principled life. And he seemed to possess the heart and soul of a dreamer.

He had dreamed of a better life than scraping out a living on a patchwork farm or an underground coal-mining job. Back in the thirties and forties, the coal mines were like slave camps. Dad's family weren't the poorest people in town, but they were certainly working-class folks. My mom's dad worked in an underground coal mine; they lived in a company house in a coal camp and truly were little more than indentured slaves, trapped in the culture of a rural Kentucky coal camp.

So this house, the airplanes, the boats, and the healthy bank accounts, in retrospect, sound more pretentious than they were. Dad believed in working hard and was a poster child for the American dream. I never heard him boast in his entire life. And I never saw him pass by a need and not respond. He didn't talk about generosity, ever. He simply WAS generous, and his example was our teacher.

So on this day, I was lying in that bedroom that my parents had allowed me to snuggle in so many times. I can still remember the way it felt to be in the middle. Yes, I was that kid. The "oops" baby that came late in life, number four, and the baby.

The house that built me: with shiny copper-tone built-in appliances, a full-sized basement that I skated in, and a place where my brother also did science experiments that I'm confident were illegal. He used to tell me he was building bombs. Ha-ha! That was before we had terrorism, I might add. And furthermore, Danny Ray was anything but a terrorist. What he was, was a bright kid who loved science and math, who also loved to torment his little sister. So his story to me back in 1961 or 1962 was that he was a bomb builder. Building bombs with his chemistry set in the basement of Jean and Elaine Coppage's home on Navaho Drive.

But now it's 1969 and my brother is no longer there building bombs. He's now a twenty-one-year-old with multiple struggles. My dad? He's not there either. He now resides at Elizabethtown Memorial Gardens—well, at least his body is there. Buried in the shadow of a ridiculously huge monument that we must have decided to erect immediately following his sudden death—for some reason it HAD to be huge. I have to believe that we were subliminally competing with the Vanderbilts or some wealthy family. I suppose that this large "rock" somehow made it better for us, the ones who had to deal with the loss and pain . . . apparently we bought the biggest, gaudiest marble monument that this cemetery had ever seen, thinking that the appearance of this thing would somehow be impressive to Dad, that he would know and appreciate the effort. It looked like a monument to a governor or president. And now? Looking back? I wonder who made that decision. I don't remember if it was Mom or my adult siblings or both. But that whole "go big or go home" that I have been SO guilty of at times in my life . . . was clearly the intent with this decision.

On this particular Saturday, I was missing my dad. Playing a game of "what if" and letting the tears fall. But he was gone. As a matter of fact, his shoes were still in the closet, his car was still in the garage, and that old black rotary phone often rang and the caller would say, "Can I speak to Mr. Coppage?" It had been three months since we lowered that casket into the ground on that windy March day, but the news traveled slow that Mr. Coppage, aged fifty, had passed away from a heart attack while working at his office on the property of his construction company that bore his name: J. E. Coppage Construction Company.

Back in the fifties Dad had realized that there was going to be a huge demand for pipeline companies. Local municipalities and state governments were realizing the need to offer the convenience of "city" water and sewer, and the ability to raise funds through taxation and federal dollars had truly taken hold. So every small town in America was replacing the concept of well water and cisterns with running water

8

from a community tower. My dad had predicted the boom and was the recipient of the American dream because of his intuitive business sense.

But today, Saturday, June something or the other? He was gone.

I wasn't wearing a cat gown or puppy pajamas; I wasn't schooled on the comfort of old gowns just yet. That would take a few decades, I suppose. I had worn my clothes all night. That's what people do who don't sleep, typically. They keep their street clothes on—that seems a bit more like fighting clothes than pajamas. And people who don't sleep? They're fighting. Trust me on that, folks. There's a daily battle going on in the cerebral activity of a sleep-deprived person, be they young or old. THAT phone call on a Sunday afternoon, March 2, 1969, THAT call that said, "Your dad just had a heart attack and he didn't make it," changed me forever. One of the by-products of the trauma was the inability to fall asleep. I was thirteen and still a child in every way, except my mind. I looked eleven; I was not physically developed, nor was I one of those thirteen-year-olds that everyone thought was eighteen. Nope. I didn't wear makeup and I weighed about ninety pounds. I looked like a child, acted a bit like a nerd, and walked in total insecurity. But the demons torment nerds, and they thrive on the insecure.

Somewhere between the graveside service and this Saturday in June, the demons showed up. They were the demons that bid for our mental health, the demons that romanticize suicide, self-destruction. Yes, those demons. They pique our curiosity for knives, needles, guns, and the craving for numbness; their orders when they are dispatched are simple. Paint a beautiful picture to the weak and vulnerable. Paint the picture of self-harm in beautiful earth tones, paint it easy, paint it peaceful, and most of all, paint it as the ultimate answer.

On this Saturday morning, all was not well at 104 Navaho Drive in Elizabethtown, Kentucky. I had been awake all night. Well, most of the night at least. Momma was there, my sisters were there, and I could hear their muffled voices as they drifted from the kitchen and woke me from my short nap.

I was thirteen and I was in trouble. The demons had found me. My innocence was in my favor. I had no images to unsee, no experiences to torment me, but oh my, the demons knew. They knew that I was confused, insecure; they knew that I felt unsure of who I was, where I would live, who would love me, and they knew the deep dark fear that I had. Would ANYONE love me? I had started to dream of being old and alone, homeless, and afraid. I was thirteen. That's not a normal recurring dream for a child. Those of you who know me, those who question why I have thrived in an environment of the "BIG" family, the blended and bonded village in which I live? God. That's how funny He is. The girl that feared being alone, and what did God do? Surround her with a village, a huge family of chaos and love. Yep. That's how God does it. That fear of being homeless most likely explains my inner need to own real estate. Seriously.

Back to the story. My Dad died on March 2, 1969. After the funeral, I refused to go back to school. I think that's probably normal. I missed a full week of school. After he died, I had an odd sense of being different. I wanted to hide in the closet and never come out, or go to sleep and never wake up. But neither seemed a viable option, so, reluctantly, I returned to Mr. Arms' seventh-grade class at Morningside Elementary. I was completely numb that Monday morning, but I remember the pity, the whispers, and oddly enough, I hated the sympathy. I didn't want to be pitied. I can remember THAT feeling to this day. I have worked hard to NEVER be the girl who people view as a victim. Victimhood was not for me. I'm not sure if that's pride or some sort of internal pretention, but I couldn't accept their condolences. I didn't know how.

When that day was over, I ran into my room, threw myself on the chenille bedspread, and cried. I had put up walls and my friends didn't try to tear them down. It was awkward. I felt their pity, yes, but children don't always know how to reach into complicated emotional situations with grace. They didn't. They distanced themselves. I didn't know how to process the loss. I didn't know where to plant my feet, for Dad was my security. I was wading in different waters, mentally. MY friends were nonexistent and I craved numbness. I craved nothingness—escape, if you will. As I remember the thirteen-year-old me, I am slapped with a new reality. The chance of my becoming an addict was about 99 percent. No boundaries were in place, no guidance, mind-numbing grief, and those demons. They visited daily. When the Kentucky sun went down, hell dispatched them to Navaho Drive.

The details are sketchy, too much pain to resurrect. At times, the brain hides the info to protect our sanity and our hearts. This is one of those times. I've tried to write about this for three years. I couldn't. As I type there's a war inside me. I fear the pain of my sister, who truly didn't want this told. She's not great with truth if it sheds a negative light on someone she loves. That's why we love her so much. She will always be on our side, even if we're wrong. But this time, this book, I must go there. For many reasons I must.

Three weeks after Dad died, I was doing little more than breathing. My school day was a blur, my clothes always felt a bit frumpy, my hair was a bit mousier, and the hump on my nose felt bigger. Insecurities had swallowed me up. I was in the beginning stages of withdrawal. I now hated school. I actually hated everything. Everyone.

On this particular afternoon a neighbor dropped me off in front of my house. Since Dad's death three weeks prior, Mom's whereabouts had been unclear. She was a mess. We were all in trouble. As I walked up my sidewalk in my normal state of misery, I saw it. The mailbox had a different name on it. Instead of saying Coppage, it now said Wright. What? I stormed in the house yelling, "Mom, who changed the name on our mailbox?" Her response was simply, "We did. Kathy, I got married today."

I screamed something at her like, "He's been dead for three weeks and you got married?! WHO in the world did you marry? You don't have anyone to marry, you ARE married!"

The rest is a blur. I was devastated. So was she. She cried like a lost child. She WAS a lost child. We almost had a role-reversal relationship. I was often the adult, and she was the child, from an early age. Dad spoiled her terribly, and even though their marriage was not good, it was what she knew. She was comfortable in her descriptive unhappiness with my dad. Trust me, she voiced her daily opinions of her marriage, her obvious distrust of Dad's friends, and her ability to constantly draw me into his shame. I was the face of his shame on most days. That's another story, reserved for another day, I suppose. But her normal breakfast table comments included infidelity accusations. This was the daily bread for me. I don't have memories of before it started, because it had always been, always. It was truly the nucleus of our life. Mom spent countless hours sneaking down dirt roads with her lights turned off, occasionally nearly running over a cow, all in the pursuit of the ultimate goal: to catch Dad in the act of this filthy affair she claimed he was having.

Mom accusing Dad, and Dad responding with silence. Talk about making it awkward to have a relationship. My dad gave up on defending himself many years earlier. He also gave up on meaningful conversations with me, for the most part. I always felt that when he looked at me, he heard her accusing voice, and I became the face of shame for him. I was never sure if he was ashamed he cheated or ashamed he let her talk to him like that. Either way, it wasn't a very pretty picture. Either way, it eroded the relationship that I so desperately needed from my dad. The thirteen years that I had him were so much less than they should have been. He fed my confidence as it related to intelligence and taught me to be generous, but the intimate conversations about family and life weren't there. I quote him on many things, but they're not warm and fuzzy things. Mom was territorial about me. I was her baby of four. I came later in her life, and she was the queen of everything. And she had made it clear to Dad that I was on her side. I truly didn't have a side, but no one corrected Mom. You just didn't do that.

In the fall of '67 she left Dad. She bought a trailer and moved it to my Aunt Mary Elma's backyard in Centertown, Kentucky. It was then I met my best friend, Linda Beth. We were in Mrs. Overhult's class together. By Thanksgiving Mom decided she was wrong, and we moved the one hundred miles back to Navaho Drive. Dad seemed thrilled that we were home. She sold the trailer and left that dead patch of grass in Aunt Mary's backyard. Not to worry, though—it wouldn't last long. In the fall of '68 we moved to Aunt Mary's backyard again. Once again I went back to Centertown Elementary. And once again the dead grass was covered by Mom's newly purchased 12 x 60 home on wheels, and, yep, you guessed it. By Thanksgiving we went home. Sold the trailer again. She lost a small fortune buying trailers and selling them for pennies on the dollar.

So, by the spring of '69, when Dad died suddenly, I was already a candidate for the "I move schools more than any kid in the world" award. I hated it. Other kids didn't have these problems, so I thought. They had birthday parties, cheerleading outfits; they went to football games and movies. Not me. I had my dysfunctional breakfasts with my parents and my music. I always had music.

Back to the Saturday in June. On this day, I was LIVID! I didn't care what DAD'S truth was; I didn't care what he did or didn't do. ALL I knew was he was dead, the dirt was fresh on his grave, and this WRIGHT person's name was on my mailbox! This was MY house. MY dad built if for US. NOT this person that stood there like a salivating animal . . . ready to feast on our flesh. I found a fighting GIRL inside me that had never been unleashed. But on this day, she busted out. She inhabited the girl with the tears and mousy brown hair. She took over. Mom wasn't used to confrontation from us, but on that day she got more than she bargained for. I had a Kentucky hissy fit. And I should have. It was deserved.

The saddest thing was that Momma had been completely hoodooed by a con artist. She was weak and vulnerable and had never made a single decision for herself. So when this buzzard came to pick the bones of her finances, she was an easy target. She cried, I cried, but he won and she left with him, and the mailbox was a daily reminder of my weak momma. In today's world we would consider her mental status and say she was having a breakdown; we would hopefully get her to a professional and salvage a few heartaches for her. But this was 1969, and this was Mom. She wasn't open to many suggestions.

So while my momma had a public nervous breakdown that manifested itself in an embarrassing marriage after being widowed for a mere twenty-one days, the family suffered in silence—well, everyone but me. There was no silence up in my world. I was suffering and pitching a fit, kicking doors, crying, screaming, and anything else one does to act out. I didn't know much about profanity. My family didn't use profane words; we weren't cussers. But everything short of profanity I was saying. I remember saying, "I hate you. I hate him, I never want to see you again!"

So this thirteen-year-old misfit, the girl who had never been referred to as pretty in her entire life, the one who had spent most of those thirteen years feeling confused, lonely, and sad, was in full-blown depression. Momma moved to Henderson, Kentucky, then on to Owensboro, Kentucky, within a short period of time, and came back to our home on Navaho about every other week. In the meantime, I had no real supervision. Anneta was in the same town, but she was a twenty-seven-year-old with a job, two kids, and a full-blown life crisis as well. Dad's death did a number on her; Mom had married a random stranger, and her marriage fell apart, all at the same time. She welcomed me daily, and I stayed there a lot, and I for sure ate there a lot, but there was no one connecting the dots. No strong-fisted adult was in charge of my life.

Danny, my brother, was a full-blown alcoholic with a broken heart. He loved Dad. They were joined at the hip, and then he died. Danny spiraled that year. As I remember the details from this side of life, with the logic of a sixty-two-year-old, I realize that his life was forever changed as well. Danny never recovered from Dad's untimely death. The addiction impacted everything he did, and the addiction was a result of the pain. He was medicating the pain, all of it. I cry as I remember my brown-eyed brother. Momma used to say that Danny's eyes were as big as her fist. They were. My great-granddaughter Addi has similar eyes. They pull you in when she looks at you. Danny was the same way. His eyes told it all. They were the window to his soul, and they had seen far too many whiskey bottles. But what a good soul he was. If you get nothing else from this book, I hope you take this away: good people do dumb things. God's love isn't confined to those who are well, and I'm speaking to mental health as well as physical health. The Bible tells us that He's close to the broken-hearted and saves those who are crushed in spirit. Bingo.

As I remember and write about this part of my life, I realize that it's so painful I have rarely talked about it. I'm not sure my children completely know these stories. God kept me. It was a miracle. Nothing short of it.

Back to 1969: So here I am, barely thirteen, and there was NO one that the buck stopped with. I had a blank check, a checking account with money in it, and nothing and no one to keep me from me. Our home wasn't normal before, but it was consistent. I knew what to expect. But now? MY life was void of direction, purpose, rules, parenting. No direction. And honestly, I wanted to die.

For a month or so after the marriage and Mom's absence, I found myself hanging out late at a city park, a bowling alley, walking down the street on the public square. But God. When I think of the potential for disaster during that season of my life, it's chilling. I wanted structure. I probably didn't say I wanted structure, but I did.

Within a month or so I had new friends. They were there because it was raining money. I had money to spend and no one to supervise my decisions with it. My pattern of being used started early in life. It actually started here.

And on this Saturday, Mom was in town. She was at our Navaho house. She went to bed by 6:00 p.m., which was her norm. It's obvious that I rebelled with the late night patterns. I HATED the fact that she wouldn't stay up with me, go places with me—I hated it! She went to sleep on this particular Friday night, and I spent the night trying to find a means with which to end my life. I was there: hopeless, helpless, and thrust into an adult world that I didn't sign up for.

I didn't watch cartoons as a child; I was a serious type who lived squarely between Momma's ideology of "television and movies will send you to hell" and Dad's ringing laughter at Red Skelton. I occasionally enjoyed a TV show with Dad, but it wasn't guilt-free. I didn't understand children—I had never been one—but I wasn't emotionally mature enough to understand the adult world of death, or abandonment, or empty houses either. So here I was. Caught between life and death, childhood and adulthood, tears and laughter, enjoyment and anguish. For God's sake, I had never enjoyed a television show without the hovering feeling of doom and guilt. I didn't have the tools to deal with this; no one had shown me the way, and I was only thirteen. Most thirteen-year-olds can't deal with a dead cell phone, much less a dead parent, an empty house, and an empty heart.

My mind twirled, flipped, and made me want to scream. I cried a lot, but the tears didn't do much. I just ended up with a blotchy face and an unattractive rawness around my nose. As Momma slept, the demons came. They spoke. I listened. They bid me come and I did.

Mom slept and I walked. I headed toward downtown, at first walking through neighborhoods and familiar areas. I started about 8:00 or 9:00 p.m., I suppose. The world felt safe at that moment. But as the night grew long, I suspected it was closer to midnight by this time; I was walking down Highway 62 and nearing the high-traffic areas. Elizabethtown, Kentucky, is a neighboring town to Fort Knox. Walking the streets on Friday night at midnight isn't exactly a safe place for a bouncer, much less a little girl. But I did it.

I am mortified of dogs, the outdoor kind, and as it grew oh so late, I was beginning to dread the walk home. The barking had started and I was starting to feel my thirteen-year-old self. I walked and talked to unsavory characters: the homeless, the street people, the drunks, everyone. I was openly and obviously tempting the fate of destruction. I listened to the demons. I walked until my feet hurt. No one missed me, no one knew. Mom was asleep.

I went south of the square and ended up in front of the county jail. This was a familiar area, but it wasn't safe. South of town was where Dad's shop was. I walked the tracks and headed toward his shop. My dad would have been mortified. He warned me about trains and the danger of walking the track. He had several acres with a welding shop, an office building, and a big back lot that stored dozens of bulldozers, dump trucks, backhoes, drag lines, ditching machines, and a boat or two. As I neared the shop, I knew I was in danger. I was defiant. I dared death to try. I walked on the shoulder of that two-lane road, I thought about Dad in that grave, and I cried.

The demons taunted me. They encouraged me to step in front of a car. I panicked as I had a sudden urge to obey. I fought for my sanity on that night; I also fought for my soul. For, you see, I knew enough to know . . . that life is a battle. I had very little figured out at this point, but this much I knew. The devil had told me to step outside and duke it out, and basically, that's what we were doing. No one raped me or tried to hurt me during that season of my life. You would have to know what I know to understand the depth and width of God's protection.

The demons suggested that I find someone to give me drugs. They suggested I try to find a gun. They suggested many horrific things. Let me detour for a minute. If you think for one moment that this isn't the same army of demons your children are fighting or your grandchildren are fighting, you've got rocks for brains. They are in constant warfare for their sanity, their sobriety, their tomorrow in general.

But somewhere in the fog of that night, a night spent walking miles and miles . . . alone and weirdly unafraid, I started to dig deep. I didn't know much about praise; I didn't know much about anything. I was no Bible scholar. But I remembered an icy creek, an old fat preacher that dunked a ten-year-old in that frozen water, and the shout that came from my lungs. I remembered. I remembered the times I entertained in my living room, no one but God and me, as I played "Sheltered in the Arms of God" alone, singing with all I had, crying until the tears soaked my shirt. I remembered. For even then, when the world was crushing me, when those that should have protected me weren't there, I knew what I knew.

Temptation was introduced to me that night. The devil himself came to me. He spoke to my soul. He made me thirst for what I had never drunk; he made me hungry for what I would NEVER taste. But on this night? A lonely little girl walked out the front door, alone, looking for an escape. Today as I write, I retraced my walk, and according to MapQuest, it was over eleven miles, round trip. The unsavory characters were there. The danger was ever-present. I should have been the next body waiting to be identified in the morgue, but it didn't happen.

I won't pretend that I had a full-on theological foundation, and I won't pretend that I wasn't headed for many days of struggle after this night, but what I will tell you is this.

The enemy of my soul introduced the idea of every destructive thing he had in his bag of tricks. I walked the streets of Elizabethtown, Kentucky, all night, by myself, daring death to grab me, almost wishing. But somehow, someway, that GREAT big hand of God reached down and put that unexplainable hedge around me. The man who should have harmed me didn't touch me. The car didn't hit me. The drug dealer didn't offer. The dog didn't even bite me. I went home and crawled up in the bed just in time to see the sun rise.

I've never told anyone this story until now. You're the first to hear it. I tucked these stories away in a deep place. The pain of my childhood is intact today; yours probably is too.

So as my sisters and Mom whispered in the kitchen of that brick house; they had no clue that I had been MIA all night. It wouldn't be the last time, actually. But somehow I survived the drama and trauma of being thirteen, fourteen, fifteen, sixteen, and so on and so on. I survived without ever tasting a drop of alcohol or drugs. That's God. Nothing prevented it BUT God. I told you in *Stronger* that I didn't attend high school, and it's true, I didn't. But for today, this is about as far as my heart will let me go. I will save the rest for another day, another writing session.

The devil put in a high bid for my soul that night. It was so real that I remember it in detail forty-nine years later. So every time I hear of a child who dies from a drug overdose or a suicide, I identify to the core of my soul. I get it. For that should have been me. Why did I live? Mercy. Why me and not other children? I don't have an answer. I don't pretend to have one.

Some of you are wondering why I would write this chapter. I can hear you now. I want you to look at my story and baptize yourself in hope as you read it. My circumstances were a bit shaky, and I made some terrible relationship choices, several of them. But I'm here to deal some hope and faith to you. You may start off with a rough patch or two, but you can still finish well. I had such a bumpy start. I have no doubt that I was the talk of the town at times. Didn't matter. God will use the willing. I was willing. Still am. I recently had a prophecy from a prophet. I didn't know this man, but clearly, through the Spirit he knew me. He nailed me on several fronts, read my mail. But then he got to this part . . . and I began to weep. He said, "Others have doubted your love for Him, but HE never doubted. He knows how much you love Him." Nothing but tears. The good news is this. Even when life is so wrong, and our choices are so wrong, and we're deemed worthless, uneducated, unworthy . . . HE still knows what we have that's worth saving, and He loves us through it, and this part blessed me so much. He knows we're loving Him back . . . through our tears, through our depression, through our suicidal thoughts, through our addiction, through our struggle, He doesn't stop loving, and truly neither do we.

When the word of God and the story of Jesus is planted, it's there to stay. My mom didn't get everything right—I suppose that's an understatement. But, oh my . . . she had faith. If you haven't read *Stronger*, read the chapter titled "43 Stitches." It tells about me getting my throat cut when I was seventeen. I was in a parking lot at the hospital in Hartford, Kentucky, when a random stranger tried to overtake me with the intention to rape me and kill me, I suppose. My momma didn't know this. She was at church several miles away. No phone, no communication at all. It was 1973. However, she jumped to her feet and said, "Kathy's in trouble. Something has threatened her life and I'm going to the emergency room, she's at the hospital." Faith. She had it. She was never uncertain when the Lord gave her a word. She didn't question. She believed.

They stopped the service, prayed, and all came with Mom to the hospital. And yes, I was there. I walked through the shadow of death. But God said, "NOT today. She will live and not die."

We can be full of purpose and still be a jacked-up mess. He's not looking for perfect people. He's looking for willing people who understand faith. There was never a day that Momma doubted God. She doubted men; truly, she was a bit of a man hater, but oh my. In her most flawed state, in her season of complete failure, she still peddled the Jesus story, His being crucified, resurrected, and rising on the third day. She loved Him. I've seen it over and over in her life. She spoke so many uncanny things, that only GOD could have let her know. She knew Him and He knew her. She spent time with Him, daily. She prayed for a hedge around her family. She got lots of things wrong. So did I. But she got the Jesus thing right. So did I. The generational curses rivaled the generational blessing, but in the end, we won. The blood was enough.

The lack of normalcy made me a strange duck, but that's okay. God uses strange ducks. My wounds became my scars. And we all know that scars remind us that we were there and we MADE it out. If you too have always felt like the misfit in your school, your family, your workplace, your church, remember that the best souls are those who have walked in the shadows, never feeling like they belonged. Those people can FEEL the pain of others. They think deep, love deep, and are typically the least pretentious people in your life, and they always make the best friends. A person who understands personal pain can cry with you, laugh with you, pray with you, and eat cake with you. And somewhere in the mix, everything feels like it's going to be okay. Usually after the cake! Ha!

So to all my fellow misfits, let's just keep marching to our own drum, loving loud, remembering what He did for us, and telling everyone who will listen: for we are the club that never concerns ourselves with political correctness or popularity. We crave authenticity and truth. Our motto is this: You can talk it out, cry it out, or scream it out; you're allowed to do all of the above. But you can't quit. We don't allow quitting.

Tonight, as I write and feel so much thankfulness for the broken road . . . I see the ministries of all of my kids, I see countless faces, a sea of people . . . washed in the blood as a result of hearing the gospel from my family. And I am proud to say that I didn't fall into the devil's trap of addiction. Nope, sure didn't. That's nothing short of a miracle. It's a testament to a hedge. It's not my righteousness, trust me—I'm truly filthy. But God will see HIS purpose fulfilled. I could have, should have, and would have been an addict at a very early age. But God. He completely removed my adolescent curiosity about drugs and alcohol the night I took the eleven-mile walk. I'm thankful.

If you're reading this and you have an addiction, I plead with you. Get help. No judgment here. Let Jesus be a part of that help. Psychology is amazing, but psychology plus Jesus is healing. You can be free. You can be clean.

Put on your fatigues, strap on your weapon, and learn to fight for your soul. Define the enemy and get in his face. Shout him down. You must. It's life or death this time. Let your mess turn into a message, not an obituary.

Okay, I'm speaking to those in a struggle: Take the needle out of your arm. Clean out the cabinet where that vodka is stashed. Get all of those pain pills out of the bathroom and confess your addiction to someone who loves you. Honesty and accountability are a must if you're going to survive. Call a family meeting and tell them the truth of your struggle. Seek out those who will make you accountable, not those who will join you. You're not a victim; you're a fighter. And always know this: you ARE loved.

In my opinion, drug use and abuse is possibly the most heartbreaking problem facing America today. How did we get here? So much pain in the world. I contend that most addicts are people with soft hearts that can't deal with ugly truths.

The church is as pained as the secular world, statistically. In many pulpits it's the "unspeakable" and the "unthinkable." In many homes it's the elephant in the room, clearly because there's abuse and the family is in denial. In other homes, many of which are made up of amazing Christians, it's a daily, unending heartbreak. Every late-night call brings a panic that is indescribable to those who haven't dealt with an addict. There are no words. So I will stop my attempt.

If you're reading this and you're struggling with addiction? LISTEN to me. There is hope for you. No matter what your last chapter has been, your next one can be better. Grace is enough. Persist, sister, persist. He's waiting for you.

It's a battle, but it's worth fighting.

Come, let me take you on a journey or two. Let me tell you about the shenanigans that He's walked through with this girl. Pull up a chair, pour some sweet tea or a Diet Coke, and go with me. I am truly in awe of a God that has kept me all these years. The year 1969 seems like an eternity away, but the SAME God, SAME word, is alive and well to this sixty-one-year-old granny.

Here we go.

The Storm Is Calling

The palm trees are swaying, the sun is oh so bright, and most of Florida is suffering today. Hurricane Irma blew in last weekend like an angry ex-wife and left the Florida Keys in shambles, Jacksonville flooded, and folks from coast to coast to coast in various stages of disaster.

I watched the news and saw refrigerators floating down canals, million-dollar boats strewn like matchsticks, and entire areas of the Sunshine State that were decimated on this Tuesday, September 12, 2017.

But here on the beautiful Emerald Coast? It still looks like a postcard. God was amazingly good. The locals are proclaiming it. GOD protected the Redneck Riviera this time around. I tend to agree with them. There's not a single remnant of Irma.

I'm here quite by accident. My daughter Kelly and her husband Mike were supposed to vacation here this week, and I had every intention of spending the week at home in Tennessee. Irma was brewing, her path was uncertain, and like most angry women, it was far too dangerous to gamble on Irma's choices . . . so they decided to go home to Nashville and try the beach thing another time. You see, my husband and I, along with our adult children, bought a family beach property last summer. We keep a family calendar and draw our allotted weeks in each season. This was Mike and Kelly's week. Whoops. The struggles of weather can be very real when you own an ocean-front property. These intense hurricanes have served as a dose of reality as it relates to beach homes for many a proud owner. We pray a little more about hurricanes than we used to, and we watch the Weather Channel now. Before I owned a beach property? Not on your life.

Now? The Weather Channel is on my favorites list. There's a message there kids: it's different when it's OUR house that's in trouble, right? We will preach that one another day. But you get the point. The hurricane season this year is a big deal and we know it.

Most weeks you will find all of MY kids, fully engaged in raising THEIR children, caring for their individual ministries, and fulfilling all of their adult commitments back in Hendersonville, Tennessee. But me? That's another story. I will pack a bag in a New York minute when the opportunity presents itself, and according to my family, it presents itself quite often. On Sunday night, September 10, 2017, once again, opportunity knocked, and I answered.

For, you see, I've been raising kids or working 24/7 since I was eighteen years old. I'm sixty-one. You do the math. Granted, my kids have been grown for several years, but those pesky obligations that come with a full-time job can bridle an old woman who has wanderlust problems. So I recalibrated my employment obligations a couple of years ago so that Granny Kathy could keep a bag packed and be ready at all times to jump on a flight or a train or into a boring black SUV if that was the best I could muster.

This particular opportunity was in the form of a text that came from Kelly. She said, "We're not going. The path of this hurricane is too uncertain. We're heading the bus toward Nashville and we will spend a week enjoying our home that we never see."

For those of you who don't know us, Mike and Kelly are in the family business of music and Jesus. They travel on a tour bus about 150 days a year. So on this day, the beach was vetoed for them, and the bus was heading north on I-65. So . . . I could go to the beach if I wanted. I started to feel THAT feeling. It was Him. I knew it. I had an appointment.

It was beginning to feel similar to an appointment that I had accepted in 2014. Then? He spoke to me while I was watching Fox News. He being God. He simply said, "Go to the mountain and I will meet you there." Clearly, I'm not a person who makes vacation plans with God every day. Do you? I mean seriously. I pray, I love Him, I live for Him, I trust Him. But how often do you plan trips around His schedule and tell your family, "Hey, y'all hang tight. I'm going over to Kentucky Lake to spend a few days on a boat with Jesus."

Anyone? I didn't think so. So to minimize these appointments would be somewhat disingenuous. It's not my daily gig.

I consider myself to be a commonsense, no bull kind of woman. Super spiritual people typically get on my nerves. And I am confident that I'm comic relief for God on most days. I'm confident that He's amused at most things I do and say, and I rarely feel like I'm the most spiritual person in a room. I've been told that my blessings were simply because I was in close proximity to anointed people. Until 2014 and that mountain visit, I suppose you could say that I had received the memo, read it, and believed it. I wasn't spiritual, I told myself. After all, so-and-so told me straight up that I didn't know the voice of God. I was told by Mr. So-and-So that my strengths were fighting the fight for OTHERS. Okay. There's possibly some truth to that. I was ambitious, a fighter, a Momma Bear if you will.

I had the guts of a comic who wasn't the least bit funny, the blind ambition of a hooker who needed drugs, and the tough skin of an army general. That was me. The good news? I've strived to use the ambition for kingdom work.

So it's no wonder that most eyebrows raise when they hear my story that explains that God came to me while I was watching Fox News in my leather recliner, and He told me to go to a mountain and HE promised that HE would meet me there.

Yeah. That.

I had never put on a super spiritual mask in my life. What you saw was what you got. I lived in the moral zone. I didn't believe in cussing, chewing, drinking alcohol, spitting, or smoking. I had all of that covered.

But the truth? I was jaded. I had seen SO much hypocrisy! I was spiritual burnt toast. My soul was parched and dry. The God of my alone moments, the God that heard my groaning and wiped my tears was real. But when I tried to put that into a daily, walking, churchgoing, preacher-trusting context? I couldn't.

Remember, this was before the mountain. Before my healing.

The struggle was real. I was a crumb eater. I had been told that the floor crumbs were all I deserved. Why? Because I didn't prophesy, I didn't pray for the masses in a prayer line, because I didn't have the "gifts" that so easily attract the world at times.

Bitter? Nope. Honest would be a better description.

Back to the mountains and the beach.

And remember, I had an onset of laryngitis that came on that night back in 2014. I am a chatty person. Laryngitis is devastating to my life . . . When it strikes, I may as well put a sign on my forehead that says, "Closed until further notice."

I'm a verbal person. Everything includes conversation. Everything. This generation that doesn't talk? It makes me crazy. My entire life is about words, and, yes . . . words matter, so the laryngitis was and is a big deal.

Oddly enough . . . as Kelly was informing me of her plans to NOT go to the beach because of her Irma fears, my voice began to leave. Once again laryngitis had set in. I quickly realized that I hadn't had it since the last book, 1,030 days ago. Yes, as I wrote *Stronger* I hadn't the ability to whisper on most days. He took my ability to chatter away, and when He did? I got down to business.

This meeting? It would be at the beach. I booked a flight and packed a very small bag. I didn't want anything I didn't need. My computer, medicines, a dab of makeup, a couple of T-shirts, a pair of shorts, a housedress, and yes . . . my cat gown.

Most of you know that I take that pink, tattered gown everywhere I go. Truly, I want to be buried in it. I want my hair fixed and my makeup on, and some great pearls would be good. But, kids, don't buy me a new dress for viewing. Pull out the cat gown. That gown has traveled to most of the continental United States with me, as well as internationally. It's seen the good, the bad, and the ugly. It's my security blanket in the form of a Walmart gown, circa 1999. So with the cat gown in tow . . . and my trusty Mac, I headed to Florida. Millions were leaving, but I was going.

I was anxious. Cause you see, I know how God wrecks me. I remembered the mountain.

The last time? The mountain? It was the beginning of a journey that will last until I close my eyes for the last time. It was the reckoning of a lifetime of pain. The nine-year-old Kathy cried on that mountain, the thirteen-year-old cried harder, and the forty-nine-year-old heaved and vomited. A lifetime of pain, and unresolved rejection and abandonment, required that those broken girls, of all ages, height, weight, and hairstyles . . . come together, in one place, and learn about the true love of a Good Father. I couldn't imagine what it felt like to be pretty enough, skinny enough, you know . . . worth enough, until the mountain experience. I had lived to be fifty-eight years old and had no clue who I was, and I certainly had no clue who HE was.

So. That was my last vacation with God: Just Him and me. It was traumatic, wonderful, awful, and oh so freeing. Some people live an entire life and don't cry as much as I cried on that mountain.

So now it's three years later. Irma has hit, Florida is in peril, and God has invited me to the beach. As with the mountains . . . I was nervous. What now, God? Am I a mechanical writer? No. Do I have notes and outlines? No.

I decided I would go and see what HE had to say.

So I arrived empty-handed. I scrapped every single word I had TRIED to write over the last couple of years, and I showed up with my little duffle bag. Just God and me. The pretense of intellect was gone, the truth was obvious. I needed Him to speak, or I would go home with little more than a tan line and a few pictures on my iPhone.

This time felt a bit more like a battle than the mountain experience did. The mountain was coming to terms with my truth. It was more like a "cry fest" than a war.

But tonight, as I sit and listen to the intoxicating sound of this ocean, it feels as if I'm typing words that are specifically for you. I'm preparing my oral argument to convince you to fight one more day. I know you're tired—so am I. I am plagued with many things that so easily beset a sixty-one-year-old.

But make no mistake, friends, this sister is on a mission. I will persist. I will give you what He gives me.

I love a storm. I'm sure that tells much about my underlying personality. I also love the underdog. Most underdogs live in varying degrees of storms and may rarely have sunshine on their face. I get it. Most underdogs fight demons for their brief moment in the sun. Most of you are shaking your head to this—you ALSO identify.

I've been disciplined. I haven't had my toes in the sand yet. I'm currently sitting here overlooking the pool. Most folks have decided to pack it up. There's no sun at all. But one granny with a distinct smoker's voice is yelling at Brian about his water gun, Brandon about picking up his toys, and in general she's annoying the entire Emerald Beach with her redneck approach to grandparenting. After hearing her yell at her grandkids for an hour or more, I'm confident that she's probably spent more money on cigarettes than a mortgage, she's probably an enabler, and she's probably picked the battle of raising these grandkids. After observing this makeshift family for an hour or so, I would bet you a farm in Texas that granny provides for these little ones. I bet she is their soul caregiver, and it's clear that she has chosen a rough road for a sixty-something-year-old. The story is so familiar and my judging isn't really judging. I know too much about her kind. Her heart is huge, yet her ability to stand isn't great. She needs a good dose of Jesus most likely, based on her language. Additionally, she needs someone to encourage her, like me.

Let me explain. I am that old woman who looks at "people" and then I imagine their lives, their stories, their pain, their insecurities. I color these stories with images, truth, and I look for signs to fill in the blanks. There were many with Sister Marlboro. Now, I'm not dissing smokers—don't accuse me of such. I'm simply telling a story. I'm going somewhere. Hang on.

I haven't always been that old woman who stopped and looked at the relationships between people at the pool. My breadth wasn't that wide. I watched MY people, maybe ridiculous people, and occasionally famous people. Now? My people-watching game has stepped up. I hope you're thinking why? Because I'm getting prepared to tell you.

I used to feel that I knew people. But I really didn't. I knew people that I CHOSE to know. I knew people that I needed to know for the furthering of my agenda. Don't judge me—you're probably guilty too. But I couldn't honestly say that I had EVER opened myself up to anyone and everyone. For you see, to KNOW people is to walk with them. And that's the difficult part. It's called GIVING. The more people we let in, the more we are prone to give. So most of us limit the people in order to limit the giving of our time, resources, and energy. After all, our obligations are clearly first and foremost, and when most people are asked, "How are you?" the number one answer is "Busy. I'm SO busy."

So, like you, I was SO busy and SO closed off when the circle expanded beyond MY people, MY longtime friends, and MY necessary business relationships. I've often said, "I trust no one. I don't have time for lots of friends."

Holy cow. That was about to change.

In November of 2014, I wrote *Stronger*. I checked out completely while on that mission. I rarely bathed, ate five-minute meals, lots of cake, and became obsessed with the journey of the story. Just God and me. We were pretty good traveling buddies. We finished it and had it edited by January 2015. I didn't know if I would let a soul read it beyond the family and a FEW close friends. The kids had read their reference chapters. The grandkids read their info, some of them over and over and over. Ha! I was pleased. I thought this might be a book JUST for my big, loving, blended family. I thought it would serve to remind the grandkids HOW we came to be, after they were older, and the bloodlines became clearer. I envisioned a day when they would marvel at what God had done. How He minimized blood to a zero and maximized love to a ten. It's a beautiful story of love, and I was proud of the finished manuscript.

In January I wrestled with the "what now" of my dilemma. This was new turf. I was a realtor. I had been the top-producing realtor at my Century 21 office for seven years in a row. I understood a contract and negotiations.

I understood songs, records, pitches, promotion, and the working of a traveling music ministry that often resembled a circus, but I always brought people to a bloody cross and the truth of Christ. Millions had been saved, dozens of the songs had been hits, and well, you know the story. I will go easy on the brag. I'm sure there are others who need the "bragging" oxygen today. I will leave it to the professional bragger's club to fill in the facts about song success and such. I will stick to the generalities.

So my point is this: I was in new water. I had on my bathing suit, but I wasn't sure how well I could swim. I felt a bit like Peter. I knew Jesus was walking. I knew He was a water walker, a miracle kind of Jesus . . . After all, He had clearly performed a miracle or two in my lifetime, most likely to get my attention. There WAS a Crabb Family because of the miracle that He performed when I was thirty-seven, back in the early nineties when GOD divinely healed as an answer to my prayer; that was a fleece, and He easily overrode MY know-it-all responses to HIS knock. The miracle sealed the deal.

This God of 2015 was the same—I knew that. That SAME GOD saw the heart and soul of my fifty-eight-year-old heart. Yes, I was a different girl than the innocent thirty-seven-year-old had been. I was a bit more jaded than she was; I had acquired many sags and bags, but my gift was still the same. I had the gift AT TIMES of being fearless, almost in the "ignorance is bliss" kind of way. And guess what, He knew it.

After I wrote my first book I pondered for a few days. I didn't ask for opinions. I didn't want opinions. It's obvious that not everyone who slaps you on the back and says "I love you" really wants you to win. They measure their own lives by others and often feel the need to diminish the accomplishments of others in order to feel better about themselves. It's called jealousy. Envy. These same people struggle to share the spotlight, no matter how dim your light is or how bright theirs is. So I was careful. I didn't go outside my circle. I didn't want haters circling with criticism just because they FEARED the content of this book. No need in causing a hater to waste their hate on something that will remain in my closet until I die. Ha!

I believed that GOD would speak directly to ME. I believe in prophecy, of course. But here's the truth. Prophecy will confirm your vision. But another man or woman can't birth a vision in you that you're going to carry and deliver. YOUR pain must be felt. Those BIG-God visions MUST be birthed with pain and blood. No shortcuts, kids. God can speak to us directly. He does not need a prayer line. Now, I love me a prayer line, don't misunderstand, but the hard work of birthing doesn't come by the labor of another. When I was pregnant, Momma used to say to me, "Oh, Kathy Jo, I wish I could do this for you. It's the most awful pain you will ever suffer. I don't know if you can bear it."

She meant well, but she scared the holy smokes out of me with that kind of rhetoric. But this part I never forgot. The "NO ONE can do it for you" part. It was my baby, my body, my choice, and my fate. I'm the one who chose to get pregnant. I'm the one who chose to create a new life. Momma couldn't alter that, no matter how hard she tried. She couldn't do it for me.

Ministry births are the same. So with this book thing? I was the momma. NO ONE else was telling their story, sharing their vulnerabilities . . . nor had they devoted hundreds of hours on the side of a cold mountain. It was my baby, and God could speak directly TO me. I had great support, but I had to woman-up and deliver the baby myself.

I waited. I ran laps around the same scenarios in my mind. Daily. The "what ifs" of change were in full force in my head.

In the middle of the night, sometime in January if my memory serves me, the Lord woke me. I had already done a photo shoot for this book. My granddaughter Edie insisted that I stop and take the time. I had a cover designed. Micah, my photographer/designer randomly did one when he was sending me the proofs. He did a mock-up that took him five minutes. One attempt, and seriously it probably took him five minutes, and I liked it and said, "We're good. This one works."

Two things. Micah has a great eye. That doesn't JUST happen. Also, I'm not terribly easy to please, but this book cover? I didn't care. I felt a bit like a self-promoter during this part of the process. But Kelly and Edie insisted on the photo. I was intent on using a stock photo of some kind, maybe of a mountain, and going in that direction. I remember Kelly saying, "Mom, let them see your face. Let them not only hear that you MADE it. Let them SEE that you made it." I received it. Terah, my youngest, had given me the title. I love one-word titles, but I was unsure. She sent me a text one day and said, "The best word to describe your journey is STRONGER. That's the right title for this book." My response was, "Okay. *Stronger* it is."

So these kids had spoken wisdom to me, forced me to be prepared, but I got nauseous every time I imagined people reading *Stronger*. I thought they would be disappointed that I didn't have a college degree. I thought they would judge my sometimes chaotic life. I thought they would put me in the category with the "crazies" and stop taking my calls. I FELT vulnerable.

So on this night, the God of the universe, the God who parted the Red Sea, the God who knitted me in my mother's womb . . . He woke me. There are many nights that I can't sleep, but this was definitive. The book. He had communication to share. No, it wasn't an email from Jesus@aol.com, it wasn't a loud voice booming from the bonus room; it was a simple introduction of thought, but I knew that I knew: it was Him.

The introduction thought was simple: post the book on a website, tell your friends about it, and watch what happens. I was a bit taken aback. I know it wasn't my thoughts, for I had dreams of a BIG book publisher, a long advance season, and a media blitz to match the in-store release week. That was the advice I would have given to any writer, or so I thought.

My immediate thoughts were, "But, God, that is so amateurish, and I don't really have a website. I have a blog, but I haven't built a website." I mean, why would I? I was a realtor. We had a real estate website, Steve and I. But I had nothing that would make sense for a recalibrated Kathy that was back up and running in ministry, per se. It had been a mighty long time since I had managed a ministry idea, much less a book about my crazy life.

God spoke distinctly and I knew it would alter the roads I traveled if I listened. I listened. I stopped and sent an email to my web buddy from Crabb Family days. I hadn't talked to him in six or seven years. I explained to him that I needed a website. Now. I wanted the book cover that I was attaching to be posted to a website when he could find time to build it. Remember, it was around two in the morning. I went and explored my PayPal account that I hadn't used in years, because I knew he would have to link it to have a commerce page. It still worked. I had obtained the domain www.kathycrabbhannah.com several years ago. Now I would use it.

I told God that if I sold a hundred the first day, I would move forward with printing and self-publishing. If I didn't sell a hundred, I would refund the money and keep it in my closet under my boots and let my kids find it when I die.

I sent VERY detailed instructions and went to bed. The next day, to my surprise, I got the call from Mississippi. It was Lance, my web guy. He said, "Well, how about let's build a website real fast." Wow. I was shocked. I can't recall exactly when I posted it, but I posted that the book would be available at a certain time that day—I think it was noon. Lance got the nuts and bolts figured out, and I went on about my day. I expected 101 orders. My fleece was for a hundred. I was a bit disappointed with this route of selling it myself on a website. I mean Barnes & Noble or Lifeway was a bit more what I had in mind. But I knew better than to second-guess. The favor of God can do more in five minutes than a lifetime of my labor.

The text came from Lance saying, "It's up. The preorders have started." He was a couple of hours ahead of the promised time. So it was clear that someone was watching the website closely. That was encouraging. And then I started getting messages. We can't order. There's a problem.

Oh Lord, help me. WHAT happened? And then I logged in and saw a struggle with PayPal. The orders came so fast that I maxed my expected amount within ten minutes. PayPal needed more financial information because the amount was now approaching tens of thousands, rather than hundreds. What? I realized I could get PayPal on the line and talk through this quickly. I did, and then I watched the orders flood in. I knew the statistics for books, and writers with lofty aspirations. Like so many in the world of art, music, and books, I wanted to believe that the potential was there, but in reality the average U.S. nonfiction book actually sells less than 250 copies per year and less than 3,000 copies over the lifetime of the title. And very few titles are big sellers. I was keenly aware that most writers write because they love it, not because people buy it. Writing is a first cousin to singing. And Lord knew I had seen that movie. I knew that many folks who had beaten the roads their entire lives didn't have a pot to pee in or a window to throw it out of. I wasn't expecting a financial return for my time or tears.

I have a newsflash to insert about here. BECAUSE we don't expect it, God feels a bit more delighted to give it.

PayPal was hopping. I was giddy. The numbers rose by the minute. I was humbled to tears. Steve was lost for words. I think he kind of considered it to be a personal diary—you know, a journal of sorts. No more than a newfound hobby for me. He hadn't actually read anything at this point, with the exception of the chapters about him. What was this? A book about my life? Who would want to read that? A girl with a big nose and no real accomplishments? With no marketing or advertising, but a simple Facebook post and a few hours to allow God time to stir a few folks, and we were up and running, with competing numbers for titles from well-known writers. We surpassed online sales for many musical artists that I had the backstory on their Internet sales data. There was no marketing team, no interviews, no publicist, no build up to the release. Nothing. Just a bit of God's favor and a great group of friends who had walked through some hell with me. That's all I had.

We sold thousands that first week. Now we had to get busy and get it printed. We did. And actually, as with everything in my life, I did it a bit backwards. But I got it into distribution after the fact. We hit the bookstores, the promotional trail, and the interview circuit. That should have been six months in advance of the release. Instead it was five months after the release. Of course it was backwards. Would you expect any less from me?

I was so glad that I had chosen the battle of facing MY insecurities and truth. IT remains one of the most difficult things I've ever done. On this day, as I watched the

LORD and PayPal, I was thankful that I went to that mountain to battle the demons of silence. I had found my voice, and you were readying to find yours.

And by the end of February 2015, the Hendersonville, Tennessee, U.S. Post Office hated me. We were bringing huge boxes of books to mail. He did it again. He told me it would happen, and it did.

However, nothing in my life prepared me for what would happen next. God didn't give me a heads up on this one. Holy smokes, if He had, I would have had a nervous breakdown.

The Girls

On February 26, 2015, the printing company emailed me to say that they had a run of books ready. Steve took his truck and loaded the entire bed. They were heavy! Who knew books weighed that much? I suppose I had never seen anyone put several hundred boxes of books in a pickup truck. Steve asked if he could own the first one as he cut a box open, and for the first time I saw it. He handed me a copy of *Stronger*. I looked at it, and, strangely, the first thing I noticed was how big my hands looked in the picture. It made me want to giggle. I felt suddenly nervous. What if no one liked it? Unlike making a record, where there are a dozen or more people involved to bask in the glory if it's the perfect recording with the perfect song selection and performances or share the blame if it's a trip to hell for the listener, this wasn't that. This was called flying solo. It wins or fails, all on my watch. The end.

So on this day, this writer was doing everything in-house! Ha! My daughter Krystal and my granddaughter Cameron spent about three days sorting and preparing packages. I signed books until I thought my arm would fall off. They worked around the clock nearly, and by Wednesday of the following week, they were in the mail. I breathed a sigh of relief. In record time we had accomplished the nearly impossible. I was out of book-signing purgatory and I was glad. Now back to normal. Steve said daily, "The real estate office is waiting for you. Are you ready to come back?" I would tell him that I needed a few more weeks to try to promote this book as best I could. After all, it didn't have much of a chance to live.

But meanwhile in Texas, Alabama, Tennessee, West Virginia, Kentucky, Missouri, North and South Carolina, Pennsylvania, Arizona, Montana, Michigan, California, and every other state between our beautiful coastlines, as well as Canada, Ireland, England, Australia, and countless foreign addresses, you fine folks were checking your mailboxes daily. I knew. You were messaging me on Facebook, asking if "it" had been mailed. It had.

One day, I awoke and checked my phone. I had been tagged in dozens of pictures; the next day was the same, the next day more, and so on and so on. You kept ordering, we kept mailing, and you kept tagging and reading.

By early March, it started. The first one came. NOTHING I had ever walked through prepared me for the tears you would pour out to me via your smartphones, while probably lying in bed, a bit braver under your quilt with the lights off . . . Your ugly cry was hidden in the dark, the pain a bit more manageable than it was the last time you tried to muster the courage to tell. So you typed, you vomited the secrets of your childhood, you told. Talk about #metoo moments—I couldn't believe these letters.

The first one: We will call her Betty. Betty was fifty-five, very overweight, and sick with diabetes, high-blood pressure, and heart disease. Her letter started out with full-on Crabb Family love and sweet appreciation of the kids' ministries today in their various representations. She, like so many, loved my family. I loved it that she did. About two paragraphs in she started. "I've never told another person this story, in my entire life. I read your book. I finished it today, and I had to write you. I couldn't stop myself. I decided that it's time to tell my story. If you are brave enough to tell yours, I'm brave enough to tell mine. If you can walk through that, I can walk through this."

She continued, "I've been in church my entire life. My dad was a pastor. I grew up in a parsonage. My mom played the piano. Dad was a pastor for more than forty years. I am still involved in church. I lead worship and my husband is a Sunday school teacher. But I'm a mess, and no one knows. I've told myself that I can never speak it, but I'm about to tell you.

"When I was about eleven, my dad started watching me take baths. He started doing it while Mom was gone to choir practice at night. At first I didn't think anything of it. He helped me wash my back and then sometimes my hair. Oddly enough he had never been a hands-on dad. Mom did everything for me. So at first, I think I loved the attention. That feeling of being a nuisance that I often felt was pushed aside when he caressed my hair and my back. One night with the door securely locked he washed my entire body. I knew that something about this wasn't right, but the attention brought me a forbidden pleasure. The baths became more sexual by the day; an empty and entirely locked house became necessary. When I saw him lock the doors and ask me if I needed a bath, I knew it was time. I knew what he expected. Even though I could have told, I didn't. He told me that it would cause a divorce and poverty. He convinced me that it was love he was giving me and I was a good girl if I liked it."

She summarized, "The fact that he introduced me to masturbation and sex with such ease, with no remorse, and then he weekly got in a pulpit and preached hell hot and sin wrong. People would call him 'anointed' and I would be so confused. I was completely confused about this 'loving' Father we called God. Why did He allow this to happen to me? I suppose it was my fault. I didn't tell anyone, and it didn't stop until I left home and got married. The last time my dad 'had' me was three days before my wedding night. By this time, I had been his sex slave for seven-plus years. There were times that I thought Momma was jealous of me. And there were a few times that she questioned the locked doors when we were there alone. They were only locked when he was pleasuring himself. We lived in a small town. We didn't have keys or lock the house unless we were going to sleep. Sometimes we didn't lock the doors then—it depended. That was forty years–plus ago in. I think Mom suspected. But I never breathed it or confirmed. She would have hated me. He would have hated me. I would have been alone if I had told. So I didn't."

Holy smokes! AND what did she just tell me? And I'm over here . . . like, TRYING to process this letter and I'm crying my eyes out as I read. Her life makes mine look like a picnic. Wow! How in the world do you let pain like this go?

I kept reading: "So I married John, struggled to be intimate with him, but like every other time, I detached. I pretended that all was well. We moved away. I learned to love food, and I never looked my dad in the eye again until he was dying. On his deathbed he mumbled an 'I'm sorry' that was truly not befitting the crime. But like the screwed-up, needy child that I became in that moment, I sobbed and had a complete meltdown as I remembered his big hands on my tiny breasts, as I remembered the way he smelled wearing cheap cologne, and the way his white dress shirts that he preached in looked as he unbuttoned the bottom two buttons for ease of the deed he was fixing to make me do.

"I tried to forgive, but I hated him. It was over. He couldn't fix it, neither could I. I went home and cried for days. Everyone thought I was crying because my dad had passed. I was crying because I felt like he had killed ME at age eleven. And NO one EVER knew. MY husband doesn't know, my children don't know. I isolated the pain and pretended it happened to another girl. I pretend that THAT girl doesn't lead worship at my church. I pretend a lot of things. That's the only way I've survived. But tonight, as I finished your book, I had this weird urge to tell you. I trust you. MY heart was racing as I took a bath and rehearsed the opening line to this letter. I chickened out twice. But finally, after I heard my husband's snoring begin, I knew I was alone. I fished for my phone and the words came easy, but not as easy as the tears. Miss Kathy, how do I learn to fight this hatred? How do I get rid of the bitterness? I don't want to live in this hell, but I'm trapped. My silence built prison walls. My drug of choice is food. I only eat when I'm stressed. I wasn't born to be fat, I know that, but my coping mechanism is food, and more food. I mostly eat at night, alone, in my home. It's triggered by my self-loathing. I hate ME.

"My dad once told me, 'You liked it or you would have told your mom. Who is the guilty one here? You were that girl that wanted it. You didn't try to stop me.'

"I'm trapped in this guilt, and I'm trapped in this three-hundred-pound body. I know there's nothing you can do, but please pray for me. Unless God helps me, I'm not sure where this road ends. My suicidal thoughts come often, but not one single person knows this story; well, now I suppose you do, if you read your messages. Sorry to unload on you, but I had to."

And then there was a simple, "Love, Betty" at the bottom. The letter was much longer, but this is enough for you to get the core of the message. It was page after page of the description of her despair.

I cried, and in disbelief I read and reread. My spirit check and the Facebook stalking solidified what Betty had written to me. She was married, about fifty-five, and was a singer at her church. It appeared she was possibly on staff there. She looked like an average middle-aged woman on the pew beside me at ANY church in America. No weirdness or outward sign of a cray-cray. She obviously didn't choose the route of rebellion that we often see jaded church kids choose after a life-altering childhood like this one. Nor did she choose the road of truth, for that road was far too painful for her to walk alone, afraid, in her garments of shame. The easiest road for Betty, or so it seemed, was the road of denial. And she walked it with ease, or so it appeared on the outside. She was conditioned to this road. Her mother taught her, possibly without ever realizing it, to pretend that she liked little Tommy when she didn't. She taught her to be extra nice to Dr. Rich Britches—he had more money than God. She instilled the "be nice to those who take care of us" mentality in her. It's a common and at times unintentional consequence that ministry kids live in. What should be the most innocent group in America, our children of ministry, often are the most apathetic. For the controlling spirit of the folks in the pew WILL impact the home of a pastor. Every church has them, wannabe church bosses. Their control is commonly their finances. They blow in like a tornado, usually after a huge church fight with the pastor at another church in town. But now? They've found the perfect church. They want to GIVE more than they've ever given; they want to be obedient to HIS voice as it relates to finances, because they have FINALLY found the utopia—until they don't get their way.

Betty's home certainly had more issues than trying to please church people, but today, Betty is a sum of her life experiences. The most traumatic of these things was clearly the sexual abuse at the hand of her father, along with the passive nature of a mother who didn't want to KNOW anything . . . for fear that it would cost her family everything. She learned hypocrisy before she knew her ABCs. If you were going to survive in Betty's home, you had to learn to never question anything. Keep your mouth shut; don't have an opinion, and learn to like it.

The adult Betty got away geographically, but she was still oh so attached emotionally. The root system was intact. The good news is that she didn't molest or harm others—she harmed herself. Her hatred was mostly leveled at the mirror. Throughout her young adult years, Betty showed up for birthdays, Christmas, and family events if she had to. She put on her smile and pretended, sometimes with ease. Betty wasn't the perpetrator. In this story, she's the clear-cut victim. How do I know all of this? I exchanged many messages with her.

She told me that she had often shown up at revivals to hear her father preach, at her mother's insistence following a guilt-ridden conversation. She would be physically ill, but she went. Her mother was very concerned at what "looked" good to the onlooker. However, she wasn't all that concerned with WHY she had emotionally lost her daughter oh so many years ago.

Right about now I need to insert some Kathy opinions into this chapter. When YOU give a reprobate a photo op that is clearly going to be used to normalize HIS ministry—think Betty and her dad—you become a prop in his sick choice to prostitute the gospel. Just say no. You can forgive without an apology; you actually need to, but you can't be healthy if you're walking in his/her manipulation. Without truth and true repentance there's never going to be a relationship. That's the bad news. And the truth about Betty? If she had done what she SHOULD have done, she would have called law enforcement at some point. What else had her father done?

How many others were there? If he so easily violated his biological child, that little girl that he had dedicated to the Lord at two weeks old, how many others were there? How many nieces, nephews, children of neighbors, children that he had counseled, how many were now damaged goods? Authority figures are commonly above reproach in a community. They live in a best-case scenario for a pervert. I'm convinced that Betty's dad destroyed other little humans. After many messages back and forth, I'm convinced that she wasn't the only one.

Read a dozen letters from heroin addicts and you will continue to see this pattern. Abuse by someone in authority is a death knell to a soul. An uncle, stepfather, older brother, dad's friend, or sometimes it's good old Dad again. Second verse, same as the first.

The next letter reveals a very different outcome; THIS church girl is checking out. We shall call her Lisa. Lisa didn't wear her robe of hypocrisy. She put on her leather pants and started having sex at thirteen. By fourteen she had been with fifty-plus men, and alcohol was her afternoon delight. The sex came after the alcohol most of the time; it made it easier. The family called her the "black sheep" and she proudly owned it. She would rather be a black sheep than a hypocrite. But like Betty, she remained silent. Well, until now. She described the night that a lady on her Facebook feed wrote a post that caught her eye. Someone was buying books and giving them away. On that particular day the post from Myra read, "I'm buying Kathy Crabb Hannah's book to give to three girls today. If you've ever struggled with addiction, I want to send you a book."

She thought, "I don't know this Myra chick, and I don't have a clue who wrote this book, but what the heck. If it's free, I will take it." Lisa put her address in the comments, and lo and behold, three days later the book was in her mailbox. Lisa worked hard in spite of the alcohol consumption. She drank after her day was finished, and she kept a job most of the time. She used weekends to party and rested on Sunday. Her mom nagged her about church, especially on Easter and Christmas, but she knew too much. She wasn't interested. Yes, she loved God she supposed, and yes, she cried when she remembered her grandmother's late-night prayers that could be heard outside the raised bedroom window. Lisa knew plenty about the word, and she knew that her granny had warred on her behalf and petitioned for her soul.

Lisa poured it out in a message that night, and then she hit send, and boom, just like that . . . it was in my inbox. When I got up to go to the bathroom, I saw it. It was an epistle, the life of Lisa. A story of a church kid who became a bitter, angry, self-loathing girl when she should have been playing with Barbie dolls. The shame owned her. The choices now defined her. She had children, but social services took them away a decade ago; they were grown now. She had gone through a husband or two, but now she lived with a man who wasn't good to her. She was scared of him and told me so. Poverty was her norm, the guilt attached to losing her kids was more than the alcohol could erase, and the self-imposed scenes of immorality constantly flashed through her mind, daily, in living color. The most vivid and painful? Her brother. He was ten years older, and he was the first. She was eight, he was eighteen. It continued until she was about twelve. He found a girlfriend, and it stopped. She never told. The shame served as a gag, and the pain served as a chain. Her young soul was a prisoner to the images and memories of the touch of her brother. Her dad died without knowing; her mom now had Alzheimer's and she would never tell her. She knew her heart couldn't take it and her mind wouldn't absorb it anyway.

Lisa's letter was heavy. I could hardly sleep these days. The Lisas, Bettys, and the rest of the class of "Stronger 2015" owned me; their pain consumed me, my prayer life changed, and my car became a prayer closet on wheels. I would drive and pray, sometimes pretending to be tasking and living a normal suburban life. But it was a joke. I would never live the life of the innocent again. The box had been opened and Kathy was the one who untied the big pink bow. The dirty little secrets of the church were out.

The bitter souls of a multitude of women had been accidentally gored. A book that was no more than my simplistic journey to find truth was like a sword to the soul of the Lisas and Bettys. The sword cut deep and began to do the first work of removing the toxins. She had allowed the sword of truth to motivate her to start typing; the first step to freedom is to admit that it happened. The memories and stories must be spoken to someone. The truth must be validated for the victim to start down the road that leads to hope. I don't claim to be a psychologist, but I know what I know. And, yes, I know PLENTY of psychologists. They will confirm this theory.

And to complicate Lisa's story even more, the brother committed suicide the year she turned eighteen. He was twenty-eight. The fate of her secret was NOW solidified. She could NEVER tell. After all, he was now dead. And dead people can't be evil, can they? Maybe it was her fault. Maybe she was equally to blame? She wondered.

There were SO MANY Bettys, so many Lisas, and so many that were hybrids of these two. One young woman wrote me and told me that her father was a pastor who had molested her for many years when she was a child, and her mother knew. She told her mother when it first started. She said her mom told her to never tell anyone or she would be forced to take his side and her fate would be a foster home. Kari's dad pastored a church in a well-known Pentecostal organization.

Kari left home after high school, told no one the dirty truth about her dad, and like so many others she married and buried it. Well, for a while. But there was a distinct difference in Kari and Betty. She married for love and she eventually told her husband. She learned to talk about it, process it.

Kari's dad was still alive and they were still pastoring. It wasn't easy. When she married, she moved a comfortable fifty-plus miles away from the town her parents lived in. She was remarkably normal. She had been honest with both of them, begged them to stop living a lie, but to no avail. Her mom was a slave to the opinion

34

of her dad and clearly wasn't the kind of mom that a girl needs. She turned her head to the molestation of her child, repeatedly. That's not only shameful—it's criminal.

Her sad story resonated with me to my very core. Like any good "Gladys Kravitz" type would do, I stalked her Facebook. She had the cutest little family for her profile picture. She had an incredibly handsome husband, two young daughters who were as pretty as their momma, and she possessed a smile that would light up a room. She looked like the perfect "mommy" with her daughters in matching hair bows and dresses. She hid the pain very well.

Soon after this letter came, I was asked to speak at an event in the town Kari lived in. She came. She came to the product table afterward and stood in line to take a picture. I hugged her. She said, "Do you know who I am?" I told her she looked very familiar. She reminded me of our messages back and forth, and she said, "I'm the girl who was molested by her father." I was thinking, "Girl, you're one of hundreds who have written to me." But we hugged and I recalled her complete story. God has blessed me with a memory for small details. I asked her how she was doing. Tears filled her eyes and she said, "I would give anything to have a family that loves me. My parents are still pastoring. I haven't had a conversation with them in many years. They're not a part of our lives and no one in their world seems to notice or question why. They paint me as the villain to all of their church people. How does a mom do that to her child? Now that I'm a mom, my feelings for her are more severe. I don't understand the level of betrayal that my mother chose."

I cried with her. The people in line waited. I remember thinking, "Okay, Kathy. You're no longer sitting behind a computer typing your paragraphs of opinion, your epistles of truths, your spin on encouragement. This is a real person standing in front of you, in the flesh."

My years in ministry, back in the day, were consumed with business, management kinds of things, decision making, sending the family army out to the stage to sing, pray, worship, and present this message of hope. But me? I was a backstage girl. Don't be handing me no microphone. I knew my strengths and I knew my weaknesses. I sometimes say that I was born to boss people and herd cats, cause it's sort of the same. And the last seven years of my life? I had been a realtor in Nashville. I had walked away from ministry completely so that I could avoid my offenders. So I was unsure of how this should go. I was a bit rusty and unsure of how the "recently freed" Kathy was going to respond.

So now Kari is standing in front of me with a story that would blow the minds of this audience if they knew. They had just listened to my story and wept. Holy macanoli! If they had heard her story, they wouldn't be able to breathe.

The eyes told it all. Now, what would I do? God help me. I don't know how to "throw down" and pray the fire down from Heaven on the spot. And what happened next surprised me as much as anything I had EVER done.

I looked at her and spoke with a newfound authority. I said, "Kari, I don't know how you're going to get through this, but I know you will. I don't know how you forgive someone who refuses to acknowledge their choice to violate you, their choice to confuse your feelings toward men, all men. I don't know how you can forgive someone who abused their position of authority toward you when you were an innocent child. He muddied your ability to trust all of humanity and made it next to impossible to imagine how God could be good. Kari, you've struggled to grasp the concept of a "Good-Good Father" and it's no wonder! But tonight, I want you to LOOK at me and listen to me. You deserve to be free. I will pray for you and request others to pray. I want to explain to you that you have a license to divorce them. It's on them, not you. You're not obligated to live in this. Forgive them and then cut them loose."

She looked at me and said, "They're my blood." I couldn't believe it, but I said, "So what?" She said, "How do I do that?" I said, "You ask God to help you, but you do it. And you need to consider calling the authorities. He's a criminal. She's an accessory. If they decide to make this right with God, you will be their first phone call after they repent. Until the phone rings and there's an apology and they validate your truth, you're all done here."

Lord help, I was bold. Was I right? Oh my word, I was speaking some STRONG opinions.

Kari seemed to get it, though. I told her, "Tonight I'm giving you permission to give them the gift of goodbye." She shook her head and said, "You know, if I don't I'm going to lose my mind. The fact that they pretend to be super spiritual ministers is like someone is erasing my existence, my life, my pain, and my story. Their hypocrisy is killing me, literally." I got it. Completely.

She left. I finished out my night. Today, she is still pushing through it, one day at a time. No apology, no admission of guilt from the sperm donor and uterus. I can't bring myself to call them parents. She said to me recently, "It's like they're dead. If they died, it changes nothing. My kids don't know them; I don't remember what it was like to sit at a dinner table with them."

God help the Karis, the Bettys, and the Lisas of the world.

You want the sad truth? As I try to wind down this chapter, as I gaze at this beautiful sky with an interruption of a palm tree here and there, as I marvel at the beauty and majesty of a perfect God, who sees it all and can compare the heart to the deeds, my mind is struck by the severity of fallen man and woman, of sin, of the selfishness of humanity. A man who studies all day long for a sermon yet molests his darling daughter. That's about as fallen as fallen gets.

I try to wrap my brain around this level of betrayal that so many of you have suffered. In the opinion of this old Tennessee woman, we're talking reprobate. I'm not the judge, and it's a very good thing that I'm not.

The letters kept coming. Not every broken heart was from sexual abuse. Many of these gals had been abandoned by their husbands. One in particular was Opal. Now remember folks, these are church people for the most part. Opal read my book in March of 2015, as soon as it came out. A week or so after she read it, I got a very sad message from her that went something like this. The names are always changed to protect the innocent.

Kathy,
I don't normally send messages to people on Facebook. But last night my world completely fell apart. I can hardly breathe. All I can do is cry.

My husband of forty-nine years told me that he needed to come home early because he had something he wanted to talk to me about. In three months we will be married fifty years. We've pastored for forty-eight of those years. We've been at this church over thirty years. Our kids are grown and many of our grandkids are grown too. We have four children and nine grandchildren. Most of the kids and their families attend the church that he pastors.

I would tell anyone that asked me that we've been blessed and highly favored. But as of last night, that all seemed to change. He walked in and said, "I don't love you anymore. I am in love with Susan. She makes me feel alive again. She makes me feel good about myself."

Susan has been the pianist at church for more than twenty years. Her husband died a few years ago. My husband seemed to fall into a trap of sympathy that turned into lust. Susan is fifty. My husband is seventy-one. I found a Viagra prescription a few months ago and asked him about it. He became angry.

So after all these years of serving Jesus together, nearly fifty to be exact, he lost the battle. A woman in a tight dress and a bottle of Viagra took my husband, took the leader of our family, and come Sunday it will devastate an entire congregation. He plans to announce it to the church.

He says it's worth it. He's stepping down. But tonight, as I sit here in the dark after a day of trying to console my daughters and calm my sons, I remembered your book and your story. I had this sudden urge to tell you about my heartbreak. I can't remember my life before him. But he's gone. I'm not sure where I'm going, how I'm going to get THROUGH this. I honestly don't think I will make it. But for tonight I'm playing tough for my kids and grandkids. They're devastated.

So Kathy Crabb Hannah, all I'm asking you for is prayer. Somehow I felt led to ask.

And thank you for writing the book. It means more to me today than it did three days ago.

Love you,
Opal

I was sobbing. God bless the abandoned. God be near those who are used and then dropped into the nearest garbage can.

Holy cow. I wanted to get my hands on this man. I wanted to throat-punch him and possibly shove those Viagras down his throat and see if it's possible to overdose on them. My mind delighted for a few minutes as I thought about what THAT emergency room visit would be like! I knew that Sister Tight Dress wouldn't even want that old man once he no longer possessed the position as pastor over those two hundred unsuspecting people. Most likely she was a preacher-chaser and he was a weakling who had forgotten why he started on this journey called ministry. The sad truth is this: this isn't an isolated story. I have received several letters that are similar. The names, years married, and details vary, but there's a common theme. Selfishness. I've got a newsflash for all you married people. When you got married, you didn't sign up to be stimulated. You signed up to be faithful! You won't always have days that are full of romance. Passion comes and goes, and Viagra and a cheap night is no substitute for a godly woman who has prayed for your sorry butt for decades.

And, yes, there are a few pastors' wives and associate pastors' wives who have pulled the same shenanigans. Women in general are extremely capable of the selfish approach to life. It's not rare by any stretch. Men write me too, folks. Actually, they are brutally honest when they stop and take the time to write.

The letters kept coming. I ate cake and read letters. Several women wrote me that they had recently lost a child. SO many were in their teens. I couldn't deal with it. I would say, "God, what's the deal? How do YOU expect these women to get out of bed in the morning?"

I had daily sessions of straight talk with Him. The abandoned, the broken, the grieving, the sick—I had a nice garden variety of women in struggle.

Many had aborted their own children. Others had an addicted son or daughter who was in jail or rehab or on the street prowling for drugs. The number of these women who were raising their grandchildren was startling. Many had enabled their children (the user) and now they felt like it was their fault. So they continued in passivity and lived lives sprinkled with poverty, despair, and a grandchild or two to live for. They worked at Walmart and waited tables. They lived in cheap rentals and drove junk cars. But somehow they were hanging on to hope, somehow. My story made them hopeful for better days, and they told me so.

By sometime in March, I was overwhelmed. I'm a fixer, a control freak of sorts. I needed to fix these girls, or at least I thought I needed to offer them some hope. Clearly, they were sprinkled all over the map. This wasn't an easy fix. I pondered: How can I do more? Write another book? Do videos? Most of them needed to have the roots pulled, so to speak. The bitter roots had poisoned and infected their souls. Their souls were very sick. Many told me of suicidal plans, thoughts, and occasionally an attempt.

Lord, what had I done? I didn't sign up for this, or did I?

Once again, around 2:00 a.m. the Lord woke me. I went to the living room and started reading. I like to read stories about problem solving. I constantly ask God to help me be a part of a solution and help me to not be THE problem. I was simply saying, God, how do we do this? These girls are in trouble. And, yes, I'm referring to old women as girls, I suppose, but pamper me. It makes me feel good to be called a girl, so I suppose it's a habit.

I was having a conversation with myself and God was eavesdropping, I suppose. I was trying to think of an affordable way to get these girls in one place so some REAL ministry could happen. One-on-one, up-in-it kind of ministry where we're going for the root and God's changing fruit. They would need to stay a couple of nights. The travel would be a long distance for many. Could they do it? Would they do it? How serious were they about being stronger? Were they ready to put on their gloves and fight for their sanity, their home, their children and their grandchildren? Were they tired of the path of a victim? We would soon see.

The scene was unfolding in my living room on that March morning. It was approaching 3:00 a.m. I hadn't slept much at all. The girls were on my mind. As always, the evening's haul had included letters from various girls who were facing everything from addiction to eviction. Time was of the essence, and I knew it. The Lord often invited me to work at night because there were no calls, group texts, or interruptions. We could hash through ideas together.

I had cabin rentals pulled up on my iPad, a different resort pulled up on my computer, and on my phone yet another resort. And then the light bulb went off in my head. We needed STRONG girls to mentor the weak. Well, actually, I think it was the second light bulb; the first light-bulb moment was about ten minutes earlier when I finally realized that CABINS and community-type lodging could be my answer. We could bring these girls together . . . from Texas to Michigan, from Florida to North Carolina, from Arkansas to Virginia: they could drive to the Smokies, make it a bit enticing with the mountain view, great pancakes, and a "slumber party" atmosphere, infused with some hard-hitting word. I wasn't sure who would do the ministering at this point; I just knew that God knew. I felt the hair stand up on my arms. God was working out the details at that very moment. These were the moments I lived for. I felt like I was half travel agent, and half evangelist as I was calling these cabin rental offices at 3:00 a.m. Ha!

As Steve slept and rested up for his work day, I worked all night. Typical. The many years on a bus with my kids certainly turned me into a third-shift worker. I learned to work after they slept as that bus floated down an interstate and I could actually have enough quiet time to think. So here I was, on hold with a reservationist at 3:00 a.m. trying to envision a hundred cars pointed toward Tennessee, with their bags packed, and their boxes of pain tucked in a shiny box beside them in the passenger's seat. They could haul that box to East Tennessee and leave it at a makeshift altar at one of these cabins that I was currently trying to rent. IF THAT girl would just take me off hold! Doesn't she know this is BIG KINGDOM business and she needs to get on the line and help me? I wish she knew that it's not a cheerleading squad needing all of these cabins or a bunch of gossiping women at the Nashville Bridge Club. It's the broken girls' club, and they NEED a place to see their miracles come to pass!

PICK UP THE PHONE PLEASE!

She finally answered and I asked, "The two large cabins at the top, do they have a full view of Mount Le Conte?" She said, "Yes." I followed up with, "Can you give me a discount if I rent enough cabins to sleep one hundred women?" She answered, "I can give you 10 percent, that's all." I said, "You have half-off specials all the time. This is on a Monday and Tuesday, not a weekend. Why can't I get a better deal?" She replied, "Those specials are always last-minute cabins that are still vacant. The discounts are never on advance sales or multiple-cabin events." Well, I need an in-advance booking. I'm having a retreat! Fine, let's do it." So just like that, I rented the cabins and spent more money than I would spend in a decade on clothes. I mean, I'm the woman who still has twenty-year-old gowns. I buy my underwear at Walmart, not Victoria's Secret. But on this night the $10,000 seemed like seed money. It felt like an investment in the girls with stories. I was in. I don't let money rule me or let PEOPLE with money rule me.

So, Lord have mercy, I was going to have a retreat! I liked the ring of that.

I looked it up. *Merriam-Webster* said this: "Retreat: a place of privacy or safety, a refuge."

Oh Jesus, let us create a refuge!

So in the wee hours of the morning on this March day, 2015, Jesus and I were plotting. We had defined the event. It would be a safe space, it would feel private, and it would be a refuge for the exhausted, disgusted, busted, and those that NO one trusted . . . to EVER get it right.

The Lord said, "Build it and they will come." I said, "God, that's a movie. I guess you didn't see it, but that's a movie about baseball. Pretty good movie, best I remember."

I wrote it down. "Build It And They Will Come." And then God said: "The THEY will include your Edie."

Edie, my redheaded grandchild who was a hot mess.

"Whaaaaattt did you say?"

For, you see, Edie wasn't in a good place. I knew what I knew, and it was too much. But NOW the God who had never lied to me, the God who had NEVER enticed me out on a limb and left me there while a man with a chainsaw cut the limb off, the God who knows EVERYTHING, THAT God just told me that MY reward for my all-night planning sessions and the hundreds of hours spent responding to the broken would be Edie. She was coming. She was going to lay it down. I could have done what we call the "helicopter" about then. You Pentecostals know what a helicopter shout is. The rest of you, just keep reading. Ha!

But I literally broke when it sank in. Tears began to fall. My Edie. Now there was a soft spot. Edie: the redhead who had tried to figure out "who" she was and "whose" she was since she was a toddler. That first grandchild who was more like my shadow when she was a toddler. If I went, she went. Occasionally the mood would strike around the house, and by day's end, she would be the inspiration for songs like "Two Little Feet." I can't describe my emotion as I type this. My underlying question is always, "How can people do that?"

She was his light, until she wasn't. Until the "script" changed.

By Edie's eleventh birthday she had been abandoned, not once, but twice. Every girl wants to think they matter to the man who promised to love her and protect her. Dads, grandfathers, and uncles play the major role in forming our daughters' self-esteem and self-worth. Don't I know that firsthand. If you had told me on Edie's fourth birthday that the little redheaded girl with curls and massive blue eyes would have her self-worth obliterated before she was a teenager, I wouldn't have believed it. She had it all, it appeared.

If Edie hadn't had amazing uncles to show her that love could last, and a new stepdad who had signed up for better or for worse, she would probably be a man hater. I know there is a battle in every girl that's been damaged by abuse and abandonment. I am one of those girls. My dad didn't choose it, but the result is still there. He left me. I suffered. And now the generational curse of daughters without fathers had made it on down the branches of my family tree.

When a parent or grandparent makes a conscious choice to walk away, never see a child again, never tell them goodbye, never call, never text, just complete CRUEL abandonment, it's too much. And frankly, I've seen far too much of this coldhearted cruelty in my life. I've seen too many children feel worthless, all at the hands of a parent or grandparent. Intentional absence is crueler than death. And for Edie, it was more than her foundation could handle. It's difficult for adults to handle this type of cruelty, but a child? She cracked. She says it was like a death. She cried, she changed. Overnight she seemed to fall into a dark place. Didn't we all. But she was a CHILD! There were so many nights I could feel the spirit of suicide on her. We were all struggling. We were all hurt. But an eleven-year-old? She didn't understand that God and the offender weren't one and the same. How could she?

So now I had the responsibility resting squarely on my shoulders. I had insisted on blending and loving, putting this entire family in a "love" box. I shook it up and then poured it out, hoping that the love breading would cover them all alike. Think Shake 'n Bake chicken. HA!

Edie had loved with everything her little heart possessed. She would cry and say, "What's wrong with me?" I was keenly aware that NOTHING was wrong with her ability to love. It wasn't her, but words don't mend hearts—actions do.

I felt SO guilty when her heart was crushed. I felt that somehow my choices had impacted her all these years later. I brought the kids into this situation of pain by saying "I do" oh so many years ago. Oh Jesus!

There. I said it. I owned the guilt and she owned the pain. I would look at her and wish for a "do over" at times, an opportunity to rethink my decision based on a look down through time, and attempt to protect her heart from selfish adults who would choose to hurt her. But we all know, that ain't how this life thing works.

There was no re-do available. So on this day, my redhead had survived to be a twenty-one-year-old with a lot of scars, a strong will, several tattoos, and a new husband twenty years her senior named Doug. We weren't thrilled. I thought she was trying to fill the gaping hole in her soul that was left by others.

I had prayed more prayers for her than all of the other kids combined. She had totaled multiple cars; she ran a car into a pond in the middle of the night on a country road no less. So my Edie ritual went something like this. I prayed, I sowed, sometimes I yelled, but I always loved.

I would pray, "God, I'm going to do for others, sacrificially. Now, please send someone to Edie. MY seed is for her." I wrote it down in books, I wrote it on checks, I wrote it on prayer cards, I made it plain. No vague prayers from this granny. I called it what it was. It had been a rough few years with her. She seemed to be on a mission that often looked like self-destruction, but we persisted. We prayed. I was straight with her, always. I wasn't interested in being popular; I was interested in her hearing truth. I knew our relationship was made of steel and love, and I knew it could weather some truth. I was right: it has.

I often say that I never found satisfaction in being the BFF parent or granny. I want to be the person who CARES enough to speak the hard things. The world is more than willing to be the pandering "yes man" and truthfully, there are plenty of relatives, including parents, who will ALWAYS jump in on the popularity train. They will buy their kids alcohol, cigarettes, and birth control pills. They are more interested in their being popular than their being saved. And later, when they're married, that same momma who stood by and said nothing while her seventeen-year-old cheerleader had sex with a dozen guys before graduation is now the convenient alibi for her thirty-five-year-old who cheats on her husband nearly every weekend. Girls, listen up. That ain't love! If this is you, I need you to listen. God didn't call you to be an enabler. He didn't give you a child to be the boss around your home either. Children shouldn't run the home, the parents should. Who is the boss around your place? If you have this confused, I beg you. Stop. Reconsider. If you're more worried about your child's invitations to social events than you are about their commitment to virginity, you're the problem. Repent.

Rant over. Back to retreats and redheads.

So on this night, or early morning, whichever you consider 4:00 a.m. to be, God included her in my promise. I was almost scared to believe it. Could I get my hopes up and then possibly be crushed? Was that really God who spoke it or was it me hoping it? I knew that God didn't lie. And in my heart I knew it was His voice. Okay, I was going to claim it. It was a promise. My "build it and they will come" promise now had a PERSONAL clear-cut purpose. Edie needed a turnaround. It was coming.

So in the wee hours of the morning I rattled off my American Express number to a girl named Jessica and paid for enough cabins for a hundred women. Alrighty then. I couldn't WAIT to explain THIS to Steve. That should be fun. He would awake owing $10,000 more than he did when he went to bed. Nice. There are times when my choices lie squarely between spiritual and stupid. Truly, I wasn't 100 percent sure which way this decision was leaning.

But I quickly talked myself off the ledge and told myself that it was JUST money. I'm sure I quoted the "He owns the cattle on a thousand hills" scripture to myself, and probably the "You trust Him or you don't woman" slogan that I speak to myself about three hundred times a day.

I really believed that He was going to MAKE A WAY for these broken girls to get there, and I truly believed that it would be a game changer for them. So we were all set. May 11, the day after Mother's Day was the appointed time, a mountain in Gatlinburg, Tennessee, was the appointed place. Now to see who were the "appointed" girls. Hmmm . . . a Facebook post was a good idea about now.

I posted something like this: Who would be interested in a mountain retreat in mountain cabins, with our special guest Jesus, and lots of friends and family. We will eat cake and do a lot of singing. If interested comment below.

And finally, I went to bed.

When I awoke, about 9:00 a.m. or so, I had hundreds of responses to the cabin trip/retreat idea. I knew I needed to think it through. I had to base the price on the room type, and I had to think of a name for said retreat.

After writing down three or four ideas, I liked "Miracle on the Mountain." The name said it all. And, Lord have mercy, these women needed miracles. So I posted it, explained how you could sign up, and waited. It sold out the first day. We expanded it to 125 women, and it sold out again. We were rolling.

A few days later I decided that I needed to go there and survey these cabins. I wasn't sure why, I just felt compelled. My youngest daughter Terah offered to go with me. I knew this plan was a plan that involved my girls, all of them. I remembered Terah telling me of a vision that she had back in 2008. The vision was clear to her. There was a stage, a congregation, and she was singing and exhorting. She sang every week. Stages were common, audiences were the norm, but this "vision" audience was completely different: it was all women. Terah shared that vision in great detail back in 2008 when it happened, so on this April day, as we rode to the mountains, we talked about promises, visions, and timing. The fullness of the vision had come.

When the vision happened in 2008, there was much disarray. Everyone was looking for a footing, the Crabb Family had retired, and Terah had formed a group with her brother Adam but had decided to go home after a year or so of travel. There was much change, many moving parts in our lives. And to be honest, I had almost forgotten about her vision. But she and God reminded me. When the confirmation has been marinating for five or ten or twenty years, it's good and strong. This was a strong confirmation. It made it extremely easy to walk in the dark, because I knew what I knew.

As we rode and talked about God's timing, we realized that the vision was exactly seven years earlier. He had shown her the plan but had required her to walk the long route to get there. We had ALL taken the long road it seemed. But on that day she refreshed me on the vision, and I marveled at God and how He is so inclined to make things happen on the seventh day, the seventh week, the seventh year, or sometimes the seventh time we march around a wall. I felt like we had marched around this wall and I DELIGHTED in the NUMBER seven, as always.

We arrived in the mountains and drove up to Gatlinburg Falls. They gave us a map of the properties we would be using. We drove up that unfamiliar mountain, slowly and in a bit of awe. That view, though. Holy cow, that view. By the time we got to the top to the BIG cabins that would be our anchor cabins, we had a FULL-on view of

Mount Le Conte. I was unsure as to where we would have services. We now had 125 people and there wasn't a living room that would adequately seat that many people. I was interested in a community-type building a few miles away. That seemed to be the best we could hope for. Not my first choice, but the expansion had ruined my plan. Reason number one that bigger isn't always better. Bigger is more difficult to manage. Options become limited. But in this case, the number represented a woman, a struggle, and I was a numbers girl. I knew the higher the number, the greater the return. So the community building would be my next stop.

We parked behind the big cabins. The parking lot was BIG. We got out and there it was: Mount Le Conte. The best view I had ever seen of it, right in our face. Terah said, "Let's have our night services here. Outside. Like the old days. Let's look at that mountain while we're praising."

I agreed, what an amazing idea. It was coming together, starting to be a reality in my mind's eye. We got out of the car, positioned the imaginary altar, rows of chairs, and imagined the music ringing through the mountains. I remember thinking, "God, you told me to build it, so here we are, building it."

I called the management office and said, "Can we have our services outside? Is there a noise ordinance?" Their answer, "No problem. Try and be finished by ten o'clock if possible. That's when quiet hours start, but people break them all the time."

We left that mountain full of hope about what was going to happen there. Oh my, we had no idea.

The idea came to us that we should offer makeovers. You know, take a tired middle-aged woman and treat her to a full-blown makeup artist kind of makeover. Make her feel like a queen. The girls loved the idea. They wanted it. Edie had a job managing a Sephora store and she was a great makeup artist. I was wondering how God was going to get her there. She had done several photo shoots, including the shoot for my book. However, I didn't expect her to be interested in doing this. I thought she would be opposed to that much time with us, trapped with the "church" and passionate preaching that was sure to be there. She was a runner, typically. And I thought she would run from the invitation, but surprisingly, she didn't.

I threw it out there and she bit. Before it was over, 90 percent of the attendees had signed up for a full-face "Nashville Style" makeover from Edie and her crew. She was coming and bringing other makeup artists with her. So the Lord was working and moving things around. He had a little plan in place with Edie's name on it!

The day arrived. We went to the mountains a day early to prepare. I was excited. They had driven from about every state that serves grits, plus there was a Canadian girl or two. Some had fought devils to be on that mountain. They had stopped and fixed radiators, dead batteries, and flat tires. One or two actually came on a Greyhound, and a few chose to fly. They packed church clothes and red heels, yoga pants and sneakers—they came prepared for everything it seemed. Some packed anointing oil and snacks, and, yes, they all packed their troubles. Jesus help, they had their bags bursting at the seams with trouble. JESUS be a fence.

Kim Bowling, Kelly's sister-in-law, was preparing food and Annette, an old friend, agreed to help me with check-ins, etc. After all, this was a small event compared to the old Crabbfest days that I had managed. We had five thousand people a night at Crabbfest, so this should be a walk in the park. Check-in was supposed to be at 4:00 p.m. for all attendees. At about 3:30 they started rolling in. I am ashamed to admit I didn't know half of them when they arrived in person. I had never met many of these girls. My only reference was their Facebook profile picture. And if we will all be honest here, that is a bit deceiving at times. So in they came, and it felt a bit chaotic, crowded, but oh so purposeful. Finally, I began to recognize a few familiar faces from the Crabb Family days. My support was kicking in. A few jumped in to help Kim in the kitchen; others started to sort out the rooming assignment charts and helping the older ladies with their bags. It was organized chaos, but I loved every minute of it. I lived in organized chaos, so I was right at home.

I had placed these girls in rooms and cabins together, using a combination of common sense, the occasional nudge of God, and a small attempt at a first-come, first-serve policy. And of course, they got what they paid for. A twin bunk versus a king suite was a consumer choice. They chose and I placed based on their choice. Occasionally I knew that this sister and that sister would get along well, but for the most part I relied on my "gut" to guide me. You know when Christians say they have a "gut" feeling? That's REALLY code for "I'm trying to walk as the Spirit guides me." It is the preferred choice occasionally so that we don't sound like a Sister Super Spiritual.

I remember a few distinct things about that first hour of this FIRST event. We had a set of bunks that were on the floorplan, but they had been removed. We had one no-show, so I was only short one bed. I kept trying to figure this out and finally realized the beds in the cabin next door were gone! I had sold two beds that did not exist. Whoops. It wasn't my fault, but it was still MY problem. And it was poor Laura's problem too.

Everyone was placed, everyone but Laura, the bedless girl. I kept saying, "I'm going to get you something worked out soon." Always the positive fixer. And I was going to fix it. I was just trying to let the dust settle and figure out the BEST fix. And of course every time I proclaimed, "You're next," I would get distracted and forget. She sat patiently. She said nothing. This happened over and over. She patiently waited. Finally, everyone was headed to their appointed rooms and we were readying the dinner meal to be served, and I spotted her again. There sat Laura. Holy smokes! I felt like such a loser! JESUS! How could I have forgotten this sweet girl. She was sitting in the floor near her bags, still waiting. At that moment, I wasn't so sure I was in my gifting. I looked at Laura and said, "I may have to put you on a sofa, but I will make it up to you." She said, "I'm happy to sleep on the floor. I don't care where I sleep, I just want to be here, in the presence of God. I've driven by myself, from Arkansas; it's not a bed I came for."

I felt the Holy Ghost when this meek girl opened her mouth. Her words were clearly a taste of the meek and gentle spirit that we would know for the next two days.

We assigned her a sectional sofa in the basement of a cabin, and she, like the others, went to prepare for dinner. Kim had prepared an amazing lasagna recipe for us, along with salad, bread, and of course cake for dessert, and we were set. We used every chair on the property of the anchor cabin, but it went well. The girls were bonding and laughter was ringing through those mountains.

I remember looking at them, gathered on porches, rocking in rockers, and I realized that some of these girls hadn't had a break, or a breakthrough in years. The struggles that were clearly represented in that small group of 125 women could be felt. It's as if God said, "See through their eyes, not yours."

Michael Hahn, a family friend, had agreed to set a makeshift sound system up for the service. My friend Kim White was already there videoing anything and everything, using drones and hand-held cameras. That mountain was buzzing with activity. It was a happy moment. The atmosphere was a bit like a party or family reunion. I announced that we would not deal with complainers, that complaining women would be pushed off the mountain. They laughed. A part of me meant it. We were all doing the best we could. I knew that grouchy spirits would hinder God, and I knew that women are terribly prone to gravitate toward jealousy. Sister Kelly talked to her and didn't speak to me. Terah didn't remember my name. Amanda didn't eat the cookies I brought her. No way, no how was I going to work MY butt off, invest money I didn't have, answer thousands of messages, and then let the devil's little minions show up and disrupt this "holy ground" mountain that we had claimed!

I felt a bit like Caleb. I wanted my mountain. It was mine. And like Caleb, I'm not exactly known to be a pushover. On this night, the spiritual mirrored the spiritual. For I too had finally declared that I WANTED my mountain. I had told God that I would give everything I had inside me if HE would use me and forgive me for walking away from the calling of "people" in an attempt to keep the pain in my OWN life to a minimum. The reminders of the hypocrisy that had jaded me were everywhere I looked, so I stopped looking. I retired the Crabb Family and got a real estate license. If you haven't read *Stronger*, the entire story is there. But I had walked it out, always. I had LOVED Him with everything in me. And I wasn't mad at God. I was mad at men.

I protected my heart the only way I knew how to protect it. I ran away from the images and audio reminders of pretenders. I also made a list of those who didn't seem to care about TRUTH, and I cut them out of my life. Period. I had to. I was commonly lectured on forgiveness and I would quote John Hagee and say, "Granting forgiveness without demanding a change in conduct makes the grace of God an accomplice to evil."

I had no problem with forgiveness, but I had a HUGE problem with people who had NO moral compass and yet remained in ministry.

But then . . . I wrote *Stronger*. I puked out the vile poison that had infected my soul. I realized that THESE hypocrites and their games didn't change a thing about my one-on-one walk in my OWN calling. I realized that the trash talk that was so easily hurled at me and made me feel unspiritual and unworthy wasn't true, and I embraced the journey that the Lord was taking me on. This mountain was a part of the journey.

I went to the mountain and wrote *Stronger* and that recalibrated my life goals. I came home different. The devil, through people, brought me a one-two punch, and I went down. My instincts to protect myself, to stay away and nurse my wounds are reasonable; they're not without merit, but they were wrong. The postdivorce "seven-year hiatus" was over. I would no longer be silent.

All those years ago, when I was handed the nasty news that was meant to bring destruction, I should have stomped a red high heel and said, "I won't give up the calling that God has placed on MY life, not today or any day . . . DEVIL. NEWSFLASH. MY promise was to GOD, not you. There may not be a touring Crabb Family, but ministry WILL go forth. I will dream dreams and ask God to help me walk them out. I will work for REWARDS and not AWARDS. I am not here on the merit of you or anyone else. GOD put me here and I TOO worked for every single ministry goal that this family has attained. And yes, the goal for me was ALWAYS people, souls. NO ONE else HIRED me, and no one else can fire me. My name is on the dotted line, and the buck stops here. I will support my kids in every ministry they pursue for the rest of my life. Period. I will not pretend anymore. The family calling did include me. No matter how hard you try to snuff me out, you can't. I have TRUTH and GOD on my side. That's a war you may want to avoid. And YOU, sir, will not diminish my existence. I've done what's right and MY God WILL defend me. You can fool many people, but you will NEVER fool God."

But instead, I cried like a little girl and hid for a year. I allowed the degradation to take root in my heart. The ugly insults that were hurled at me, coupled with the street "smack" that was being whispered—it was simply too much. I cried all night and hid all day. So this aggressive "get 'er done" business woman became a closet recluse. Nevertheless, God knew the truth. He had my back. And somehow, with HIS help, I persisted.

And now it's 2015, nearly a decade later, and I had the pep back in my step. I wasn't sure how I would survive financially, but I knew I would. I hadn't shown or sold a house in six months. MY $200,000-a-year salary was now less than 25 percent of that. I had my book sales and the royalties from all of the Crabb Family songs I had promoted oh so many years ago. But that wasn't a fraction of what I was accustomed to. But it didn't matter. Now I had my mountain.

MY purpose was not only intact; it was in overdrive. I was chasing Jesus, purpose, and a bunch of straggling women . . . all over this mountain. As I say, I'm a bit of a cat herder.

So tonight, on this mountain, the "whispers of the devil" were NOT going to steal five minutes of this mountain joy. Granny Kathy wasn't having no mess up in here. She was protecting her mountain from the first moment until the last. It was her job. She wouldn't sit in the back of the room and wear the "you're not spiritual" badge anymore. She no longer felt like she was facilitating someone else's GOD-called journey; this time, He called HER She was flying solo, sort of.

So I read the riot act and then told them I loved them.

They complied. The beds were hard, but they didn't complain. The A/C went out in a cabin, but they didn't complain. Maybe I scared the holy crud out of them. But I think it was a bit more than that. The truth was this. The die was cast. We were truly ALL in this together. My season of living with the "I don't give a rip if I make people happy or not" may have found a home. I knew my job wasn't to make them happy. It was to lead them to truth.

Here we go.

We opened that first service on that beautiful May evening with perfect weather. It was more than I could have hoped for. The clear skies allowed a full view of the evening shadows. Oh my. The shadows created a dimension that I'm incapable of adequately describing. I would sound so amateurish if I tried, so I won't. The girls were starting to sing with the mountains as a backdrop. Michael had set rows of folding chairs, and it virtually turned that parking lot into an old-fashioned brush arbor. The air felt thick to me. Part of it was the majesty of the location. It's so difficult to take you there with mere words. The mountains invoked tears immediately. I was already a mess. Combine worship with that view, and it will reduce you to full surrender quickly. But it was more than that. Maybe some of these girls were nervous; they had driven long distances, and some were alone. Some had driven alone for the first time in their lives. Some reminded me of the woman with the issue of blood. They had to get to that mountain. They came for answers; they were fed up.

In my opinion, for what it's worth, so much of the breakthrough comes from the journey. How bad do you want it? Will you drive twelve hours alone and use the last of your vacation days? Will you sell your extra purses on craigslist for gas money? Will you work three extra shifts and clean your neighbor's house for the funds? Will you ride a smelly Greyhound bus for eleven hours for the opportunity to be in the presence of people who believe in miracles because you MUST have one or you're going to die?

For many of these girls, half of the battle was fought before they arrived. The travel didn't come easy, and the finances didn't either. Now, before you start judging me and saying, "So you're saying God is only in the mountains?" let me explain. God is obviously everywhere. He knows which one of us needs to find grace and who needs to extend grace. He knows our zip codes, our email addresses, even that secret one we're hiding. He knows your cell number, He knows it all, Sister Sue. God knows EVERYTHING and HE is clearly EVERYWHERE. But SOMETIMES, He wants US to come to terms with OUR own needs. And He wants us to ask Him to go with us to the darkest room in our past, He wants us to build up the nerve, close our eyes and just walk there. But in reality, He wants us to ASK Him to go WITH us. And SO often the journey is 90 percent of the solution.

We must journey.

The trip, the "GETTING there" part of the trip, was necessary for most of these girls. They rarely had alone time. They needed to drive, and think, and remember. It was coming. They had accepted the challenge when they signed up—well, most of them had. When Jesus asked the blind man what he wanted, Jesus already knew what He wanted. He was blind. He wanted to see. But Jesus "knowing" wasn't good enough. He wanted him to SAY it. So many of these women had tasted pain so that others didn't have to. They suffered in silence to keep the family intact, they mourned, they cried, they asked why? And the long drive down I-40 to this mountain, for some, was a process of talking to themselves and pouring out to God. Both are healthy.

And like the blind man, these girls needed to own it and THEN they needed to say it. They needed to journey, maybe alone, to those mountains, and they needed to look at the truth with clarity. They needed to be mentally prepared for the looming question that they had EACH signed up to answer when they said YES to this retreat. They knew it wasn't going to be an aerobics class with a motivational speaker. They knew that we weren't going to paint angel ceramics and exchange cake recipes. They knew that they had signed up for some hard-core truth.

They knew.

And now, at about 7:15 on Monday night, the eleventh day of May 2015, the girls knew the question "What do you need Me to do?" was coming. For now, they too were like the blind man. They would soon have a Jesus encounter. They sang and waited. They cried and waited some more. And then it happened. Terah started singing, "Looking for answers, you need a way out. You've been trapped in that trial, full of sorrow and doubt. You saw a trickle of sunlight, but you found no escape. Just hold on to His promises. He said that He'd make a way."

You could hear the physical release of pain as I heard these girls start to sob, wail, and a few were doing what I call an old-fashioned GLORY shout. Some were beginning to pray in a heavenly language, some were weeping, others were bent and shaking, but here's what I want you to remember about this story. EVERYONE was doing something. No one was checking their Facebook or their email. EVERY woman on the side of that mountain was feeling this thing.

I've heard old preachers say that there's no evidence that Jesus jumped, ran, or shouted. But EVERYONE that He touched did.

That story seemed to apply. I watched the video of this again last night. And it was as clear as a bell to me. The Holy Ghost fell on everyone who was there.

No two people respond to the Holy Ghost the same. These women were from different backgrounds and had varying degrees of experience with these kinds of services. Their common ground wasn't that they were all Baptists or Church of God or Assemblies of God members. The truth is some of them were Catholic, some Baptists, some United Pentecostal, and everything in between. Some were unchurched, some were straight-up backslidden for twenty years. That was oddly irrelevant.

That "thing" that brought instant unity to that beautiful group of women? No one was playing around. They came on business.

The spirit of a living, breathing God blew onto that mountain and touched every person there. These girls clearly hadn't come to be pampered and have their nails done. They weren't expecting a hike or a day spa. They were chained, broken, desperate women who were fed up with defeat. They were exhausted and so ready to have the chains cut off of their hands and feet. They had to get to Jesus.

The current status of the demons? They were trembling. They feared what would happen next.

After all, THEY were there when the shaky hand of a sixteen-year-old signed the abortion consent; they laughed as they clicked the lock on the chain. And now, as she trembled on this mountain, she wanted to be free. You could hear the chains fall.

Those same demons stood on the porch and watched the police officer knock on that red farmhouse door; they watched her scream and sob when the police officer said, "Ma'am, I'm so sorry," as he told her about the motorcycle wreck and asked her to come with them to the morgue. The demons jeered as her body collapsed into unconsciousness onto that gray porch that he had painted for her, just last week while she baked his birthday cake. The demons partied. Because they know ALL too well that she will now be dragging around the weight that's labeled "bitterness" with her for the rest of her life. They know that the chain of grief is their prize gift to this one. Click. While she lay unconscious, they locked it firmly around her ankle. But now, three years later, she's on a mountain. She's had enough.

These same demons watched as the blonde pastor's wife deleted the texts from him. No one knows about him—well, no one but her—and she supposed God knew too. She didn't talk to God about it much. She didn't talk to God about anything, she recently decided. Her sister insisted that she come to this stupid mountain, and after all, if she didn't, the churchwomen would judge. And Lord knows, that's their talent, judging. So here she stood, on the mountain with the saints. And when the worship of the sister beside her started, when she turned and laid a hand on her back and started praying in the spirit, it happened. The layers started to peel back. The truth? It wasn't harmless bathtub shots. It was sin. Pornography. Her teenage son had been grounded for a lesser crime last year.

She had often wondered in the dark of the night if it was all an elaborate story. Was the God thing even real? She hadn't felt Him in so long. For the first time in years she was convicted. As they prayed, she wept. And the demons trembled. Because they knew the chains were coming off. They knew that this pastor's home was going to be restored, and they knew that their hellish control over her mind was about to get an eviction notice. On this night, in Gatlinburg, Tennessee, on THIS mountain, with sisters surrounding her, with the Holy Ghost power all over her, she would take her life back. She would change her phone number and walk it out.

The chains came off.

The demons were standing in full attention the night her father raped her for the first time. It was the week she started middle school. The demons had a party afterwards. This one would NEVER be free, they thought! Click. A lifetime of chains for her, guaranteed.

But oh how wrong they were. For on this night, while she lay under the power of God, the chains were removed. Just like that, she received her miracle. The strong girls held up the arms of the weak girls; those that were well bound up the injured. We were a sight to behold, a newly assembled squad, an army of sisters, soldiering as if we had been trained for years. You just had to be there to understand it, I think. I felt like a lottery winner as my eyes soaked it in. What had God given me?

The mountain grew dark, and with my spiritual ears . . . I could hear the "clank" of chains. Some were falling. Kelly pleaded the case of the cross; she spoke to the demons who were erratically trying to avoid being caught between the bloodline and the cross. She rebuked them and told them they must take their hands off of God's property; she pled for the sanity and health of her sisters. We felt the release for so many. And along about 9:45 on May 11, 2015, about 125 women with mascara-streaked faces and disheveled "church" hair, stood arm in arm on a mountainside in Gatlinburg, Tennessee. They knew that this night was a beginning, an exciting genesis. They sang one last verse of "Holy Ground," hugged necks, wiped their tears, and headed to their cabins to eat cake. For most, sleep came easy.

Promises And Banana Pudding

I awoke on the second day of my "Miracle on the Mountain" retreat, and I was in a bedroom in a cabin that looked more like a Hansel and Gretel cottage than the typical Gatlinburg log cabin with that splendid mountain view. The big cabins on the hill were full and overflowing, which was a good thing, but I had to have a bed. As in typical Kathy fashion, I had ended up without a room. I had several event planners who told me that I could depend on a 5 percent no-show rate. That would mean that I would have a few extra rooms, so I waited until the day of the retreat to solidify my housing; I would take a room from a no-show. A leftover was fine with me. That's pretty much how I roll. So last minute, when I saw that we only had one bunk no-show, I rented a small cabin on the other side of the resort and we housed the "stragglers" there. I was the queen of the stragglers.

I am one of THOSE people who invite the masses and then I worry about it later.

Ask Steve if you don't believe me. I'm often guilty. I had invited my friend Marcia to "Miracle on the Mountain" and she was bringing her sister. Michael Hahn had driven from Hendersonville on the first day and I had decided I needed him to stay. We didn't have a single man to help with unloading and setting sound equipment or chairs. And like any woman who screams for a special southern belle brand of equality, I am NOT referring to manual labor when I talk about being treated equal. I want equal pay, but I have no intention of doing equal work if it's unloading chairs and setting sound in the hot sun. Ha! Maybe I should hashtag spoiled about now.

Anyway, poor Michael got dumped on with the usual "So, Michael, can you help me out? Can you stay another day?" And of course he said yes. So the stragglers crew on this night included Michael, Marcia, her sister Wylene and me. Marcia was there at my insistence. She's proficient on piano. She's also a gifted singer, an award-winning songwriter, and I wanted her to do a sing-along in the cabin on Tuesday. I felt it was exactly what the event called for—I knew the girls would love it. She agreed, so she drove from Georgia with her sis as her traveling companion, and they ended up on the "straggler" list without a bed. I love Marcia's gifts, but more than anything, I love the "I ain't skeered" personality that emerges when she prays. She will rebuke the devil and dare him to mess with her. I was sure that her sister was made from the same stuff Marcia was, and I was thrilled to host her as well. I wanted them on that mountain. I just forgot they had to have a place to sleep. My hosting skills weren't stellar that day. Ha!

So I had put the four of us in a little cabin tucked back into a grove of trees. It was about all they had available, and I felt blessed to get it. There was no view and we weren't within walking distance of the services like the other folks were. But oh well.

Michael had to stay on a sofa in the living room, and the sisters ended up in bunks on the lower level. But they didn't complain, and we made it. So on day two I woke up and realized we needed to head to the big cabins on the hill. It was time for the day to begin. As per the agenda, all of us went into town to Flapjack's and ate pancakes.

The cabinmates were starting to bond—I watched them. It was good. We ate the sticky-bun pancakes, repented for it afterwards, and then headed back to the big cabin where Marcia was going to lead the sing-along. Those girls sang the old songs of the church with unmatched intent. It's as if every single word was their battle cry. My church sings a song that has a lyric that says, "My feet on the battleground, my weapon will be my sound" and on this Tuesday morning, their weapon was their sound. For about twelve hours earlier, some of these girls had decided that the games were over. Some had called and broken off ten-year affairs. Some had flushed opioids down the toilet. Some had looked into their own eyes with forgiveness for the first time in years, and some had committed to a life that wasn't ruled by self-loathing.

These girls NOW knew what it was to be free, and they sang about it. It may have been 10:00 a.m., but they praised just like they had the night before. Marcia led and they followed.

There was enough God in that cabin on that Tuesday morning to start a revival that would change the world. These girls had slept on their change and it was still intact the next day.

They sang, "There's power, power wonder working power, in the blood, of the Lamb!" Then a bit of "Is anything too hard for God?" And a few verses of "Amazing grace, how sweet the sound, that saved a wretch like me. I once was lost, but now I'm found, was blind but now I see."

I surveyed the happy singing girls; they were holding coffee cups, wearing their event T-shirts, and didn't physically resemble the group of women that showed up on this mountain a mere eighteen hours before. My momma would have put it like this: "Their countenance has changed." Momma loved to use the word "countenance." I didn't understand the word when I was little and Mom overused it. But today, it was the only word that could begin to describe how clear it was what God had done. They had traded guilt for smiles. As they worshipped and sang, their newfound hope was shining through, for most at least.

Sometimes AFTER God moves, our circumstances are EXACTLY the same. We pray for God to change the storm, but the storm is still there. The rent is still late, your child is still in federal prison, your husband still has Stage IV liver cancer, and the storm is still ever present outside your shelter. But somehow, in the midst of a Holy Ghost visit that's got your name on it, He simply breathes new breath into your mind, body, and spirit, and He SOMEHOW changes you. This was that. Their storms were still in full force, but NOW these women could walk through them. They could muster the wind, they were preparing to be soaked, and they NOW understood that they COULD coexist with that storm.

Grace. They were getting a workshop in grace. This room of girls who had their hands raised at 10:30 a.m. had individually spoken to their personal storms, and they believed they could walk it out. Yes, they believed.

Meanwhile, Edie's makeovers were going well. The schedule was tight, but the results were oh so right. Those tired eyes NOW looked bright. Women who had clearly let themselves go for forty years, were staring at their images in mirrors, all smiles, and asking how to take a selfie. They lit up the room. Good makeup brings instant confidence.

Confidence is the greatest magnet there is. Men are attracted to confidence; actually, the entire world is attracted to confident people. So the confidence created a new attractiveness in these well-seasoned ladies. It was clear that many of them hadn't used makeup in years, if ever. It was totally out of their wheelhouse to be applying mascara and lipstick. But with Edie's gentle encouragement they learned; they wrote down color palettes. She recommended skin tone information, and they all loved Edie and displayed such gratitude for her personal touch and the true joy she brought to that makeshift makeover studio. For Edie was like her granny. Her gift was herself. She wasn't a singer, a musician, or a preacher. Small doses of Edie "love" were being distributed to these tired ladies who had age spots, thinning hair, and unruly brows. As Edie lovingly minimized the unwanted things they each possessed, they noticed her light-up-a-room personality and said to me, "You sure have a sweet girl there, Kathy." It was a good day. The struggles that had weighed heavily for the last ten years, the "Edie Chronicles" if you will, were about to be dumped on the altar and dealt with. Buckle up.

The music was anointed. As only she can sing it, fifteen-year-old Hope Bowling sang, "In one glorious moment of faith, though drowning in sorrow the redeemed can truly say, Boundlessly loving me, He brings sweet victory, in one glorious moment of faith." The praise began, and the Spirit was SO incredibly welcome, I believe they could have sung "All My Exes Live In Texas" and still had a move of God. What Kelly and these women had stirred up the night before was still going strong.

It was like a hurricane that had crossed the warm ocean waters and was growing in intensity and size as the warm waters propelled it. The waters were propelling this thing. These girls had their shouters turned to the on position and they had no intentions of finding neutral. We rejoiced together, a bit too long it seemed. It started to get dark and Amanda hadn't preached yet.

As she opened her message and we read scripture together, I knew we would be in the dark soon. Once again, I was skirting the perimeters of the area, looking for Kim and asking her what kind of video we would have in the dark. She answered and said, "A video we can't see." She had made it clear that we needed to stay on a schedule because of the dependence on natural light for her video crew. There was no plan B for lighting. And now, Amanda's preaching, we don't have a plan B, and it will be pitch dark in five minutes.

Dadgumit. The message was plowing. Amanda preached "The Lord Is a Spirit" and she proceeded to tell the ugly details of her life story. She convinced anyone who wasn't ALREADY convinced that they could do this thing. She talked about freedom in the Holy Spirit, a "what do I have to lose" kind of freedom! She talked about God using the unlikely after one realizes that it takes the LORD, WHO is a spirit, to have liberty. The walls fell. The unity was profound. Every single person was fully engaged. Loudly Amanda screamed, "You MAY have been in hell for the last twenty years, BUT tonight, on this mountain, you can FINALLY be free. Choose it." She paced back and forth; the word in her was alive, and so was little Eda, who would be born about three months later. Eda was a surprise, but her existence was prophesied to Amanda a few days before she took the pregnancy test. On a cold winter night earlier in the year, an old-time prophet of the Lord told this couple who had been blessed with three children already, with no intentions to have a fourth, that they would experience another birth. And so, on this warm Tennessee night, she was carrying our sweet Eda Beth. As she paced and brought the word, the form of this sweet child was clear. Kelly actually stopped and asked all of the girls to stop and pray for little Eda, for the devil had deposited fear in all of us about the health of this child and the health of Amanda.

Amanda kept pacing, back and forth, proclaiming her own freedom in spite of the plan the enemy had for her, in spite of the molestation, the personal temptation. She told that one day she decided enough was enough. And that night, on that mountain, in the darkness, her argument for the cross was convincing.

Kim and I decided to pull cars up near the brush-arbor area we had created for the church services. We turned the car lights on to give enough lighting to have an altar service. It was blinding in places, nonexistent in others. Obviously headlights weren't designed to spread a wide, even, soft light. It was better than nothing, I supposed, a little. I won't lie: the distraction of the lighting situation was clearly my problem, and it took me out of the service, completely. I checked out. I was frustrated. Why didn't I realize I couldn't MAKE folks stay on a schedule when they were leaving the premises of the cabins and going into Pigeon Forge for that country skillet buffet. I HATE BUFFETS!

We were late starting church because someone refused to leave the restaurant until she got her blasted banana pudding, or so I was told. Therefore an entire group of twenty or more stayed behind with her. So a hungry woman craving banana pudding and a full-blown Holy Ghost praise and worship session put us WAY off our scheduling track. And now, my pregnant daughter-in-law was pacing back and forth, in the DARK, in high heels, as if she were putting marks on the devil's head. And clearly, she was.

The chain-cutting ceremony that had happened the night before was now in full-blown "sequel" mode. It was happening. But I was worried that Amanda might fall while giving the devil that high-heel headache.

I finally got every car light on that would shine remotely near the girls, and I resumed my position beside Michael. By now, the girls were in a prayer line, praying for each other, on the ground slain in the Spirit, and some were simply weeping with their hands raised toward Heaven. God was doing a thing. The grace and mercy was flowing freely—you could feel it. They were forgiven, they were free, and they knew it. Well, most of them were, it seemed. There may have been a straggler or two.

One girl came and grabbed me and began sobbing as I hugged her. Her choice to abort multiple pregnancies in her youth was finally confessed sin and forgiven sin. She had cried so much her shirt was wet. This fortysomething woman, for the first time in her life, was acknowledging her choices. She hadn't told anyone. Her parents would have lost their minds had they known she used their car and their money to do it. Her husband didn't know either. This was dark. This part of her soul had never had a light penetrate it.

Well, not until now. I think I convinced her that when much is forgiven, much love is returned. She WOULD love Him so much MORE for the grace He was extending, and that LOVE would change everything about her life, I told her. So as the car lights penetrated the dark mountainside, the light of truth and the Spirit of the Lord penetrated this deep place in her.

She was my poster child for this retreat. She embodied everything that I believed I was currently called to do. She was a "church" girl, with an outward appearance of normalcy. Normal family, normal career, normal husband, normal commitment to church—she had all things "normal" covered. But the truth? Her soul was festered with infection. It had been untreated for twenty-five years. She hadn't repented; good grief, she hadn't even admitted it yet. She was in complete denial, until the mountain. She represented the VERY reason that God had changed my life course six months earlier. She was dressed right, she talked right, but she was the walking dead.

The infection of unforgiveness had come very close to taking her out. See, if you're going to kill the fruit, first you must kill the root. Her fruit of self-loathing was never going away on its own, never. The root had to be exhumed. Only Jesus and truth can pull that root out. The root was deep and it had wrapped around her heart. But tonight, like the blind man, she too would tell Jesus what she wanted. She wanted to be FREE from the guilt of choosing to kill those babies. She had to say it, and she did.

There was a commotion in a dark, unlit corner of the area. I walked over to check it out. I was terrified that someone would fall, and it would certainly be my fault, so I sashayed back and forth between my roles as maintenance man and prayer warrior. That's pretty much the story of my life. But here's the truth of the matter. Ministry can ONLY move when there's support. The man or woman with the microphone is the face of the ministry, agreed, but the hands, feet, brain, heart, are usually somewhere unstopping a toilet, in a back room praying, replacing batteries in microphones, handing out bottles of water, serving in the nursery, or playing an instrument on the back row, completely out of sight. These folks are the REAL ministry movers.

They're not always on the marketing piece, the church billboard, nor are their names easily remembered by the masses. But they're still the heart and soul of ministry. They row the boat, in synchronized fashion, knowing that if just ONE person stops rowing, the boat will not move in the straight "on course" direction that is necessary to get to the destination. The loss of a rower makes the boat start to cut to the left or right, depending on which side suffered the loss. Ultimately the vessel will start to go in wide, inefficient circles, never landing on the shores intended. The destination isn't obtainable without synchronized rowing and a complete team in place. The body of a church, or a God-appointed group of followers is akin to that boat full of rowers. Each is given a position that must be executed or the boat starts to circle, and the ministry cargo never reaches the shore.

That night, I was responsible for moving ministry, and I didn't have adequate lighting. I had failed. But God knew.

The car lights cut through the crowd and the silhouettes danced back and forth, all shapes and sizes, their hands still raised toward Heaven as Amanda laid hands on them, one by one. Kelly, Hope, and Terah had managed to make this mountain music sound a bit like I believe Heaven's music will sound. With their nearly perfect song selection, and a heavy anointing, they kept the atmosphere in full worship mode.

And then it happened. I spotted her. A redhead who clearly resembled Edie was being prayed for. I had missed it. Those dad-gum lights. But it sure looked like her. She was in the prayer line and Amanda was laying hands on her. Oh yes, Terah spotted her, Kelly spotted her, and NOW they're helping Amanda pray, they're with her. OH GOD! The PROMISE. I had been SO distracted with the workings of this day I had TEMPORARILY forgotten about the promise! How could I forget?

I was invested. I believed it was going to happen. I had tucked the promise away in my mind and soul where faith stories are cataloged under "He did it" or "He's GOING to do it." It was tucked away safe, in the latter.

I accepted Him at His word the night HE promised, and I forgot it, literally. I know how God rolls, so no sweat.

But as I remembered THAT promise that seemed oh so impossible, as I watched her body bent with emotion, I knew that this was it. This was the end of the pain of her youth. Enough was enough, and she was coming to take her stuff. The child who had described her life to me as a chalkboard painting that had been slowly erased was now standing at the foot of the cross.

Her little life, her chalkboard picture life: at first only a small corner got smudged, then a wide strip down the middle was gone, and then the part with him—swipe—erased. Her first day of school, gone. And not even a memory remains. The day she learned to ride a bike? Same. The tears of the eleven-year-old painfully told the story of adult pain that came way before its time. And finally, the chalk painting of this baby girl's journey becomes little more than the smudged black slate with streaks of what used to be there. But now? Just the streaks remained as a reminder that there used to be a picture of a story.

The confusion in the mind of a child as to why she can't remember her seventh birthday. She wondered why the memories were spotty. When the family dynamic changed, the smiling family photos of a "used to be" were tucked into the box in the garage, with all of the other "I can't deal with it" items, waiting for a better day, a day when everyone would be strong enough to look. Edie had lived to see many special occasions end up in the box of "can't display that." The result? She felt invisible.

I often say that pictures are a reminder of the reality of our lives. Take them, look at them, and allow them to be your gateway to remember what God has done. For I know that when I'm securely tucked away in a nursing home or assisted living home, when I am roaming the halls on my bedazzled walker, trying to organize a get-together in the social hall, I will be wildly waving my iPhone, hollering and annoying everyone in my path, saying, "Look at my grandkids, people. Look at this service back in 2017: they were praying for the sick, and see that woman in the red dress? She got healed! Look at those babies. They love to go to the beach together. Look at my great-grandkids, folks. Aren't they the cutest kids in the world? Look at those eyes."

You see, my memories are jolted by those pictures. I look at that seventeen-year-old girl, and I remember her battles. I look at the fifty-seven-year-old who is headed to open-heart surgery, and I remember her fear. My peace of TODAY is dependent on my ability to allow the little girl inside of me to coexist with the thirteen-year-old who was abandoned and also the thirty-three-year-old divorcee who did everything the wrong way, and even the sixty-one-year-old who battles herself more than others and loses more than she wins. ALL of these women must choose to live in one body, in one mind, sharing one soul. They must figure out how to make peace with each other and live in it. I realize that this sounds a bit schizophrenic, but it's still true.

So the Edies of every age had struggled with the peace. The child was crying, the teenager was rebelling, and now the young adult was tired, just tired. The shame was like carrying a bag of rocks. She wanted it. She was all in. But she had to allow the Lord to heal the Edie of every age and every experience, and they would have to learn to live together in peace.

The large chunks of chalk erasing had taken a toll. She was tormented. There were far too many pictures of a little girl with braids in the box in the garage. It's impossible to have change without a consequence. The depressed eleven-year-old Edie was a product of divorce. There is so much I could say, but I won't. It's her story. Clearly, generational curses were manifested in a textbook kind of way. The devil won lots of battles in those days, too many to name. If you haven't read *Stronger*, this may be a bit gray. Our lives were VERY impacted by the choices of others. EDIE would never be the same. No one would.

But a child who is developing her value system, a child who has clearly been jaded by the loss of so many who claimed to love her, all by age eleven; what was her next? There's lots of shared blame in this story. But as I often say, let the pictures tell the story. They will.

Who is there, who isn't? Who prayed, stayed, and somehow made it to the end with her? Those of us who did are immensely blessed to be in her life. She's beautiful, smart, creative, works like a man, looks like a movie star, and is Mommy to the most beautiful little girls you've ever seen. I don't regret my years of investment. She was worth it.

To those who walked away and never looked back. No birthday texts, no graduation gift, no Christmas gift, no nothing. God will settle it.

If you've never experienced complete abandonment, this may not bring tears. But those of us who have experienced it, we are wiping tears and feeling this child's pain. There are no words. Right? When a human being attempts to snuff out your VERY existence in the pages of history, pretend you SIMPLY don't exist; it's an unexplainable brand of pain that is unbearable at times.

I rest my case.

Today Edie candidly described to me the moment her life completely unraveled. She explained the spiral that started in a little house in Hartford, Kentucky. We relived the hell of her fate. I said, "Edie, you always knew I would give my life to make you better. Right?" She knew. But somehow, it wasn't enough. She confessed to me that for two years, starting at age eleven or twelve, she was a suicide risk. She described the "cutting" and mutilation. I wept as she told me stories. I've read the countless stories from the parents and grandparents of children who had made this dark decision. I've read them and lost sleep for weeks after reading. There is no greater pain. Period. I knew that this story COULD have ended SO differently. But God.

Edie also felt that somehow the mess that she woke up in was HER own fault. I told her it was NOT. She said, "I know that, but my eleven-year-old mind truly thought that every bad thing that had happened to me was completely my fault. And the eraser kept erasing, and I truly wanted to die. After all, I was already invisible, so why not?" I listened and I wept. Thankful doesn't begin to describe it.

I used to beg GOD to put a hedge around her. I knew that without a hedge she was no more than a statistic waiting to happen!

I wept and listened as she walked me through her life from her perspective. On days like this, I'm thankful for FaceTime and phones. She explained that the shame of being so broken was intensified because she felt like people would judge her more harshly because she was from a ministry family. After all, her little five-year-old self was on the cover of the album that contained the signature Crabb Family song "Through the Fire." She said she felt like PEOPLE believed she had it all together. Well, this granny knew she didn't have it together, but of course I didn't publicize that. I knew there had been a WAR for her soul since she was born. I knew that her disappointment in men would very likely affect her in a critical way. I prayed she wouldn't be a lesbian. Sorry if that doesn't set with some of you. It's my book, and I'm being honest. I'm allowed to be.

I prayed protection over her—I actually begged for it, every day. And then she would have a wreck or run her car into a pond. I prayed harder. I told her truths. I hung up on her, she hung up on me. We battled. She moved in and out of our home several times. I would scream at her for sneaking out during the wee hours of the morning. We had no clue what she was really doing, and I prefer to never know. She was SO secretive. She was delving into the deep. Almost daily, we would have a brutal conversation that would end in drama, but by dinnertime we would move on. I would take her to dinner and she would order the entire left side of the menu. We would laugh and talk as if THE BIG fight hadn't happened four hours earlier. Two peas in a pod. The relationship was strong enough to be tested.

We knew about fighting through darkness and putting on a red lipstick that somehow made it better. We understood how to wipe our snotty noses and faces that were dripping with our own tears, all the while slapping on makeup because we MUST go to work. Work mattered.

It kept her sane, as it had her granny, always. People will fail us. But patience, persistence, and perspiration won't fail. Edie and I share that trait. The more we hurt, the harder we work. Men left, but the work stayed. The spineless pretended that it didn't happen, but not us. Edie and I screamed about "it" and cried about it. I remember a day when she was about seventeen. I caught her in my closet with a bucket of old pictures strewn on the floor. I walked in and saw the top of her head. She was sitting Indian-style somewhere in the midst of the shoes and purses. She looked up and I saw a quivering lip, tears streaming, and the soul of a girl who had been devastated. Pictures. They're the trigger, good things and bad things. The image of her tear-stained face is so vivid to me as I write today. The story of Edie sadly overlaps with my story. How sad is that? When selfish people make selfish decisions, the list of victims is always long. She was an eleven-year-old victim.

By the time she was eighteen, the path was somewhat forged. She had turned left.

The lies and deceit were beginning to own her. I feared for her. Her choices were now hers, and they were poor. She says that she would never want me to know the entire truth of her teenage years. I don't know if I could handle her truth. But I knew God could in fact handle her. I would pray for her to avoid the swamp of addiction, and I prayed that she would always know that I loved her, no matter what she did, wherever she may roam, or whomever she chose to be with.

She wasn't a paper plate that would be tossed in the trash. No. She was fine china. No matter how many chips or cracks she might acquire, she was STILL china. No matter how many times she cut her arms and legs in an attempt to release the hatred she felt for herself, she was still beautiful. On days that people called her "trouble" or "a little tramp" God still called her virtuous. He saw WHO she would be. He knew.

So that day, as we talked, she described the mountain experience to me. She said, "I was late to the service. I had to take all of my makeup and supplies back to the cabin. And even though I was a bit afraid to be in the presence of Amanda with a microphone, I went. I knew I was supposed to. I stood in the shadowy dark, in the back next to the ditch. I liked it being dark. It made my shame easier to hide. I listened. She was speaking directly to me. I knew that this would happen. Every single thing that she said about herself and her shameful childhood was me. I was freshly ashamed when I looked around and realized that these people had no idea how messed up I was, how messed up I had been my entire life. As Amanda said, 'Most preachers had preached to the fruit, the sin, but no one knew how to get to the root—well, until now.'"

Edie said, "I was sobbing, but still standing in my little dark corner. But then came Wylene. I didn't know her, but I soon would. I knew immediately that God sent Wylene to that mountain because I needed her. She read my mail. The thoughts that were already concrete in my mind, she spoke them to me. This woman was reading my mind! I would have a new thought, and, boom, she would speak that too! She was on it, this Wylene lady from Georgia. She asked me if I wanted to go to the altar. I said yes. I remember how dark it was, but then I turned my head to the brightest light I had ever seen. From dark to light with a slight move of my body. Granny, the most intense God moment of my entire night was that night. I finally gave it to Him."

This girl who always felt like the "black sheep" of our family, the girl who felt she had no value in ministry, the girl who didn't sing or play, wept unashamed before God for the first time. The painful shame of my choices, the confusion of my seemingly "blotted out" childhood, the feeling of SOMEHOW being responsible for someone choosing not to stay . . . on that mountainside . . . she was dumping it all out.

She said, "I felt the shame of the child of divorce, the grandchild of divorce, and the great-grandchild of divorce. I was the child that was never sure WHO she really was. I left ALL of that on that mountain. My self-loathing had to go, in Jesus' name."

64

Realistically, it's clear to see that kids don't create this much pain, but let me tell you, they think they do. They carry it.

Edie continued, "That night molded me for the rest of my life. I finally experienced deliverance. Since that night, I have walked with Him. I'm far from together, but He's with me. I plan to raise my girls in the presence of God and teach them about Him. I think that mountain was the first time in my life that I was brave enough to own my truth and let God help me accept the things that weren't my fault, and HE helped ME to forgive myself for the things I chose. It was a combination of accepting grace and extending grace. But it happened."

I cried and told her goodbye, trying to disguise my emotion. I got off that phone and fell on my face. I hadn't properly thanked Him for making good on His promise, Yeah, I had said, it, I had written it, but I needed to do it in a ceremonious way.

And that day, I did.

Girls, please listen to me. Edie is a strong girl. A short two-plus years later, she's walking in worth and grace, full of the Holy Ghost, and she's a warrior in the most important ways. I don't like her tattoos, and she doesn't like the fact that I take sleeping pills to help me sleep sometimes. But those are side issues. To each his own. We're both VERY human. We're both brutally honest. But please, let's not sit in the seat of scornfulness; let's examine the miracle.

It was clearly JUST an obedience issue. I had to obey, plan the mountain event. Amanda had to deliver what GOD told her to, no matter how difficult, Wylene had to step into the mix, unafraid of offending Edie's granny, unafraid to READ her mail. It takes a bold person to go to the pastor's daughter, the event planner's granddaughter, or the boss's wife, and plow a while. But it's necessary. If you have that gift, stay on track.

There's nothing worse than a self-absorbed person claiming to have a word for you. But in spite of the sometimes "garbage-y" prophecies from the narcissistic, there are still a few Marcia Henrys, Wylene Bloodworths, Lily Isaacs, Aaron and Amanda Crabbs out there . . . who will shoot it straight, step up into your personal space, tell you what GOD told them to tell you, and end by saying, "Doth sayeth the Lord" and leave it between the receiver and God. That's exactly what Wylene did. She did what HE told her that night.

And me? I got my promise. The obedience was SO much better than sacrifice.

The truth is, Edie sat outside for hours with her aunts and me, allowing the pain of many years to be exhumed. She spoke her feelings in candor and says for the first time in her life that she wasn't afraid to speak truth.

For, you see, Amanda had preached, "The LORD is a Spirit" and where the Spirit is, there is liberty, or in this case, let's just call it freedom.

Finally, this child of bondage was free.

As I finish this chapter, it's 1:37 p.m. on September 19, 2017. My tears have soaked me. I needed to hear Edie say it in her words. I'm thankful for mountains and banana pudding. I'm NOW thankful for Sister Banana Pudding throwing us off schedule and into the dark. The darkness was part of the plan. God knew. And truly, a little banana pudding just may be well worth the wait.

Smoky Mountain High

After "Miracle on the Mountain" I was on a high. John Denver may have sung about his high in the Rocky Mountains, but this chubby chick was high in the Smoky Mountains. We had seen GOD do things that wouldn't be a little "puff" of spiritual powder, dusted on and washed off with the first good bath. We had seen these girls wade in. First to their ankles, then their waist, finally up to their chin. They were swimming. My girls were swimming. They were headed home to slay devils, and I for one believed they could do it!!

I wasn't the only one who was on a mountain high; most of us were. We had found a new thing. Terah's vision had become our newfound cause. Before the mountain was sold out in May, I had journeyed to a different location. Again, Terah went with me. We spotted a massive fourteen-bedroom lodge that was overlooking a wide, clear creek that originated in the mountains. The mountain water was clean and bid you to come wade. On this day we didn't wade, we had to truck it back to Nashville, but we worked out the rental details and swiped the trusty American Express card.

The cabins have a four-night minimum, so at first, we thought it impossible to make any of this plan work. But, lo and behold, Kay, the manager of group sales, said, "Kathy, I can do July 1 and 2. These two days are sitting there with long reservations in front and back." The first was on a Wednesday. Hmmm, that's a church night. Terah said, "Don't you get it?" That's the five-year anniversary of the bus wreck. Kelly needs to preach on that creek bank in her high heels! In case you missed the memo, the doctor told Kelly when she broke her back that she would never wear heels again. She does. Nightly. So this had become her symbol of her miracle of health. Her high heels prompted a rant something like this to the devil: "God wasn't through with me ol' boy, and I WILL wear these heels every time I minister and sing . . . just to remind YOU that I can."

So in Terah's visionary thinking, she had Kelly in a creekside camp meeting on July 1, 2015. I agreed. "Bam! GREAT idea!" We would bring all of the girls in the family. I was blessed with many grandchildren, but girls far outnumbered the boys. I could see all of the girls standing on the creek bank, singing and praising, and in my mind it would be reminiscent of my childhood and the creek where I was baptized. I could see the granddaughters singing, playing a guitar or two, and I was elated. How God had used church, music, and ministry to bind this family together, and I knew this "Stronger" season of events was an extension of that bond. We girls all knew it, even the granddaughters.

I said, "Let's do it." We secured a dozen cabins and would add more. I knew it was a church night but Aaron and Amanda, my pastors, would be as excited about this as we were. The task at hand was becoming more defined by the day. The depressed, the downtrodden, the broken in spirit and the broke as a joke financially, the grieving . . . oh Jesus . . . the grieving, now that was a big one. I had a dozen girls who had lost children to death. It was heavy. I wasn't prepared for the stories that these poor girls would tell me. Many involved car accidents. As I type this, I'm fighting back my own tears; I can't imagine their tear count on a daily basis.

So on July 1, 2, and 3, a mere seven weeks after our first mountain experience, we were going back! This time, we had 250 women who had registered. This time "sponsorship" was birthed. A man in Tupelo sponsored a grieving mom in Tell City, Indiana; a wealthy woman in Arizona sponsored three women who were victims of sexual abuse. A pastor's wife in Cleveland sponsored a pastor's wife in Arkansas. A pastor in Michigan whose wife had walked out on him, the kids, and the church, now felt led to sponsor a woman who had been abandoned by her husband. A recovered addict in Alabama who now owned a flourishing real estate office wanted to sponsor several church women who were closet addicts. And on and on and on, every imaginable scenario. The sponsors came from the four corners of MY world. Saved, heathen, and about everything in between. That's when we knew it was a move of God. We were lifting HIM up, and HE was drawing all men.

This was a very different animal. It had organically evolved . . . completely accidental and yet so effective. The giver could follow their OWN heart and choose a recipient they totally identified with. They could choose the field they wanted to sow their seed in, so to speak. Some chose the field of addicts because THEY should have died in 1998 when they overdosed but mercy rescued them; someone was praying. Some chose an abuse victim because they KNEW what it felt like to have Uncle Raymond's hands in their panties at every family reunion.

The list of struggle that the readers identified with would have stretched from my Hendersonville driveway to a farm in Texas . . . and back.

When people whine about a lack of ministry financial support, I sometimes scratch my head. My belief is now, and has always been, money follows ministry. Period. God's will? God's bill. Now listen up. God's not an ATM, nor is HE handing out lottery winnings. Ministry is hard work. I could list many examples. I've worked hard all of my life, and the ministry years were no exception. But the important things to convey as it relates to THIS ministry season of my life are as follows: I personally communicated with every person who was a sponsor or being sponsored. That was insanely ambitious. I answered thousands of your messages, directed the donations; many times I helped choose the recipients, occasionally arranged travel to and from, mailed gift cards for gas and food, and on a couple of occasions I sent shoes and clothes because the objection from the woman in need of a spiritual breakthrough was also in need of finances and had nothing to wear that she deemed nice enough. These women were living on a prayer, financially; well, some of them were. Some were working two and three jobs, raising grandchildren, and their budgets DID NOT include shopping sprees. They wore yard sale or Goodwill clothing. So occasionally we bought clothes and shoes and sent in advance of their travel.

I became a servant to the cause. It wasn't a job that could be delegated. It was my job. My eyes had to read the stories, my heart had listened to the pain, and these blue eyes had to shed buckets of tears as I journeyed with these broken people. They were mostly women, but occasionally I got a letter from a man who just couldn't stop himself from telling me his story. I listened. I answered many of them with an invitation to the mountains . . . knowing that the funds were going to come from my personal checking account.

The Lord impressed on me to sell our boat and sow the money. We rarely used it and it was a rich man's MONEY PIT. We weren't rich. I was convicted. There was no return for this depreciating item. I was smarter than that, plus it made me a nervous wreck the entire time we were on it . . . if the grandkids were there. When I was about ten, when I lived in Elizabethtown, Kentucky, my neighbor was critically injured when he swam up under the family's boat and got caught in the motor. I was scarred for life when it came to boat safety. I was a Nervous Nelly every time we took the kids. It was a BIG cruiser, and I screamed every time Steve backed it into the slip, because it would require someone to be on the back; sometimes his skills were less than stellar, and sometimes the danger of that person falling under a boat that was in reverse and being jimmied into a slip . . .was MORE than I could handle. It was the perfect storm for an injury or a death, and I knew it. He struggled. A big cabin cruiser isn't a great "first" boat.

But it was Steve's first. So this relaxing hobby wasn't so relaxing. The boat made me crazy and I made Steve crazy, and to be honest . . . anyone caught in the crossfire of that crazy can confirm this. There were many witnesses. HA!

Back to the sponsors. In the spring of 2015 I asked Steve if I could sell the boat and use the money to move ministry. It was paid for. We had paid $60,000 for it a couple of years earlier. I told him that I wanted to put it on craigslist for $55,000, and if it sold within a week, we would know it was God. If you own a cruiser you know that the market isn't fast turning for that type of boat. You can't trailer them, therefore you have to have a slip at the lake. This adds tremendous costs and reduces the number of potential buyers for the seller. I lived in a lake town. I had friends who had been in the boat business and I knew the ropes. I also knew the price I had set was a full retail price, AND I knew that it would probably SIT on the market for months like most boats that size did, unsold.

Steve knew it too. So he agreed. If it sold quick, we would sell it. If it didn't sell quick, we would take it off the market, use it and enjoy the screaming and look for a referee. That boat truly brought out the flaws in us: his lack of maritime skills and my crazy fears and the memories of my childhood friend who spent a year in the hospital.

On day three I got a call from a couple who lived in Kentucky. They wanted to see our boat. They came. The next day they called me back and wanted to know if we would hold it until Saturday. They planned to come and get it and bring a cashier's check. They came, the boat left, and the money went into a checking account that would be a cushion for my "Stronger Women's" fund. About now some of you are saying, "She's crazy. Why would she do that and why would that silly husband allow her to do that?"

Thanks for asking. I knew what I knew. I knew what I felt. I had walked through a life assessment of sorts, after the mountain, after it was clear that I wouldn't return to the real estate office. And I quickly realized a couple of things. I did not have the finances to retire, and I didn't have time to go back to work if I was to continue walking out the walk of "Stronger" the movement. It took twenty hours a day it seemed.

So, could I use the $55,000 as a cushion and operating capital to leverage and move this new vision that God had dropped on me? This had to be in addition to my regular giving to my church. That was an obligatory 10 percent because that's where I eat. We are fed by Restoring Hope. So they get the first fruit, always, plus weekly offerings. That was not going to change. But now I am taking a large amount of our nest egg and earmarking it for additional giving, and to top it all off, I NO LONGER have an income-producing job. I have a FULL-TIME ministry, in my heart, but no paycheck.

Could we do this? Take our savings and sow back into girls that hadn't escaped the dark generational curse that I had escaped? This was the "there but for the grace of God go I" scenario. This was heart, not head. It was faith, not doubt. It was me, the crazy woman who is too much ministry for most businesspeople and too much business for most ministry people. These broken women were my passion, my newfound purpose. Reaching into the jaws of hell and pulling people out, one broken life at a time. This was a new thing, but I knew that it was God's thing. I was merely the hands and feet of His master plan.

Ultimately, I also knew MY decision to take the funds from the boat sale to upstart the "Stronger" ministry was like throwing a hydrogen bomb into the plan that the enemy had for MY life. The devil wants you to be fearful, insecure, and selfish. He wants your main concern to ALWAYS be you. The devil doesn't tell you to give large offerings or to take on the struggles of others. That kind of talk is a foreign language to him. And the truth about most folks as they enter their retirement or pre-retirement years is this: they obsess about money. They start taking the jelly packets from Cracker Barrel along with the butter and Sweet'N Low. They begin to speak over their finances and they claim their lack as if it were a trophy. They often say, "We're on a fixed income now." My response: "Who isn't on a fixed income? If you work at Walmart for $300 a week, do they arbitrarily pay $600 some weeks, $1,000 other weeks? No. They pay you $300, give or take. So, wouldn't that be the same as a fixed income? So when Granny has her sixtieth birthday, typically the spiral begins. She starts the conversations with others about retirement and picks up the lingo and rhetoric that creates mental images of poverty. She fears what's coming.

You want me to GIVE you some truth? Sure you do. Here goes.

There is NO reason on PLANET earth that our years shouldn't be MORE productive after we celebrate fifty-five, sixty, or sixty-five. I'm smarter than I was at thirty. My wisdom, thank you Lord, has increased. The wealthiest people I know are past eighty and working every day. And as for you, the reader, examine yourself. Have you bought into the lies of the devil concerning this season of your life? Do you think you have to live in lack, somewhat of a second-class citizen, as you age? You don't. If you are a participant in that conversation, I rebuke it in you now! The word tells us over and over that the latter shall be greater than the former. Why is that? There is a reason. It's called managing the process of choices. I KNOW at my age what matters and what doesn't. I've made enough mistakes to avoid "bad" investments, and I also know about GOD and His favor. I have come to realize that HIS favor on my finances will bring exponential increase. Period. I am a testimony to this philosophy. I live it.

So now, here we are, and I had a choice to make.

The choice to sell real estate and completely *REJECT* every aspect of the ministry/music that had been my life's work came with a price. It also came with a paycheck. And the devil reminded me often that I needn't consider going back into ministry. He said, "Worry about yourself; no one else is going to. You know what it's like to be thrown under a financial bus, so protect yourself. You, my dear, are getting old, and you must prepare to settle in and get ready to live out your life in a quiet place. There aren't many battles worth fighting, because no one would fight for you, Kathy. Remember the ones who walked to the other side of the street when you were the bruised one. Remember ALL those ministry people who pretend to NOT know truth when it's easier? You weren't on many ministry lists when you were holed up in that closet for a year. Why would you try to save the world? They didn't try to save you. If you're smart, you will buy real estate, sell real estate, and watch the market propel your pennies into dollars."

He had a case. The market had recovered. The "stay in your current occupation" argument was strong. The "why would you want to get hurt again" argument was stronger. For the pain of the last year of the Crabb Family had taken a huge toll. Everyone loves you until they don't. The rejection that came with the end was painful. When the family was touring and I owned the "entity" the Crabb Family, I was often treated as royalty by the pretentious, the well-known, and of course, it was agenda-driven. Isn't everything in the world of competitive people? But once the family thing was over, once I said, "I'm out, let's call it the last season," I felt the ice. Once again, as with many other seasons in my life, I was painfully aware that not everyone who says "I love you" really does. I was aware that hypocrisy was alive and well in the green room.

If you were one of the loyal ones who walked through that transition with me . . . if you were there when the nights were long and the demons were rejoicing, we're still friends. That's pretty much how I do "life." Loyalty trumps stupid, and broke, and sexual preference disagreements. Loyalty was my litmus test, always. I don't throw people away who stood with me, ever.

The people who rallied behind truth and subsequently me, are MY forever friends. They earned their place at the front of the line. I've gone to some in the middle of the night, multiple times. Others, I've flushed their drugs down the toilet and talked them off the ledge. I've played counselor, financial advisor, and banker more times than I can count. I've written checks when they walked in need and handed them out as gifts, not loans. I've opened my home up for months at a time without thinking twice. I'm not that nice. I'm *THAT* loyal. Loyalty trumps blood at my house.

And these same people made sure I made it, they made sure I didn't take a bottle of pills, they made sure I had a great lawyer, they babysat me, listened to my endless, annoying stories about "you know" and continued to pray. They prayed and they listened. That, my friend, is what got me through.

I don't want to confuse you into thinking that EVERYONE was a pretentious jerk— they weren't. But 95 percent of the world was. That's common when they no longer NEED you, I suppose. The other 5 percent that STOOD on truth? They were my treasures. I didn't care what they did or WHO they did it with—I had their back. Kathy's my name and this is my game. Gay, straight, white, black, fat, skinny, saved, lost: if you protected me and were on the team that made sure I survived the vicious attack on my vision, if you were there to wipe my tears and subsequently tell me that you knew what truth looked like and would stand with me, you're on my "good" list.

I will fight for you. I may not agree with everything you do, but my job is to be your friend. That's all. You are keenly aware of my opinions. I am keenly aware of yours. We have often agreed to disagree, but we love. So I guess the summary for my "good" list goes something like this. We understand unlikely loyalty, and we love no matter what. I have my list.

But the pain that came with being "tossed" into the back alley trashcan was raw, real, and the devil's favorite argument. I've avoided MANY events that my kids were participating in. Why? To guard my heart. The whisper would start the day before and become a loud shrill by the day of, and I would beg off . . . blaming a headache or a last-minute client. But the truth? My fifteen years of butt-busting work had been purposely minimized by a couple of factions and occasionally completely denied. The buzzards that ate my flesh were various . . . I won't elaborate. But the truth was still the truth. I knew, the kids knew, and anyone with one eye and half sense knew. But the opinions of a few big mouths would always blow my way.

So now the boat is sold, the fleece was fulfilled, and the devil is whispering an essay in my ear. The essay was eloquent and contained a few truths about the unworthiness of humanity. The essay reminded me that people are selfish and usually use your assets, until they use YOU up. They want you to fight THEIR battles in proxy for them, they will use you for a rescue plan, or to CREATE a better life for themselves . . . but then? When they GET what they want? They abandon you. Garbage can. This much I had lived, I remembered. But this essay, it contained an expanded list of arguments. There was additional information in the devil's oral argument this time. He had upped his game.

There was a paragraph about addicts and sexual abuse victims. He told me that addicts never REALLY come clean and were a waste of my resources. And he said girls who have been raped by their dads and brothers are never going to be able to unsee the images; they can never forget the FIRST time, and how it felt, how he held his hand over her mouth so that her painful moans couldn't be heard. They can't be free, he whispered. I wondered.

Why would YOU, of all people, at fifty-eight years old, take a portion of your retirement nest egg and spend it on people who are going to do what PEOPLE are going to do?

It was a great question I suppose. But I'm a hard head. And nevertheless, I persisted.

The River Runs through It

I was scurrying to catch a flight to Orlando, where I was slated to do three days of whirlwind radio, television, and blog interviews. In a nutshell I was on this crazy trip alone to promote *Stronger*, the book. I did book signings, and all of my interviews, staying one day late to do the show with Dr. James Dobson. It was early morning of July 1, and I checked out of my hotel room at the Rosen Center and pulled my carry-on bag with me to the last morning interview. I had no time to waste. My flight left Orlando Sanford International Airport at 1:24 and I was due to arrive in Knoxville at 2:55. Yes, that was cutting it SO close. Steve was going to pick me up in Knoxville, and assuming we took the back road from the airport through Seymour, I thought we could make it close to the check-in time of four o'clock.

For today, July 1, was the first day of the retreat. It was the fifth anniversary of the bus wreck. Remember? We were going to have a service under a big white tent down by the creek and have Holy Ghost breakthrough. I could see it in my mind. The skies would be blue, with big fluffy clouds, and then at dusk the air would get crisp and the smell of the creek and night air would make this night perfect. The BIG white tent, that reminded me of tent-revival days, would be stark against the green grass and the trees. Oh my, I could see this. It was truly a picture!

So as I finished my morning at CBA in Orlando, as I said goodbye and headed to my rental car, my phone was abuzz with texts, calls, and many details that were contrary to my envisioned blue skies and fluffy clouds.

It was raining cats and dogs in Pigeon Forge. Kim White, the video producer, was calling, Kelly was calling, Terah was calling, Amanda was calling, Steve was calling, Mike was calling. We had problems. The tent was up, but the rain was so heavy that no one could safely walk down the hill to the tent. It was sitting by the creek where other folks had set tents before, but on this day, the only way to get to it was to slide. SO MUCH rain. A friend told me it was the heaviest downpour that Pigeon Forge had experienced in a six-hour period of time, ever. So here I was, I was trying to get to my car that was a country mile from the convention center. I walked hurriedly, imitating my momma's fast walk of my childhood, rolled my overnight bag, and was talking on the phone the entire time. I was extra fatigued. I didn't feel well.

So the news from all of the family and Kim, my trusty production expert: the sound and video equipment was under the tent, as I had insisted it be. After all, God gave me this idea . . . I was pretty sure . . . and the rain was GOING to stop, the sun was going to pop out and dry up the grass, and we would resume plan A, which was fluffy white clouds, blue skies, and a Holy Ghost hoedown like the old days, by the creek. Hey, I envisioned baptizing people in that creek. No kidding. I know this was "the" plan, so I insisted they keep the faith and I would be there SOON to help God and everyone pull it all together. So I thought. My inner control freak was in takeover mode. She totally shut the other Kathy down and began barking orders at everyone, anyone. I mean, surely there was SOMETHING that we could do. After all, these women were coming to drop off their burdens, their problems, and I just KNEW that the altar of the week was UNDER that blasted white tent, which currently had so much water puddled on top that it was a hazard. The monsoon had decided to hit Pigeon Forge. And I was one confused woman.

I finally arrived at my rental car, tried to take a deep breath as I loaded my tiny rolling bag and told myself to relax. I looked for the text with the airport address, put it in my GPS, and all it did was twirl! Round and round, and by this time I'm leaving the parking garage and must go somewhere. The patience of Orlando drivers is questionable. They started blowing their horns. So I chose to turn right, found a drugstore, and pulled over, retried the GPS on my phone, and still no dice. Twirling was all I got. Finally it popped up and said, "Service not available." WHAT! Are you kidding me? So I then proceeded to yell at Siri. Trust me, she deserves to be yelled at. I said, "Take me to the Sanford airport." Siri also told me that all GPS information was unavailable! Heaven help me. I got out and asked the guy in the drugstore. He didn't speak English and he motioned to his phone when I said I need directions. He was telling me to get them on my phone! Duh! Einstein didn't get it that AT&T had an issue on this glorious July 1, 2015, and he didn't realize that it was raining big cats and dogs in Pigeon Forge, and he didn't realize that I had broken women coming on planes, buses, cars, and every other form of transportation to get there. I had women from Idaho picking up women in Illinois. I had women from South Carolina picking up women in Georgia.

Didn't this man know that the frantic woman in front of him had KINGDOM business and HAD to find the airport? Apparently he didn't. Neither did the next person I asked. The shoulder shrug and lack of communication between us was unbelievable to me. Where in the heck was I? Iraq? NO one spoke English, no one.

So I got back in my car, prayed for GOD to help me, and decided to call Steve. I was yelling, and he was yelling back. I said, "I HAVE NO GPS and I need you to find the airport from the street I'm on, stay on the phone with me, and tell me every turn until I get within sight. If I don't get this resolved within a few minutes, I won't make my flight." He started trying to follow my instructions, and lo and behold, his GPS wasn't operating. Again, AT&T. Yay!

I called a few other people and tried to get them to walk me through the directions, but they were slow to understand the direction, or they weren't proficient enough to actually do it. Steve was trying to find a map of Orlando to help me, but he was already at Hidden Mountain, in a cabin. He didn't have a printer, just his phone. He tried, I yelled, he told me he was considering a divorce, and finally I realized I wouldn't make it.

Steve said, "Keep trying." Suddenly, I saw a sign that said "Airport." I knew it wasn't the big airport that I was accustomed to using, because I had driven several miles from that area.

I giddy-upped, I ran through toll booths, I broke the speed limit in a pretty serious way, I prayed, and finally I arrived. I looked at the time, and it was 1:50. My flight was gone. I turned the car in and walked to the Allegiant ticket booth. Allegiant flies to Knoxville—that's why I was at this small airport to start with. We usually fly Southwest, and they have a hub in Nashville, but they don't fly to Knoxville. Hence I'm in Timbuktu at a small airport watching my plane cut through the blue skies that Florida, NOT Tennessee, was blessed with on this July 1.

I had needed to pee since 9:00 a.m., but I hadn't had time. I still needed to go. I pushed to the front of the Allegiant counter and said, "Can I get to East Tennessee today?" She quickly replied, "Not unless you want to wait right here and be a potential stand-by passenger on the flight to Chattanooga." Yes! I told her yes!

Holy cow, my phone was blowing up. Curtis, my retreat piano player, fell as he tried to navigate the mudslide and walk down the hill to the big white tent. They were taking him to the ER in Pigeon Forge. And, whoops, my ride who was picking me up in Knoxville was worried because I didn't show. In the DRAMA of the day I had forgotten to call her when I saw I had missed the flight. Geez. What a loser I had become. I was still standing at the counter, afraid to go pee or get food, or a drink, or any of the many bodily things I needed to handle. I stood there in my personal Kathy misery.

Suddenly, it occurred to me. If I don't get on this flight as a stand-by passenger, I'm going to miss this retreat, at least the first day of it. The Southwest flights to Nashville were completely sold out, and the airport that Southwest flew from was close to an hour away, but there wasn't a single seat on tonight's flight anyway. I had just called them.

So now I'm realizing if I don't get the Chattanooga flight, I will have to rent a car, rent a room, and try to fly out tomorrow. So I will miss tonight, tomorrow DAYTIME events, and potentially be late for the last evening service. MY body started to hive. The stress of the day was beginning to punch hard.

It's time to board for Chattanooga. They boarded for twenty minutes or more. I watched. I even tried to buy a seat from a lady; no dice, but I tried. There was a small disruption at the other counter. Some real unhappy folks using some strong language. THEY had oversold the flight by three seats.

HOLY COW, WOMAN! I said, "I've stood here for over an hour, I need to pee so bad I can't uncross my legs, I need water more than I've ever needed water in my life, and I would tell you how hungry I am but I'm sure you wouldn't believe me . . . and you had me wait for over an hour for stand-by for a flight that was ALREADY oversold?" I was having in implosion of sorts! Jesus! Help me. I called Southwest again, and the reservationist said, "That flight is full, we have one available seat tomorrow, but you need to get it now. Shall I reserve it for you?" As I was ready to say yes and cry, she said, "Let me look one more time. This is the Fourth of July week, and people change their plans frequently. OH WAIT! Someone just canceled their seat on the 6:30 flight to Nashville. Give me your credit card number!"

So I bought a $423 one-way ticket and was SO happy to be doing so. Now the bathroom—I had to find a bathroom, and water. I took care of the necessary and then ran to the cab line. It was 4:30 p.m. and she recommended arriving ninety minutes early due to the long lines at security, holiday travel at its worst.

So that meant I had thirty minutes to get there, and it was a full hour drive, or more, with traffic, I was told.

I got in the car and completely melted down. The driver seemed concerned. He said, "Do you need a drink? I can recommend good places in town to drink and party." I replied, "I don't drink and I'm hurrying to get to my flight." He asked if my boyfriend had walked out. I said, "Not to my knowledge." He continued to dig: "Does he hurt you? Does he not appreciate you?" I told him something like this: I don't think he ever hurts me, maybe just when we arm wrestle. I showed him my big hands and told him that I could take any man down with those hands. I told him that I was supposed to be in a Holy Ghost revival and I was upset that I had missed my flight.

His look changed. It was somewhere between shock and fear. Ha! All of a sudden, he started telling me that he didn't drink either, he went to church, and he was very glad that he had a passenger like me who understood the spiritual side of him. So Mr. Cabbie went from a possible plan to send me to a bar to do no telling what to being an ALMOST pastor. Whatever it takes to get the tip. The comic relief was welcome. I breezed into the airport, had a "precheck" ticket, and walked past hundreds of people to get through security. Now I was starting to see the prayers kick in.

I got to my gate and saw a little restaurant that served salads. I had been to this airport many times, but I had never seen it this crowded. But this little joint was cleared out. Jesus. Thanks again. First the security line and now the food. LORD you are good. I ordered a panini (of course I didn't get a salad) and a drink. As I ate it, a couple came to me and said, "Are you Kathy Crabb?" I told them I was. We had a quick conversation, but I knew I had made a kingdom connection. They were in the world of Christian television, and I wasn't sure when this piece would get placed in MY puzzle of life, but I knew it would.

I finished my panini, grabbed a water for the plane, and headed to my gate. Meanwhile in Pigeon Forge, the ducks were happy. Kim sent me a video. As I stepped onto the orange and blue Boeing 737 that would take me to my beloved Tennessee, I started to cry. I needed to call Steve to come get me. Geez, it would take him longer to drive than it would take me to fly. He had headed to Chattanooga in anticipation of the stand-by flight. Now, I was calling him after the fact and saying, "I'm not on the flight that just landed in Chattanooga. I'm so sorry I didn't call you.

My brain has checked out. I'm headed to Nashville. I will be there in two hours." His stress was mounting too. HE had dealt with a hundred fires that needed to be put out already, and the rain, the blasted rain . . . he said it was hazardous and would slow him down, but he was headed that way.

I had a dozen texts come through while I was talking to Steve. More videos of rain, and the girls were saying, "What do you want us to do? We can't do this. People will get hurt. We will be soaked." Equipment had to be moved; it was getting soaked. The piano player, Curtis, is still at the hospital getting a CT scan because he hit his head on the concrete; mud, slick grass, and hills don't work well together.

The tears became a river. People were staring, I was gushing, and I had to accept that "night one" of STRONGER, and my lofty ideas of the mountain meeting that would be outdoors and under the tent would clearly not be under the tent. It was thirty minutes until church, and there was no place to go.

The girls texted and said, "WE got this. We will figure it out."

I turned my phone off, and for two hours, while that Southwest pilot was navigating the airspace, I too was navigating the space between that airplane and the throne room. I cried and prayed. "God, did I miss you this bad? MY tent and chairs that cost thousands won't be used, Curtis is injured, the women are wet, unsure of where they're going now, the girls are discouraged. Did I imagine that this was YOUR will? Where did I miss you?"

I cried the entire time I flew. I was disheveled in my appearance, and I was so disappointed. But meanwhile back in the mountains.

The girls had always listened to me without questioning the command, but now they must devise a plan. There was this huge porch at the big cabin at the top of the hill where the tent was sitting. The girls gathered those women, all 225 of them, as torrential rain showers continued to pour; they brought the chairs and ushered the women into the deep rows that they created with the chairs. The porch was long and narrow, but they made it work. They didn't have high-dollar speakers. Brenda Ruppe and her daughters Heather and Valerie didn't even have anything to play their tracks on, but they improvised. Here's a note worth taking folks: real professionals are not slaves to production items, nor are they slaves to their environment. A real singer can sing anywhere. A real minister of the gospel can minster anywhere. A real doctor can doctor anywhere. Granted, you can't make a live recording in these circumstances, but you can certainly let the Holy Ghost know that He's welcome. You can certainly open your mouth and allow the amazing harmony that is SO distinctly reserved for family to penetrate the night air.

They did. With the rain falling, and the GIRLS all pulling the wagon up the hill, together, they had a move of God under an overhang that was built for rocking and eating. But tonight, this big family porch was standing-room only in the back and had more than two hundred women crunched on it, somehow resembling sardines, but it didn't stop God. God knew, and HE allowed the rain, the missed flight, the pandemonium of the day. He allowed it all.

When my flight landed, they were in full church mode. I was getting reports. God was moving. Someone sent me a video of Brenda and her girls singing "I'm Going to Make It, He's Already Said That I Would" and I just let the stress of my day dissipate. Lesson learned. My overcommitting self caused this problem—well that and AT&T. I vowed to not allow anything to take me away from that which God had put in front of me. The publicity tour was too close. I should have come home the day before.

Secondly, as always, God proves that He will get the glory. I watched a video of Amanda preaching, her ever-growing belly on full display this time as she brought truth and convinced these girls that God was able. Even on a porch you can have an altar. And clearly, they had. They prayed for hours as I rode from the Nashville airport to Pigeon Forge, too tired to understand much, but somehow knowing that I had learned a lesson, and that MY girls had proven to me that they were full-fledged professionals. They made it work.

By morning the owners of Hidden Mountain had invited us to use the lodge for our services. It was a nice building that was equipped for events such as ours. Mike, Kelly, and Terah had done a video there back in 2010 right before the bus wreck. I loved this room. It was pretty, self-contained with a kitchen, and perfect for what we do. It was also positioned right beside the pool and hot tubs. So on this rainy morning we commenced our sing-along, and held all of our daytime sessions there. If memory serves me, Edie and crew had moved their makeup booth from a cabin. The makeup artists could be a part of the service; they were in the corners of the room. It was a big open space and we loved it. The day event ended, and I was SO tired. I hadn't the time for rest. I started to visit with these girls who had come from all over the country, and a few from Canada.

The girls opened the night service with amazing music. Hope, Cameron, and Terah led us to the throne. Kelly brought the word, "A River Runs through It." She told of the river that runs through the days of trouble. She made us all realize that when we look back, Jesus was there. When you're lying on a stretcher on I-85 and your back is broken, He's there; when the helicopters are flying overhead and your six-year-old is in one and your critically injured husband in the other, He's still there, holding your trembling hand, whispering in your ear, "This is THAT peace your grandmother spoke of; this is the freakish calm that comes when you have to live what you've preached."

Strangely, the creek that was supposed to be our baptism creek was high, out-of-the-banks high; the monsoon rains had destroyed the possibility of our going back to the tent/creek area. The lodge it would be.

As Kelly pleaded with these tearful girls, as she begged them to look for Jesus in their pain, find Him in the shadows, as she convinced them that He didn't abandon them like their moms did, their husbands did, as she pled the case for the cross, as she wept and gently led the new class of "Stronger 2015" to an altar of raw truth and repentance, I realized that this was a movement, not a one-time experience.

As I often do, I walked the peripheral. I froze. I photographed it: I would remember. The sexually abused girl with such serious health issues that she had a feeding tube, she was on that rug that was our appointed altar. The suicidal girl . . . who was fighting, fighting hard to overcome the pain of an older brother who had raped her repeatedly as a child. She had walls, but she was brave when it was just she and her computer. I knew the backstory, in its entirety. I looked at her, I wept. I prayed from a distance and she finally walked to the front. The cancer patient who was desperate for a touch. The girl whose husband was having an affair with another man, and she knew, but for the sake of those little girls . . . for the sake of "forever" and ever, she wanted God to turn him away; she wanted God to miraculously break the spirit of perversion off of him. She was ashamed, but I knew.

And then there were the depressed pastors' wives, three of them. Carrying the burdens of thousands, but no one seemed to carry them. We tried, we STRONGER women, we were gaining our stripes, learning our game, and we tried. And then the women who were raising grandchildren, the children of addicts, who happened to be their children, their first attempt at parenting that didn't go so well. So now? They worked multiple jobs, lived in mobile homes, and attempted to right their wrong. The guilt drove them, but they desperately wanted to purify these homes; they desperately wanted the generational curses of addiction, rebellion, and perversion to be broken off these grandchildren. They found hope and they took hope home to those rented trailers and inner-city apartments.

The sponsors were going to be blessed. I just knew it. For on this night the spirit of the Lord had blown in like a cloud and hovered over that 8 x 10 oriental rug that on this night doubled as Holy Ground. Once they got their feet on that rug, they were under the spiritual cloud. It was amazing to behold.

The service was winding down; again, the makeup struggles were real. Streaked faces and disheveled hair was the consistent look. Those makeovers that Edie did were long gone! I went to do my normal "Are all hearts and minds clear? You want cake and then a soft bed?" My lady that was deeply tormented with her sad story raised her hand and very timidly said, "I need to be baptized. Can we do it in the pool?" I answered, "Of course we can." I turned to the girls and said, "Get ready to get wet." I asked the audience, "Anyone else want to be baptized?" Hands started popping up, a dozen, two dozen, three dozen. I wept a bit more, for you see I knew the backstory on almost every single girl.

I knew that they had been baptized before—most had multiple times. But I also knew that this dip in the water would signify a clean start with Jesus, granted. It would be significant to wash away the hurt, pain, bitterness, self-loathing of years or decades, whichever the case may be. But as I wrote in *Stronger*, when I described my creek experience, as I described the icy baptism in that cold Kentucky creek, I realized that it was more than a commandment for me. It was a physical marker that I could TAKE to him on THOSE days that he wants to TAKE me to the pain, the shame, the subtle reminders of what he did, when he says, "This Jesus stuff ain't real: if it WAS real, there would be punishment for the pretenders and abusers that occupy a pulpit, there would be vengeance for the babies who are abused. Where's your Jesus, Kathy?"

And for the better part of fifty years, when THAT argument presents itself, out of nowhere, while I'm driving, washing my hair, or sitting alone at 2:00 a.m. . . . I go there. It's a bit like a bus tour in the hallways of my mind. I load that rotten guy on the bus and I start out at that icy creek in Kentucky . . . and I say, "Okay, scum bag. See that little ten-year-old girl that's just stepped into icy water because she wants to follow Him, because she innately knows in her ten-year-old gut that she will need him to be a hedge? She knows. And next, devil, look at the seventeen-year-old, lying in her own blood, and look at the thirty-seven-year-old, the forty-nine-year-old, and the fifty-nine-year-old . . . Leave, you must leave. For this girl knows WHO she belongs to, and why she belongs to Him. And yes, the cold-water experience was my genesis!"

And every time I take him to that creek, he runs. For, you see, when this ten-year-old came up out of that water, I came up shouting. That fat preacher put me under, but the Holy Ghost raised me up. My momma wasn't Pentecostal, my grandma wasn't Pentecostal, but on that winter day, in an icy Kentucky creek, this girl got a taste of the Holy Ghost, and it has kept me. When men failed me, Jesus didn't. When the world used me, He loved me. When I wanted to find a bridge, He stopped me.

So as they lined up like little ducklings following their momma duck, my girls were going to get a fresh experience to remind the enemy that they meant business.

I watched them and I cried. For the promises of God had come to fruition. I saw a creek, HE saw a hot tub. I saw a tent under a blue sky, He saw rain, clouds, and a beautiful log-cabin lodge. In the end, the result was the same. But the lessons learned were priceless, and now I was watching the vision happen.

One by one, they were going under. The oversized hot tub was perfect. It was the first body of water they came to, and they were so anxious they jumped in. It would hold several people at one time, was plenty deep, and it is THE place that dozens of women use as ground zero for their NOW victory. Terah and Hope both got baptized in that hot tub, along with so many girls that I had grown to love.

As with most things, I'm walking the peripheral, crying, making a video, and watching through a special lens that God has allowed me to see through. The lens of "Won't HE DO IT."

I went to my room and wept for hours. Thankful is a lame word for what I felt, but it's about all I have. He had made all things new. The ministry that had been buried alive in me through no real choosing of my own had been restored times ten. Not only had he restored it, it was richer, more life changing. I was over the whole quantity thing, the awards and fame. I had been to hell and back and all I cared about in 2015 was rewards, as in souls. The "NEW" calling was certainly not my idea, but I am always up for anything that allows me to live in the land of favor. This was that.

And how blessed am I that this movement allows me to include ALL of my girls, daughters, granddaughters, and even the boys and Steve. For God has been SO very good that he has continued to bring the increase. The spring retreat is now in a convention center, and my boys typically attend and are musical guests. Blaine Johnson is my faithful band leader, bringing the most amazing talent and arrangements you will ever hear on a stage, anywhere in the world. We've been blessed with the stories and talents of so many musical heroes and personal favorites. In my heart I know that it's just the beginning.

For truly, we are Stronger together, girls, always.

As I close this chapter, as I sit on this balcony overlooking the gulf, the rain is pouring much like that July day in Pigeon Forge. I reflect. Rain? It's a bit like Jesus. It never changes. It always shows up.

In Leviticus we are told that we would have "rain in our season, land shall yield its produce, and the trees of the field shall yield their fruit."

I have declared many times that these women shall be my fruit. When I stand before God I want to hear Him say, "Thank you for bringing Donna to that mountain, for the first time she felt loved. Thank you for taking the time to tell Debbie that it wasn't her fault. Thank you for proclaiming healing over Iris, she has no family." And I will say, "Thank you for trusting me with this responsibility, for it was truly my honor to love these precious souls, and, yes, they made it, God, they made it."

After the July 2015 event, we did a documentary called *Stronger: The Journey.* It was a raw depiction of the movement that God had started. In the footage of that piece, as the documentary producer interviewed me, I prophesied, "These women will be lifetime friends. They will be the army of prayer warriors that will change the world, literally; they will be friends, and eventually family. They will laugh together, eat cake together, shop together, and bury each other."

Three months later, almost to the day, the girl who timidly raised her hand to be baptized, the girl who started the water revival, left this world. I speculate but will not share. She was tormented and struggled to forget the images and the damage that was a huge part of her childhood: abuse from a close family member. Insult was added to injury with an accusation from a person she loved more than anyone on the planet—it was too much. I don't know the details, and neither do you. It's between her and a merciful God . . . who was there when she was violated, who was there when she obeyed and sparked the "hot tub" baptizing, HE was there.

There are many unknowns, but here's what I know. I don't judge the whispers of suicide. I'm not God. I'm glad I'm not God. If I were, I have a list that's sitting in a drawer. It's filled with people who have committed unforgiveable wrongs to the innocent. And, yes, I will never do one solitary thing to retaliate against these "list" people. God will do it for me, and He will give me a private box in the rich people section, serve my favorite meal: beefsteak tomatoes with blue cheese, grain-fed rib eye, medium-rare please, a side of grilled asparagus almost crunchy, and molten lava cake with vanilla bean ice cream just in case the calorie count isn't high enough. In my opinion, on the day that this meal is served . . . it will be so heavenly that there will be NO calories in it.

The word of GOD says that HE WILL set a table for us in the presence of our enemies, and, yeah, I may have expanded a bit for the sake of your imagination, but you get the point. He's got this.

And my friend who died three months after the July 2015 meeting, the baptism girl, He's got her. I leave it in His hands, knowing that His mercy is real.

So on a cool September day, a group of Stronger sisters journeyed to South Carolina for a memorial service that the family of the deceased didn't see a need to plan. But these sisters, after a short three-month relationship with this broken lady, went. They sang the songs of Zion. They honored the lady who was baptized in the hot tub, the lady who God knew would need a "crew" to do what a family should have done. And God was pleased.

And then there were the moms, the grieving, lifeless moms who cried all day, every day. They posted pictures, as they relived the last birthday that they spent with their "baby." Most of these babies were teens, some older, not that it mattered. They were their babies, and it was the worst possible pain that I could personally imagine. And, yes, I felt helpless and I was certainly no match for this cruel twist that blindsided these women that I so desperately wanted to see smile again, or eat ice cream and really taste the chocolate, or simply hear a bit of hope in their voices. I wanted it so much.

He mocked me. I weighed his mockery. The struggle was real. But my rebuttals were pure reflex. I cut him, I defied his manipulation with everything in me. I knew it was a big job, I knew I was no match for the pain, but I also knew I had to try and love them through it. I knew that this old hillbilly woman was far too smart to back up on a deal with God. My instructions from Him were simple, just love them and listen. And I reminded them often that He loved them too. I could do this, well at least for a while. God had provided the means. Remember, the boat. I wasn't sure how long the funds would last, at this rate, but I was in.

So now, this "Christian music evangelistic momager turned real estate agent" had a brand new vision, and Steve no longer had a boat. My granddaughter Hope often laughs and tells me that I am the original "momager." She tells me that Kris Jenner didn't have a thing on me. Well, I don't hear much good about Kris Jenner, but Hope assures me that she's giving me a compliment. Ha!!

We moved forward. I could feel the favor of God on everything my eyes could see. He was pleased. Side note: I could also feel the fight of the enemy. He was having a nervous breakdown. I love it when that happens.

Miracles and Whistles

Stronger, the retreat, started on July 1, 2015, and lasted until July 3. The last day was on Friday. Remember, I had started my week on Sunday in Orlando promoting *Stronger,* the book, and had missed my flight and the first day of the retreat. DRAMA! Too much drama. I was micromanaging every single detail of my life and I was beyond tired. I was two years post-op open-heart surgery for a valve repair. Sometimes I didn't feel as well as I should. Stress, lack of sleep, and a life of trying to be all things to all people will do that, so they tell me!

When Stronger was over, on the Friday, I told Steve, "We must stay in the mountains another night. I'm not up to the drive back to Nashville." We got a room at the Hampton Inn on Teaster Lane. I read the sweet messages that the Stronger girls had written on envelopes to me, cried, and tried to sleep. We had passed out envelopes for an offering for the needs of women. The women had used these offering envelopes to communicate their hearts to me. They were scrawled with markers, Sharpies, and one with a crayon. The common theme was simple. Thank you for caring. I felt hopeless when I got here, but I'm going home with hope and an army of friends. Well of course, that hope was Jesus. And these friends? Oh my. As it turns out, they would be best friends in spite of distance and barriers. These notes are stored in my closet. When I die my kids will find them, I suppose. And, yes, when they're digging through my junk and remembering me, let them remember the girls that God led to me. Let them remember.

I had never been more tired, and that's a huge statement. I was fulfilled, but my lands a mercy, the price was high. Saturday we got up and had a biscuit and trucked it back to Hendersonville. That's about two hundred miles. We got there early afternoon, just in time for me to head to Kentucky to pick up my sister Anneta. I was set to meet my nephew at the Cracker Barrel at 4:00 p.m. to bring Anneta back to Tennessee with me. For, you see, Anneta could no longer drive. I covered this in *Stronger*, my first book, but for those who haven't read it, let me summarize. The year 2013 was the year from hell for us. My mom died on January 21 after being in a nursing home for a couple of years. That was a terribly trying time for me. Momma had been healthy her entire life, until she took a fall. She never had a well day afterwards. Overnight she became an invalid.

She took no meds, was healthy as a horse, walked five miles a day, could work circles around her kids, until . . . THAT day. She fell and never recovered. And a mere two years later we were burying her. A couple of months before she passed, I realized that something was wrong with me. Finally, I went to the doctor. I had no clue that I had a problem, but Dr. Smith told me after about three minutes, "You have a pronounced heart murmur that you didn't have in July. We must get you in to a cardiologist and most likely a surgeon." I said, "I've been here three minutes and I think you just told me I need open heart surgery? Are you kidding me? How can you know that with three minutes and no test?" That was Dr. Smith. He knew his stuff.

And I knew my family history. My sister had already had two valve replacements, my dad died an untimely death due to heart failure, and we all suspected that it was a valve. He didn't drink, smoke, or eat much. He weighed 140 pounds on his heaviest day, I would say. So yes, I was in congestive heart failure. I needed surgery immediately. My momma was dying. I was like . . . JESUS, really? Is this that "All things work together for the good to them that loves the Lord" scripture? Uhm . . . what's up with this? ONE of these at a time would be bad, but she's dying, and I might be . . . and that's too much at once. THIS is difficult for my family, God! HEAR me? So I kind of yelled at God, visited Momma at the nursing home, worked like a mad woman trying to close real estate deals, for the year was ending and I had goals as it related to year-end numbers. And I was growing more fatigued with each passing day. So Momma was dying, and I had finally been given a surgery date. I had elected to wait on the best surgeon in the South. He was world renowned for his ability to repair a valve, rather than replace. I wanted him. I hoped to live a normal life after surgery, without blood thinners and a mechanical valve that would need replacement in twenty years. I wanted Dr. Petracek, but there was a line. So I went to the back of the line. The doctor put me on house rest while I waited. I was never sure what "house rest" was. I had heard of "house arrest" before. Ha!

Momma died and we honored her in a tremendous way. I had a house flip going in between Momma's funeral and my surgery. So much for the house rest thingy. And on the day before surgery we finished staging that big ol' flip house. It needed to sell fast. It was pricey and we didn't want to carry it long. So a day of staging, dinner with my kiddos and family, the body scrub that's part of the prep, and off to bed. On February 19 at Vanderbilt Heart, Dr. Petracek repaired this old chubby girl's heart valve. It was a struggle. My heart didn't want to restart. My kids tell me that the good doctor came to the waiting area drenched in perspiration, white as a ghost, and relayed the struggles of the restart. There are more details, but this ain't the book for that. Next time. But the only thing that really matters is this. He did it. He didn't give up. The devil tried, but God said, "Not today. She's got places to go and people to see." So I would live another day, another year, and as I type this today, it's been five years.

So the gist of this story is this. I was recovering and wasn't driving or working yet when we got a call from Kara, my niece. Anneta, my sister, her grandmother, was missing. I'm repeating information from *Stronger*, but here is the condensed version. She was trying to pick up a honey bun that had fallen in the floor while driving on the William Natcher Parkway, in Kentucky. Yes, I said a honey bun. She had a one-car accident. She flipped her car and was life-flighted to Vanderbilt from Kentucky, all for the love of a honey bun.

They had no identification or information, so the family hadn't been contacted. The injuries were life threatening and left her on life support for seventy-three days. Anneta lived with Steve and I during this time, and I was her advocate and responsible party. That year was SO overwhelming for me. I said, "God? What just happened? I'm not sure I'm going to survive this." But I did. The devil tried oh so HARD to stop the train of truth that was coming!

So this is the story that explains why Anneta can't drive. On Saturday, July 4, 2015, as I was driving home from Kentucky, I started to feel a weird pressure that turned into intense pain. I felt like someone had a vice grip on my heart. I called Steve and said, "I need you. Something is very wrong." I couldn't drive. I was in terrible shape. It was so bad that I trusted my sister, who hadn't driven in more than two years, to drive my car home. That's big, y'all. I got in Steve's truck and started crying. I said, "After all I've been through and I'm going to end up dying in this green truck. This isn't where I want to die. Hurry! Get me to the hospital." I screamed and he drove faster. He wheeled into the emergency room entrance so fast it felt like we were on two wheels. I don't do a lot of drama in regard to my health. I've had a gazillion surgeries, most fairly minor, but I've also had some pretty awful things too. I'm a Coppage. We deem ourselves tough and a bit martyrish. Don't complain, don't let ANYONE see you sweat or fear. That's in my DNA. So when I went in for open heart? I was consoling my family. I was calmer than they were. But holy cow . . . when the pain is BAD enough, the toughest of people must deal with it. I was dealing. My loud screams alerted EVERYONE in the waiting room of the emergency room that day. They knew that this sister was there.

They immediately took me back, no wait. They got me on a stretcher, popped an IV in my arm. They started the pain meds in the IV. The first batch did nothing. I was screaming, "I'm dying. DO something, PEOPLE." The flurry of activity would rival what you see in movies for someone with a gunshot wound, or a car accident. I was creating so much havoc they believed that I was dying. The second round of pain medicine went in the IV as they pushed me into a room for an MRI. The medicine went in and I went into the tunnel. Immediately I started hallucinating. I don't hallucinate. I'm not much of a "grassy fields, butterflies, and little children running across the meadows" kind of person. I'm more of a realist. It ruins me when it comes to enjoying musicals and happyish children's movies. But on this day, I was seeing children run and butterflies fly, and I was flying with the butterflies . . . high above the mountains. I would fly high and then swoop down near the children. I could hear their giggles and I touched their hair as it blew in the wind. Think of the Disney World ride, Soarin.' It was a bit like that. I'm sure the hallucinating lasted seconds, but it seemed like forever. I was somewhat aware that I couldn't breathe. A part of my brain was urging me to move, make a noise, do something to alert them that my breathing was blocked. But the part of my brain that was soaring and swooping down in the meadow won. I didn't care about breathing. I wanted to fly.

A part of me understood in some abstract way that I was dying, but my will failed me. I didn't attempt to alert the MRI tech. But somewhere in that decisive seventy-five seconds or so . . . a thought occurred to her. And she came over the speaker inside the tunnel and said, "Are you okay?" I could hear her, but I couldn't respond—my throat was closed. Plus, I was flying. The medicine took me on a trip that I have to believe is similar to LSD. I've never had LSD, but the descriptions of hallucinations are the same. I would later learn that they gave me Stadol. When I didn't respond to the question or voice command to knock on the wall if I was okay, she quickly got me out of that tunnel. She pried my mouth open with a bite stick. I could hear her. I was still conscience, but I was paralyzed, and remember . . . she was interrupting my flying. When the bite stick pried my mouth open she yelled, "Oh my, her throat is closed! She's had a reaction to the Stadol." With the speed of a ninja she had syringes dumping into the IV. My throat felt like a balloon that someone let the air out of. It was immediate. I could breathe. And immediately my flying was over. She grounded me. The quick response and that little nudge that MY GOD gave her saved me. I would NOT be in the number of 250,000 people that die each year from medical errors. God said, "Not today. She will live and not die."

So let me put this in perspective. Hundreds of women journeyed to that mountain. MANY left and walked out their new freedom. But as they packed up their cars and headed home, as I slept in a Hampton Inn trying to muster my strength for the journey home, the devil plotted. He hatched a plan to kill me. Boom. Done. An innocent hospital error should do it. The family would be derailed for a while, and better yet, this woman would be dead. Gone.

So as I recovered at home from my week of exhaustion and my newly diagnosed pericarditis, the girls returned home. Some were so fired up they could have started a revival on a street corner beside a strip club in the French Quarter. Some were going home to straighten out a thing or two. However, others were going home just like they came. They packed up their pain and loaded it in their suitcase, put it in the car, and headed to the interstate. Life is hard. Changes are too. And sometimes it takes a smack in the face to unpack it permanently. Such was the case with one of our girls from Oklahoma.

Shelly was a tough case. Her story made me cry the first time I read it. She was damaged. A month before the mountain retreat she emailed me. Pretty much like the rest, unsure if I would ever see it. The truth gushed out of her in this Facebook message. The truth was ugly and I knew that she was to be on the mountain. I told her so. She received the love and accepted the gift. She drove a thousand miles alone. She wanted to be free. If you are willing to drive from Oklahoma to Pigeon Forge, you're looking. But the walls stayed in place. I don't remember a thing about Shelly at the mountain. She came, she played the wallflower, and she left. Her messages were clearly not the words of an overcomer. My job was pretty much done. God said get her there, and I did. I was released, so I thought. The "girls" were trying to encourage her, and I was too, but I'm too busy for time-consuming messages. That's a bit honest, but it is simply the truth. I care, but my calling isn't defined in the "pen pal" section of gifts. As I've adequately described, it's more the "build it and they will come" philosophy. I'm never going to be a good babysitter. Ask my family. I will do anything in the world for them and theirs. But I do very little babysitting. It's not my gifting. I don't love less than the "babysitting" kinds of grandmothers, not at all. But the Lord has provided me with a long "to do" list that keeps me running and gunning, and He knows that I am one person. Finally my family realized the same thing. I stay in my lane and do what I do. Now, don't think I don't want time with my kids—I do . . . I'm just giving you insight.

The Stronger sisters were doing a pretty fabulous job at reaching out to the weak girls. That was the way I envisioned this thing, and God hadn't disappointed. He gave the strong girls the patience and they shared in pulling this wagon up the hill, daily! So, my Shelly was struggling and we were praying, but it was a bit of business as usual. Until it wasn't. In early December she messaged me and told me she had pneumonia and was in the hospital. We prayed. She was precious and we loved her. And then the messages started to be a bit more severe. Like this one: "I went back to the doctor today. There's a new update. They have made a new diagnosis. Pulmonary fibrosis. I will have a chest surgery next week to do a lung biopsy."

Oh Jesus. I knew this wasn't good. She was so scared. She often messaged me and told me how fearful she was of leaving her three babies and husband. Her youngest was only twelve. The diagnosis and her estimated time left? We prayed and lived our lives. I was working like a crazy woman. Shelly Deason, one of my Stronger girls who also goes to my church, was communicating with Shelly. That made me happy. Spring was in the air and the April 2016 retreat was going to be doubled in number. We were moving to the conference center to accommodate. We were looking for five hundred women this time. I was slammed to the wall with communications, dot connecting of sponsorship money with sad stories, and I was barely functioning. Pandora's box was opened and there was no turning back. So much pain but also so much hope. Many were willing to give to make the mountain trip happen for an unknown woman with a #metoo story. So before the #metoo movement, I was over there trying to find Jesus healing for these girls.

Time passed, the sick were coming to be healed, the brokenhearted were coming, the abandoned and abused were coming, the poor in spirit and in the bank account . . . they all converged on Pigeon Forge, Tennessee. There were several women who had lost teenage children the previous year. Jesus. We needed God to show up. He did. We saw a move of God that would rival the old-time camp meeting Holy Ghost services. The Isaacs girls alongside my girls and me, we marched into hell and pulled a few out. Actually, my boys showed up too. You can't keep them away from a move of God. THEY love it. So the family had feasted on Jesus; the Stronger girls had been in the presence of the Lord. They baptized 250 women while Jason and Aaron led the rest in singing. It was oh so sweet in that place. On Wednesday morning, we did the devotion and thought we were finished. But we weren't.

Shelly Deason had bought a blanket. I think she had stopped off at the Dollar Store or Walmart to get it. It wasn't expensive . . . it was just a blanket. But she went to the trouble. She remembered. If you don't get another thing out of this chapter, get this. Sometimes the miracle starts with the simple faith that is exemplified when we stop and do the ritual act that we know to do. When we march around the wall, when we dip seven times, or in this case when we buy a Walmart blanket. It releases a snowball of faith that starts its way down the snow-covered mountain. Shelly

Deason with her blanket of obedience launched the snowball. It was a goner, headed down the hill, for the Oklahoma Shelly. Not only did it make it to the bottom, it was massive by the time it got there.

These women prayed over that blanket; the oil was applied, the tears were applied, and, I am going to be honest, I begged God. Something in my mind switched that day. I was down to business. Shelly Deason shared with us as she asked for the prayer. She told us that unless a miracle occurred, the Oklahoma Shelly only had a couple of months. So this forty-three-year-old woman, the mother of three, faithful wife, teacher, friend, neighbor, this woman who I was CONVINCED had never caused grief nor pain, was given a death sentence. And truly, she had walked through ENOUGH hell as a child. She was due some happiness. I was drawn in emotionally and spiritually at this point. I had picked up my gun. I was ready to go to war. The devil knew.

So, as I said, we went to the Hampton, I felt like death, we went home, and I had the crazy diagnosis of pericarditis, so I was a bit sidelined, for a minute. Our Oklahoma Shelly's health was in decline. Serious decline. And by along about the twentieth of April I was feeling a bit better. I was wondering how everyone was faring.

Meanwhile in Bogalusa, Louisiana, there was a sister named Donna. She was precious in every way. I first met Donna via Facebook. But, hey, don't diminish this online friendship. She was the real deal. And, yes, Donna had a story, but it's not mine to tell. Back in 2015, the first year of our retreats, the first year I was hooking up sponsors with ladies who needed a mountain experience, Donna was on my list. My old friend Melinda Baize, who knows my heart as well as I do, said, "Kathy, I want to sponsor her. Miss Donna Dean is mine. I want to get her to the mountain." I can't recall how she got here, but I believe she rode a bus. Now that's a little ride. Bogalusa is about thirteen hours in a car, and I don't want to think how many hours it would be on a bus! But somehow, she got there. She met Shelly. She was part of that blanket prayer. And, oh my . . . how the dominoes do fall. Melinda sponsoring Donna, Donna meeting Shelly, and now I must share the "rest of the story."

Shelly wasn't on the transplant list. She wasn't a candidate at that point. Unless she received a healing, she wasn't here for long. The Lord would have to heal her if she was to see her baby graduate from middle school. The Lord would need to heal her if she was to see another Thanksgiving or Christmas. It was grim.

Here's a series of messages I received from Donna via Facebook messenger. They started at 8:45 p.m. on the twentieth and end at 4:17 p.m. on the twenty-first. I won't bore you with my lame responses. Just read Donna's messages, and then pray that God trusts you to be a Donna Dean. This is a picture of someone going the extra mile, getting involved, seeing the need and responding. ALL for someone she had met ONE time. The HANDS and FEET of JESUS.

And you're about to see why I love a paper trail. You can relive the details. And FYI, Donna Dean was a retired nurse who had lost all of her earthly possessions in the New Orleans flood. She lost her house and all her stuff, but she sure didn't lose her beautiful ability to know what matters most. People. Here we go with the unedited paper trail:

URGENT . . . Do u know if Shelly in Oklahoma is on the transplant list? My daughter's friend is in Tulsa at St Frances. He's 28 yrs old + was n a motorcycle accident a few nights ago. They have declared him brain dead and have asked the family if they knew of anyone needing organs because he is an organ donor. My daughter called me because she's heard me speak of Shelly. Please let me know. He is A+ if that makes a difference. Please pray!

I first spoke with Shelly's daughter then she had her dad call me back. He spoke to someone at the hospital. They will check with her transplant people and will check everything in the morning. My daughter said they do not have to be on the list if we knew of someone it would go to them first. So pray it's a match!!

My daughter is going back to the hospital to let them know that Shelly needs his lungs. She will give them Shelly's information + her husband's phone number. Wow this has been a night! Don't know if I can sleep. I'm gonna pray, pray, pray!

~~~UPDATE~~~I spoke to Josh (Shelly's husband) this morning to get Shelly's information and have relayed it to the team at St Francis. It's a matter of time now to see if this is a match. I can say that James and Shelly have the same blood type. I almost shouted! Please continue to pray! I will continue to post updates! I believe in miracles!

My daughter just texted me that they're not a match due to the size. He was 6 feet 1 and she is 5 feet 6. I'm fixing to post on the Stronger page.

Josh, Shelly's husband said that her Dr informed them that James was Not a match But that she is now on the list and at the top of the list as a Priority!! I told him to please tell Shelly that her Stronger Sisters were more determined than ever to PUSH (I explained what that meant). God has this and we were believing for her miracle! Won't He Do It!

So for about twenty hours or so, we had high hopes! And the proactivity of one Miss Donna from Bogalusa was one for the books. Persistent. That was her. So as we gulped the disappointment of the last message, as I cried and said, "God, really?" Donna kept the faith. Also, the Stronger girls were praying. They were on a high as they watched the progress of the day, as they walked through their otherwise eventless day, waiting for Donna's updates to the Stronger Facebook group. They had so much hope. So the bad news was the bad news, but the good news, oh my goodness, just like that . . . she was moved from Shawnee, Oklahoma to Nazih Zuhdi transplant hospital in Oklahoma City. And she was at the TOP of the transplant list as a PRIORITY. What a difference twenty hours can make.

Five days later I hopped on a bus with Shelly Deason and headed to Oklahoma. I have a friend or two who own bus companies, the tour bus kind, not Mr. Greyhound.

I called them both to see if anyone was deadheading toward Oklahoma City. Bingo. I had a ride. A coach was headed to California. I met Shelly Deason at the bus lot; we grabbed a bunk on an empty star coach and woke up in Oklahoma in front of the hospital. There's a little more to the story, but we will leave it there. Ha!

I was going to see the Oklahoma Shelly, and she didn't have a clue. I Googled, I researched, I knew the odds. I knew what the statistics looked like. But I decided it was time to stop clinging to the tree trunk and get out on the limb. It was time. I rode to Oklahoma and I didn't feel great, but once again I just knew I had to go. Shelly Deason was the perfect partner in crime. She felt it too. After all, she had bought the blanket. She had started this domino of prayer and persistence.

We walked in and Oklahoma Shelly was in shock. She looked like she had seen a ghost. The visit was simplistic—there were no bells and whistles. It was typical Kathy, in and out, keep moving. We had a flight scheduled back to Nashville and a tornado warning prevented us from taking it. So we booked another route, a flight to Denver to avoid the tornado, and it cut our hospital visit time short. But it didn't matter. We came to pray and love on her. We did it. Personally, I knew the devil was on my heels. I knew he had an agenda. I was truly still sick. But I also know a bit about being the one who has the last word, that "fat" lady who sings last, uhm . . . that would be me.

We left and I shouted to the four corners of planet earth: "Shelly needed lungs!" People thought I was talking about my daughter-in-law, Shellye Crabb. I freaked them out. I had to specify that this was a different Shelly, but I kept shouting. Churches all over the world prayed, and I began to spend a lot of time talking to God about these lungs. There were several almosts and near matches, but always a disappointing ending to a hopeful day. The clock was ticking, and now we were on my watch. I was on the limb. I reminded God about every fifteen minutes that we needed Him to move. And let me say about now, yes, I realize that someone has to die for others to live. That's another entire book. Someone else can write it. It's one of the most disturbing things I am forced to wrap my brain around. The guilt and struggle is real for recipients and those who pray for organs FOR recipients. I get it. Don't lecture me. God gave me this burden. It's on Him. I knew that God had used Melinda Baize to bring Donna Dean into the picture. I knew God had used Donna Dean to connect Shelly with her miracle. It didn't take a rocket scientist to see the fingerprints of God all over this story. I felt so incredibly humbled to write the book that connected all of us. We were a community now, a STRONG community. We had a foundation of prayer and believed in truth, maybe a bit too much at times. Their truths had gotten incredibly heavy for me. Hundreds of them, one of me. But I begged God for strength, and voila, somehow I got up every day and loaded my pistol and dared the devil to cross me.

But there was Shelly. No lungs yet. She was weak, her oxygen levels were dropping daily. The six months that she had been given to live was looming. We were almost there. Of course doctors don't know everything, but they seemed to have been pretty close on this. She was still at the transplant hospital. About three weeks after our visit to see her, I decided to go to my cabin in the mountains. I needed to speak to God, up close and personal. Don't we all. I had been fasting cake since the visit to Oklahoma. Don't laugh. That's big for me. Ha! Some people were fasting meals and most of the Stronger girls were fasting something. God needed to show up. Where was HE?

I arrived at the mountain. I went to the porch and stared at those mountains. I began to talk to God and remind Him that we were out there on the limb and the storm was coming. We had claimed that He was going to show up. We had reminded Him that this was a great opportunity for the world to see faith win. And then I said, "I know she's a winner either way. I get it. I suppose I need to recognize the truth about that. I also know that we're born to die, this is ghettoville compared to the mansions You've prepared. Maybe You want her to see the splendor sooner than later."

I came to terms sitting in that porch swing, listening to the Dollywood train whistle blow. It blows pretty often and I love it. It reminds me of so many good things, mostly days gone by. But on this day it was part of my come to Jesus for Shelly. About 4:30 in the afternoon I got a business call from a friend. He's not a friend I see often. And this call was simply business in the beginning. But soon I found myself telling him the story. And I said, "Anthony, I'm not sure how this is going to end. She's weak and sick, and the clock is ticking. I'm trying to hang on to faith, but good people die sometimes, and God is still good." He boldly said, "By this time tomorrow, she will have lungs." The train whistle started blowing again, and we hung up. That dad-gum train. I processed what he had said, and I went to get food. I was working on a project and dove into that pretty deep. I distracted my otherwise twirling mind and found a place to take a long nap. I don't really sleep at night, I nap.

The next morning was uneventful. I was working, answering calls, and working some more on my specific project that was the flavor of the week. It was a nice day and I was outside again, enjoying the view and feeling like God hadn't forgotten me, or more importantly, that He hadn't forgotten about Oklahoma Shelly.

I get lots of phone calls. I don't answer them all. No one does these days. I was on the phone with a business call and I had a call coming in. I didn't recognize the number so I made no attempt to get off the phone with the current call. Then, suddenly, I realized it was an OKLAHOMA area code! I clicked over—no manners, no explaining—I left the other call high and dry. This was THE call! We had lungs! The caller said, "Momma Kathy, go get you some cake! We're getting lungs!" And guess what happened next? You guessed it. The train whistle celebrated with us! Shelly heard it and I said, "That's the Dollywood train!"

So my friend who risked the prophetic word, "By this time tomorrow" was oh so right. And the kicker, it was Shelly's birthday! Nope. Not kidding. You can't make this stuff up. God loves a nice little "what?" moment. We had one.

And ain't it just like God to show off. On Shelly's forty-fourth birthday, at precisely the SAME time she was born, they sewed in her second lung. The road was tough. It wasn't a picnic. Double lung recipients don't have a long life expectancy, granted. But as I finish this story: as I think of the blanket, the quick thinking of Donna from Bogalusa, the bus ride, the train whistle, and the dots that the LORD connected, I declare that we must extract the miracle and let it live beyond the flesh that we are doomed to die in. For the story of the girl who needed lungs shall outlive the girl, the storyteller, and the reader. Ain't that how God wants it to be? They say a good song has no expiration on its shelf life. Think of "How Great Thou Art" or "It Is Well with My Soul." I agree. But the story of a miracle will live forever. We shall praise Him until we get there, and then some more . . . for allowing us to be a small part of His big plan.

I don't care how busy I am or how cold my food is getting. If you see me out and about and want to stop me and share your story of a miracle, do it. I ain't afraid of cold fries! Especially after I've had church in a restaurant full of people. So when given the chance, I tell the story of the girl who needed lungs. If she goes before me, I will still tell it. But I have a feeling that God ain't nowhere near finished with Shelly from Oklahoma. And yes, she persisted.

Bears

Let's just put it out there, folks. My life has been one long roller-coaster ride. Much of it is circumstantial, but not all of it. Sometimes I feel like THAT person who constantly tells stories that NO ONE believes. I mean what are the chances, folks? Why does it always happen to me? I'm pretty much an organized train wreck. So let's just get that out of the way. I'm aware. And if not for the fact that I allow God to unravel the messes I so often get myself into, I wouldn't be here to tell these stories.

So here we go.

As many of you know, I love the mountains. Because I live in close proximity to the Smokies, those are my mountains of choice, I suppose you could say. We actually own a cabin there and visit often. I wrote my first book *Stronger* while sitting on a balcony looking at Mount Le Conte. The Lord told me to go to a mountain. HE was specific. He told me to find a place with a view. I rebutted and told Him that I was too cheap to pay for a view. He let me know that it was a must. I obeyed. I rented a cabin at Gatlinburg Falls in November of 2014, and write I did.

I sequestered myself in that cabin for days upon days. I would occasionally take a break and go home for a day. But ultimately, I spent most of November on a balcony, with earmuffs on my ears, a fuzzy robe, two pairs of socks, a Mac, a few snacks, and a lot of conversations with God. He didn't hang me. He met me there.

Many of you know the story. So, me and the mountains, after I wrote there, we were in a full-blown love affair. After I finished the manuscript, I went home to Hendersonville to start the editing process, and I was deep in the struggle of trying to figure out how one actually wrote a book, got it distributed, printed, available for retail, downloads, publicity, marketing. I hadn't promoted a record in nearly ten years. I was rusty. And social media had changed the game. Money was no longer the leveling agent for promotion. The new magic? Page "Likes." The reach was no longer defined by big budgets, but the smart people were telling me it was all about engagement and followers.

Hmmm. Interesting. So Granny is learning something here. Until the bus wreck I hated social media. However, after the awful accident, I learned to use it to populate updates on Mike and Kelly's conditions. I immediately realized the value after July 1, 2010. But before that? I called it hogwash.

Back in the day, the kids had MySpace accounts and I scolded them. I frequently told them that nothing GOOD would come of such nonsense. I insisted they use our websites, a controlled medium. For you see, this old hillbilly gal had lived through some days that required me to be a public relations crisis manager. Not my choosing, just a nice little gift that some lovely person dropped off in my lap. And, yes, you can insert sarcasm here. In those days there was no Facebook, Twitter, or

Instagram. Seventeen years ago we had newspaper, local television, and online chat rooms. Remember those? Oh Lawd have mercy. The drama that was unleashed in those cyber rooms. Buzzards ate flesh and most of it was under the heading of a thread about Jesus. Not. People pretending to be Southern Gospel fans bloviated about my divorce. They pretended to have the inside scoop and were more than willing to share. They critiqued my kids, insulted my management skills, and rejected us in every way imaginable, including direct slams toward a seven-year-old Hope Bowling. It mortified me. I hated this new idea that ANYONE could say ANYTHING about my family, or myself, and hide behind a screen name like "SG Fan For Life" or "Alto Singer" or some stupid handle that seemed oh so right to them but oh so wrong to me.

They were ruthless. Now I have my theories that these commentors weren't fans at all. They were what I call "bitter peripherals." Truth? I would like to call them something else, but since I'm working on walking AND talking this Jesus thing out, I won't.

My point: they were my/our enemies. You figure it out. They could attack from their king-sized bed every night right before they said their selfish nighttime prayers. When Steve and I got married, the "bitter peripherals" attacked us with a vengeance that's usually reserved for politics or street gangs. I still have dreams and nightmares about it. The pain went to my core. I was so bitterly disappointed in people. They knew the truth, yet they participated in a feeding frenzy.

It's amazing how low one's standards are when they're not the one being decimated. However, watch that same person's expectations of loyalty when they are THE one that's suffering at the hand of hypocrisy, when THEY are sitting in the seat of the rejected, abused, used, or cheated. And this is times ten if someone who's standing in ministry or authority invokes the pain.

I read your letters. It's devastating. The only cure is truth. There is a remedy, but without repentance and truth there isn't.

I see it every day. It amazes me how many people can adopt a bit of amnesia because it's JUST a photo opp. It's not our job to try to be God, clearly. But YOU are accountable for what you know. When you make a conscious decision to endorse a ministry/minister who you KNOW is out of relationship with truth, they're probably out of relationship with God. You figure it out. It's not difficult.

But sometimes the slander feels like a fight worth fighting. Sometimes it doesn't. It depends on where it comes from. Clearly, the Lord said He would fight for us. He did. But there's also a little scripture that says, "Don't let your good be evil spoken of." I'm a bit bipolar as far as the Internet is concerned. Some days I bounce back and forth, between these scriptures. There are no hard and fast rules to me. Defend what you feel must be defended; let go of the comments from people who aren't in your circle. And my best advice of the day: use the block feature. I have hundreds of people blocked on Facebook. Yep, sure do. The reasons are various, but many times I realize they're not loyal to me or mine. I realize they don't want what's best for my life. So? Why would I want to invite them into my "living room" of sorts and converse daily? MY wall is my home. It's my safe space. I don't want haters hanging out there. You shouldn't allow it either. Rules. You must have rules.

Moving right along. Back to the mountains.

So after I wrote *Stronger*, I started to dream of a cabin, you know a small, Pottery Barnish kind of place. No bears or deer for me. My dream cabin would be nestled on a mountain, with a wide, safe, paved road to get there, preferably close to Dollywood (I wanted to be able to hear the train whistle and see the fireworks) with a view of Mount Le Conte. A community pool would be nice, but it wasn't a must.

I started stalking the listing sites. I have a real estate license, and I frequently buy properties, always have. Steve and I have bought a property a year since we got married in 2006. That's one of our bonding stories. Third date: he took me to see a house he was building. It got him a fourth date. I desperately wanted to be FREE from all things music back in those days; the pain was too deep, and I wasn't in a place to deal yet. I had ALWAYS loved me a house, a build, a remodel, a property acquisition, so this blue-eyed real estate broker and I had great similarities on which we could possibly build a future.

So now it's 2014, and the wife of that real estate guy is now a self-acclaimed author. She took a little reroute that year. She picked the battle of pouring it out on that mountain. She had regurgitated her life and those mountains now represented so many things to her. Truly, sometimes it takes a mountain. So . . . the cabin hunt was fast and furious.

In 2015, we went to Pigeon Forge and Gatlinburg five times to look at properties. We struggled to see them because they were all rented. Summer is incredibly busy in the mountains. By July, we had narrowed it down. We knew where we wanted to buy; we just needed to find a cabin in that resort. There were two in our price range. Both had amazing views. One was a view of Pigeon Forge, and the twinkle of the lights after dusk, the close view of the Ferris wheel at the Island, along with a mountain view, but not Mount Le Conte. However, the night view was almost worth the tradeoff. We called and asked to write an offer sight unseen. Remember, it was rented. The response was that they had accepted an offer the day before.

Rats. We were disappointed. The market in the area hadn't recovered like Nashville had, but it was clear to me that it was coming within the next eighteen months. I convinced Steve that it was a solid investment. He's a bit slower moving than me, thank you Jesus. If he weren't, I would be orbiting the earth every day. HE keeps me grounded, and I keep him from dying of boredom. We were truly custom-made for each other. Too bad we didn't know that many years ago. But, as my grandkids so frequently remind me, we wouldn't be US. Our lives would be so very different . . .

and there would certainly be missing people at the dinner table . . . if I hadn't made every single choice I've made. MY life is the sum of the choices. Good, bad, and stupid, somehow He has managed to allow it to be a beautifully broken life.

So on this day, my little husband became "sold" when they told him it wasn't for sale. HE's like 90 percent of the world. He wants something when someone else has already bought it. Rule number one in real estate: your client will ALWAYS want the house that just went pending. So now I had a fully engaged co-buyer. We were buying a cabin! WOOHOO!

I could just see it in my mind's eye. People would come there and feel something different. They would read books of faith; they would eat pancakes, drink pumpkin spice coffee, watch the velvety shadows move across those mountains, shed tears, and decide that they could face their "tomorrow" junk back in Indiana, or Alabama, or Beaver Dam, Kentucky.

That was my vision. I went straight to God and said, "God, I will be generous, I will make this place a 'God' experience, if you will help me realize this dream." I know it seems like a very small thing to many of you. You're probably wealthier than we are. But $300,000 for a cabin, $25,000 for renovations, and another $5,000 to $10,000 for furnishings was a lot of money to Steve and Kathy Hannah.

But I believed it was a fight worth fighting. Finding a large down payment, obtaining a loan for an overnight rental, committing to a daily responsibility of keeping it rented. After all, this "mountain oasis" had to pay for itself. The costs were high: the insurance, ridiculously expensive utilities, the mortgage, the rental taxes and property taxes, and all of the maintenance and upkeep. But I knew what I knew. We kept looking.

In the meantime we moved some financial things into place and we readied ourselves to make an offer and close quickly when we found "that" cabin. There was a cabin on Lone Eagle in Starr Crest. When you popped over the hill to go down to the cul-de-sac, the view would take your breath away. It was panoramic. The best view I had ever seen. But dadgumit, it was rented . . . and it had been on the market for over a year. The realtor in us said, "Nope. If no one else wants it, we probably don't either." But that view. Holy cow, that view.

It was July. Traffic was horrible, it was hot, and I wanted a cabin. I felt like God had said yes. We had our approval and our funds, and I knew what I wanted. I knew that it was ALL ABOUT A VIEW for me. We drove up every pig path and gravel road in Gatlinburg if it led to a mountain view property with a "for sale" sign. We looked, we peeked in windows, we stopped occasionally and ate sticky bun pancakes, a day stretched into five, rooms were scarce, and Steve needed to get back to the real estate office. My random travels can cramp his work style at times. The truth, though? Most things can be done from a laptop and an iPhone. He was surviving, but tired. We were tired. We were tired of looking.

Now this is where most folks who decide that they want to be proud owners of a property close to their favorite vacation destination throw in the towel. We were almost there. The towel was in hand and Steve was ready to get on I-40 and head west. One more call, I said. One more. I said, "Let's call the agent who has the property with that killer panoramic view. You know, the one that's been listed for 376 days. "

He agreed. I called. Remarkably, she answered. We chatted. She had been a pastor's wife for decades, I quickly learned. He left her and the church for a Russian woman . . . if my memory serves me. We bonded. I told her my story, my name, the story of *Stronger*. We had common ground. Lots of common ground. Real estate, divorce pain, but both of us were still loving and trusting Jesus. I quickly realized that she was the premier agent in that area. Ain't that just like God. She had been an unemployed "dumped" ex-wife of a pastor, who had lived in a parsonage and been supported by a ministry that was NOW gone. But God. HE raised her up, sent her buyers and sellers, and had already taught her the patience of Job during her ministry days. She was amazingly equipped to be a superstar in real estate.

We chatted about life in general, our similar roads, and then she opened up about the cabin. She said, "It's still on the market because it has spiral staircases. There's no way to get the furniture out of the lower level. Well, you could if you hired a crane. The carpet down there is at least twelve years old. So is the furniture, and the balcony is on the side of that mountain. It's beautiful, but you can't throw a sofa over the balcony."

We drove back by the cabin. It was still rented. We walked around the cul-de-sac, we assessed the best we could with online pictures and walking on the porch and side yard. I say often, "The world is full of problem makers and problem solvers. You are one or the other."

I quoted my little speech to Steve. It was something like this: there HAS TO BE A WAY. Where there's a will, there's a way. We just need to be problem solvers.

The level of opinions typically gets intense during these conversations. I'm opinionated; he's very hard-headed. We clash at times, usually in the midst of a property discussion. That's okay. Iron sharpens iron. Our voices may rise, but no lasting struggle from it. We are passionate about our opinions. Once we fought in front of several people over cutting the top of a cabinet off. I wanted to do it RIGHT then. He wanted to wait and hire a cabinet builder to cut it. I proceeded to tell him that I COULD cut that cabinet myself if he wasn't up to it. HE got mad. But he cut the cabinet. He grabbed that saw and cut that cabinet; all the while I'm sure he was cussing under his breath. Just kidding. Maybe.

So we were having intense fellowship and discussing how to create an affordable access to the lower level without taking the risk of having to get a building permit.

Because we wouldn't know if the permit would be granted until we bought the property and applied, and if it wasn't granted? Not good. We would have an unusable lower level with gross carpet and the nastiest sofa known to man. So now we understood why it had been on the market for over a year. It also needed some major TLC. The décor was circa 2004 according to photos. Now mind you, we hadn't been inside yet.

But Steve Hannah and I parked in the cul-de-sac in front of that cabin, gazed at that view, and plotted to build a staircase down the side of the mountain that wouldn't change the footprint of the deck or the house. It had to be within the boundaries of what was already there, be safe, and be affordable.

He called Carl Buttry, an old friend whom I had known since early Crabb Family days. The Buttrys were like extended family to me and they had loved Steve, and welcomed him when he came into our lives. Steve loved Carl and Carl loved Steve. Carl has been building houses for decades. He wasn't a contractor like Steve; he was a framer, a jack-of-all-trades builder. He knew how to do everything and anything. Steve built for many years before the recession, but he hired subcontractors to build, while he was the boss, the risk taker, the overseer. He didn't know how to build steps on the side of a mountain. But he was betting on Carl. We talked to him, sent him pictures on his phone. Of course he could do it.

We made the offer, sight unseen. We negotiated the contract over the next few days, and boom, we had a deal. By August 27, 2015, we found ourselves sitting in a real estate closing. We owned a cabin with a straight-up panoramic view of Mount Le Conte. It was close enough to Dollywood to hear the train whistle and see the fireworks, and it was going to need a major refurbishing.

When I walked in for the first time, I knew it was right. The view from upstairs is indescribable. The fight had been worth it. The mountains of paperwork for the loan, the ridiculous struggle that the seller had presented regarding possession, the scraping to pull together a large down payment, it ALL felt very worth it the first night I watched the shadows fall on that mountain. I was in heaven. I cried and thanked God for giving me the desire of my heart.

We started lining up painters to stain the decks and furniture builders to build bunk beds, and I set a world record for trips to Hobby Lobby. I piled my SUV daily. We stripped out the expected bear and deer décor, and I went for an oversized cow over the fireplace. She was colorful, very large, and made ME oh so happy. The feel of the place changed quickly. Scriptures painted on shiplap and shaggy area rugs were brought in. The colors changed from hunter green and red to light blue and tangerine. This was going to be a happy place. People were going to come here to lose their fears. So I thought.

If my memory serves me, on Friday, September 4, Barbara and Carl were heading down to start the construction for the staircase that would stretch down the mountain. Now listen up. This was no little job. We had asked several people to bid it. We kept worrying about Carl's health and safety. I told Steve over and over, "If something happened to him on our watch, I would never recover. You could bury me with him." All the while, Carl was telling us it was no big deal—he could make it happen.

So on Friday, September 4, they left Bristol and headed our way. I had to go to South Carolina to an event. That left Steve with Barbara, Carl, their son-in-law Michael, their grandson Tanner, and Michael's uncle Robbie. They unpacked ladders, tools, and surveyed the lumber that Lowe's had dropped off. They were like little boys with Legos. They were preparing to BUILD something. I love people who enjoy creating with their hands. There's nothing quite like it. They were pumped.

I jumped on I-40 and headed toward Asheville and left it to them. I prayed a lot while driving. It was a steep drop if anyone fell, and I have a terrible fear of heights and have nightmares of someone falling off balconies, steps, or what have you. It was a good thing that I was leaving. I would have been in stroke mode.

The men worked, and Barbara cooked. Steve sent me updates and encouraging texts. He was loving the hands-on feel of getting to help these hardworking guys. Life was good. After my event on Saturday night, I wanted to go back to the cabin. My hotel was reserved for another night; my plans were to stay and head out on Sunday, but I changed my mind. I drove all night and arrived at my cabin about daybreak. I snuggled up to my teddy-bear husband and slept the morning away. He got up and returned to the hammering, stair-building with his friends, but I snoozed a good bit of the day away.

I awoke to a nice dinner and the warm feeling that a house has when old friends are gathered for a meal. It was perfect. The guys finished off the day and I think everyone left except Carl and Barbara, if memory serves me. They stayed because the next day was Labor Day, and Carl could finish shoring up and putting in the last of the steps. The framing had gone well and the most dangerous part was finished, but he and Steve had a few leftover things to do on Labor Day 2015. These two guys were living out the meaning of labor.

I can't remember much about what Barbara and I did. I think we went to TJ Maxx and Lowe's, finishing up my "need" list. Steve and I would be staying there until the renovation was complete. Once these steps were in we had to start on the basement tear-out, which included an old built-in sauna, the carpet and pad, and all of the furniture except the pool table. The painters were set to start staining that week and I had people lined up to bid floors and built-ins.

It was popping. We loved it. About dusk on Labor Day, Monday, September 7, 2015. Barbara started readying her bags to leave. Carl was finishing up and Steve was helping him. My happy meter was set at about a ten and Steve's grin told me all I needed to know. We loved our little cabin home. We knew that God had smiled on us. We loved our friends and knew that we were more than blessed to call them friends.

We hated to see them go, but they had work the next day and a two-hour drive back to Bristol. At about 9:45 p.m. we waved and watched their taillights head up the road. Steve and I looked at each other and smiled. The weekend had been a major success. He said he needed a shower. They had put in a long, sweaty day. So we started the process of moving our bags to the upstairs master bedroom before we took showers. That's when we found Barbara's pillow. Steve said, "Call her. This is an expensive pillow. They're probably not down the mountain yet. They can run back and get it."

I called her. I told her that one of us would walk outside and walk up the hill and meet them. They turned around and headed back up the mountain.

In the meantime, I had noticed the lock on the door. I asked Steve about the lock; it didn't look secure. It was simply a doorknob and the digital combination security lock had been removed. The seller had taken it off. I suppose now that it was just us. I was starting to take mental notes of things that may pose a security issue. Remember, I'm a recovering chicken. I need to know that there are locks and more locks.

He said they were installing the fancy lock on Tuesday or Wednesday. It would need a code to be opened, and we could change the code remotely for every guest. I liked that idea. But for that night we would just have to deadbolt it from the inside once we were settled in. We didn't even have a key. So if we left, we couldn't lock the door. But for that night, that would work.

I grabbed Barbara's pillow as Steve ran up those spiral steps to the shower. He was stripped down to his shorts so I volunteered to take it. I immediately noticed that the motion light was still not working. It was supposed to come on as you walked down the steps. The steps to parking were minimal: there's a small porch and then four steps. The new steps down to the lower level had made it possible for someone to go down to the lower balcony without access to the house. And I will admit, that creeped me out a bit. Remember, I'm the girl who had been the victim of an attack. I had my throat cut in a dark parking lot when I was seventeen. It took forty-three stitches to sew my throat up. I should have died, but I didn't. But I sure did live with many nighttime demons and a pretty good case of PTSD.

So my instincts are purely defensive when I'm in dark spaces. The new steps were to my left, and it was creepy dark. I surveyed with my phone light. All was well. I felt like my typical chicken self. On with the pillow delivery, so I sort of bopped down the steps to my right that led to the parking area. Four steps in the dark. I fear falling, so I instinctively held the rail on my left and put the pillow in my right hand. It was a big, nice pillow. I'm short. As I remember it, I realize that it served as a barrier. So, left hand on the rail, right arm holding the pillow, and my eager bounce down the steps . . . until, something stopped me.

At the bottom of the last step, this big old girl hit something that was solid and clearly blocking my path. The word stocky comes to mind. Pretend you close your eyes and bounce into a seven-hundred-pound Sumo wrestler. Or possibly it would be better described as a padded brick wall. I had hit a wall. Now realize, this is seconds, not minutes. It's dark out there, and my mind is trying to process what just happened. Remember the throat-cutting story. I can go PTSD on you in a flash. For a split second it occurred to me that they may have stacked lumber in the way, and that isn't a rational thought for many reasons, but that was my first thought. There were things in the driveway that didn't belong and I had smacked into something.

Then . . . the sensation of grabbing a limb registered in my brain, a furry limb, but I didn't connect the dots that fast. This is truly a split second of arm-to-arm contact. I grabbed a furry arm like you would grab your child's if you were guiding them onto an escalator or through a crowd. MY BIG hand on this furry forearm. Still not connecting the dots. And somewhere down inside me . . . that FEAR button got pushed. The fear button that signals there's no way out of this unless God intervenes. I pray you've never had "that" scream come rushing up your diaphragm from your gut. Nothing can describe that feeling. IT happened. BLOODCURDLING screams came out of this old woman—my instincts had finally kicked in. My brain hadn't caught up to my intuition, but it soon would.

As my deafening screams broke the still of that September night, my newest acquaintance decided she would show me what loud sounded like. Suddenly, there was a burst of air in my face that was like old-fashioned bellows. I remembered seeing bellows as a child. They were being used to stoke a flame. I was extremely intrigued as we played with them and blew air on our faces. This felt like those bellows. But I could SMELL breath. It wasn't a bellow, it was breathing and ALIVE, and it was in my FACE.

Before my brain could begin to catch up—it still hadn't—the most deafening sound I had heard in my entire life accompanied the end of the burst of air in my face. NO words can describe the ferocity of this roar. I ran. My instincts were in flight mode. I ran up the four steps with the pillow clenched in my hand. Remember, this encounter was in pitch-black circumstances. It was dark, so dark. And when I say I ran, I picture myself like a cartoon character that sort of bent in the middle and melts up the steps in a way that is only possible in cartoons and when a bear is chasing you!

I had on flip-flops that were also a big tripping hazard, and for a split second I freaked out and wondered if the door was locked. Within a couple of seconds I was on the porch and there was a stream of light from the kitchen that allowed me to see the doorknob. I grabbed the door, glanced over my shoulder, and sure enough, right behind me, a bear. A BIG ol' bear. Holy macanoli! The screams kept coming and so did the bear!

I would have been at home in a Barney Fife episode of *The Andy Griffith Show*. I was shaking so bad I could hardly open the door. I got it opened, all the while I was still screaming, and then I dead-bolted it—or did I? I didn't know . . . but I couldn't open it . . . because SHE was standing at the door, which had a plate-glass window, and she wanted to come in too. And to top it all off, she had two cubs! Bears rarely roar. She had. Bears never come in physical contact with a human without hurting them. I knew all of that. I screamed bloody murder, and Steve slithered down that staircase. He too was a bit like a cartoon character. I'm not sure which one, but he was down the stairs in seconds.

He came to the door and said, "What's wrong? I thought someone was trying to kill you." All the while I'm screaming and can't seem to stop.

Steve suddenly looked at me and said, "Oh my GOD! There's bears out there!"

I said, "WHY DO YOU THINK I'm screaming!?"

And then he said, "Barbara! What about Barbara. We must call her. Those bears will attack her."

Neither one of us had enough control to unlock our phone. I couldn't. I was shaking like Barney, Steve was shaking worse, and I was still screaming. Truly, it was beyond anything you could imagine.

Somewhere in all of this I realized he still had his shorts on—for that I was grateful. He later told me that I almost had a naked husband busting up in that kitchen. Right after a bear encounter is probably not the best time to see your husband naked.

So with me still screaming and Steve shaking like Barney, we hear Barbara and Carl pull up. I scream louder, Steve is in full panic. He was saying things like, "It's going to kill her! Oh God, the bear's going to grab her!" Before we could compose ourselves, she was at the door. Once again, imagine the cartoon where they grab an arm and drag a person through a small crack in a door, and the person's flattened body reinflates once they get through the tiny crack. That's a good description of what happened. We were screaming, talking, and she thought it was all a big joke!

Carl was in the car with his windows down. We screamed and tried to tell him to roll them up, and as we did, we saw a shadow of that momma bear and those babies walking down the mountain. They were leaving. No one got mauled. Barbara carefully went to her car; she called us and said they were okay, just a little shaken.

By now, I was in crazy land. Adrenalin confused with desperate panic and a burst of self-preservation isn't a good day for an old woman. For an old woman who had open-heart surgery a couple of years before? Not good at all. My body went totally limp. I cried and cried and cried. My heart was racing and I couldn't get it to slow down.

JESUS, I cried! WHO DOES that!? Who!? Steve was equally shaken. He wasn't having a full-blown PTSD meltdown like I was, but his big boy panties were probably going to need to be changed. It WAS scary.

I'm not gonna lie. I decided I needed some help or there would be NO sleep for me. I took an Ambien and went to bed. I snuggled so close to Steve that he thought he had a different wife. I couldn't get close enough. I would have crawled into his intestines if I could have found a path and I would have fit. Seriously.

I texted the kids and they couldn't believe it. Jason said, "Do you realize what just happened?" I did realize. I read several stories online that said that once there is contact, they will maul you. I saw pictures of dead bodies after mauling. I was FREAKING out.

But thankfully the Ambien worked. I went to sleep. At about 2:05 a.m. we both sat straight up in the bed. It sounded like a bomb had been dropped on us. We've been married eleven years, and we've never done that before or since. I've been roused by a noise here and there, but nothing more than a creak or a pop. This was a bomb. We were in immediate panic mode. We didn't even have a gun.

I said, "The bears are in the cabin. They're turning over furniture and breaking windows."

Steve didn't move. My normally brave husband said, "I'm not going outside and you can't make me." I didn't blame him. We sat there with our hearts pounding, I was imagining our funerals and the headline. "Steve and Kathy Hannah Eaten By Bears in the Smokies." As I type this, I'm laughing. But the truth: I was terrified. I had told the kids after the encounter, "Wouldn't the devil love to make this anointed cabin a laughing stock. Wouldn't he love to have me get killed on the front porch and ruin the vision before we have our first rental guest?"

So now . . . these loud noises had to be the bears or a deadly home invasion. HOLY cow! Either way, we were in trouble. Our breathing was heavy! I couldn't take much more. We were SCARED! Finally . . . Steve rolled over and stood up. He mustered the bravery to go to the window in the front of the house. We were upstairs. In clear view by the light of the kitchen lights shining through the downstairs windows, there was a silhouette of that momma bear and those babies. They had broken our bear-proof garbage cage, ripped it out of the pavement and thrown it on its side. Hence the loud thunderous noise. See, the berries were scarce that fall, and bears were hungry. And that momma, like many of us mommas, wasn't going to give up. She picked her battle. She knew where there was food. And she came back for it.

We spent the next day cleaning up the mess, washing out Steve's underwear, and I attempted to tell myself, "It's no big deal."

But in the end? I had to fight to get myself back on track. Fear had crowded out peace. I had to evict it. I too had to pick my battle, I had to decide that I wouldn't let bear fear ruin my getaway or my joy for the mountains or make me too fearful to come and go at night. I'm being honest when I say that it could have debilitated me when I'm there. But it didn't.

For, you see, the devil has tried to kill me more than once. I decided a long time ago that I was going to live until I die. That means LIVE loud, laugh often, eat cake, hug tight, and find adventures every single day. And, my word, some days they were doozies.

To all of you who struggle with fear: There's help. There's hope. The bottom line? You either trust Him or you don't.

No gray, just black and white. If I can meet a bear face to face and still go back to the spot, alone, and unload a car full of groceries after dark in the same place, you can conquer your fears. Right?

We got this, y'all.

Pick your battles. Living without the chokehold of fear is a battle worth the fight. Persist and resist. When the devil whispers and tells you that you're not strong enough to withstand THIS storm, tell him to FEAR you, because you ARE the storm.

Fire on the Mountain

If my memory serves me, along about September 4, 2016, Steve and I went to our cabin to fix a leak. We do that from time to time. The joys and blessings of owning a rental property can't be explained; it must be experienced. We experience it often. So we have made the annoying 210-mile journey to the mountains, settled in for the night, and looked forward to a day filled with trips to Lowe's and manly work. Make no mistake, I don't do manly work. Steve does. So my day was almost open. It was the anniversary of my throat-cutting attack. Forty-three years earlier I faced the chilling death swipe of a man with a scalpel in a parking lot. He cut me and ran. Well, he cut me after he told me to scoot over and let him drive my car. He also said, "If you scream, I will kill you." Most of you know the story. I screamed, and he cut me with a surgical scalpel and then fled on foot. I was in a hospital parking lot and made it into the lobby before it was too late. Long story. The entirety is in *Stronger* if you want the details. I ended up with forty-three stitches, a lifetime of fear of people and darkness and a big ol' dose of "I know God spared me and He has a purpose."

It's a little twisted to some, rightfully so, but I acknowledge the anniversary of this attempted murder. I've been known to go to Publix and buy myself a cake and eat it all alone while I cried and praised a God who knows the end before the beginning. A God who saw the souls that were saved this week in 2018, from the labor of my children's ministries. I was seventeen when the attack happened. Had the devil won that round, there probably wouldn't have been a ministry known as the Crabb Family; Krystal and Kelly wouldn't have been born; there wouldn't be a Bowling Sisters, a Bowling Family; it's safe to say that Aaron, Adam, Terah, and Jason would have had a very different life trajectory. So, being the sap that I am, I remember. I spend time talking to God when it's near or on September 5. This was my "thankful" week of reflection. So God and I were hanging. Tears were annoying me, for I couldn't stop them.

My thankful heart is always doing inventory of the life I've been blessed to live, a life I clearly didn't deserve or earn. That batch of tears was normal. But this new stir was different. I was a frequent political commentator at dinner, on Facebook, and anywhere I could find a willing audience. I knew what I knew. If the church didn't take a firm stand on social issues and stop letting the liberal bullying shame us . . . Christians were hiding under the bushes. The "Jesus shame" was a common theme. It was so prevalent that we now expected to be degraded on the daily news. The president was the leader of this mind-set and the amount of trickle-down permission was staggering. If our commander in chief bashes Christians and defends terrorists, it eventually changes the psyche of the young, the impressionable. It's not going to change me? I'm hard-headed and know what I believe. But I was becoming so nervous about a CHURCH that didn't stand for anything. They had been bullied into submission. They were scared to speak for fear of being humiliated, made to look like they weren't tolerant. There have always been political differences, but I saw the writing on the wall. We had regressed, as a society, to a place that made me fear that religious freedom could be a thing of the past. That, coupled with the barbaric stance that Hollywood and almost all people of influence had taken on abortion, the rabid hatred they spewed on those of us that disagreed? It scared me. Our children were being reprogrammed in university settings. The embarrassment of a professor scolding a conservative student was often the norm—it still is.

So . . . on this September morning, I was grateful for the Lord sparing me in 1973. I was grateful for my life, the souls that my family had ministered to . . . but I was heavy. And no, I'm not talking about my chubby legs or round middle; I was heart heavy. America. I was heavy for her. I love my Jesus, my family, and my country. I cry right on cue when the national anthem is sung. Count on it. And I saw a people who were being led to the slaughter.

Steve was trying to fix a leak and I was trying to get out of fixing a leak, so I told him I needed to run an errand or two. I did. I drove and talked to the Lord. I frequently ask Him if I'm crazy. I ask Him if I cry more than anyone else and if I change my mind too much. I could feel Him nudging me to listen. I had it. I was supposed to do a small winter gathering for the Stronger Sisters. The building up of the core group was necessary at times. The communication was fairly good with phones and Facebook, but sometimes the one-on-one time is a must. Sometimes it's needed to get the bonding job done. If these women were going to change their world, they needed to be undergirded. That was it. I drove to Hidden Mountain and went in to see my friends Kay and Brenda and find out what the availability looked like for say . . . early December. I wasn't looking to replace Stronger and the conference center setting. I was simply looking to go back to the cabin experience and a small intimate group. It was already September. I needed ninety days advance. So December it was. They could shop, and we could have a Christmas meal. Perfect. A little girls' trip in early December to see the lights, shop, and spend quality JESUS time with the sisters. PERFECT.

I drove back to my cabin and was ready to call Kay at Hidden Mountain and confirm the December dates. I hesitated to turn the car off. Mount Le Conte screams at you when you pull in. My habit of sitting in my car in my driveway, listening to music, talking on the phone, answering messages, is always an enemy of my time management. Today was no exception. I needed a bit more stare time at that velvety landscape, and I was possibly trying to avoid helping Steve. So I lollygagged for a few. Somewhere in that time span of five minutes I heard God say, "Election week. Call a prayer meeting the night before the election. Come to the mountain and pray, and then rejoice for I have heard you."

I was like, "Uhm, what? Election Day? Nope. I am going to be at home on Election Day. Wrong girl, God." And the truth was pretty evident. MY candidate, the only candidate who thrived when evangelicals were in the room, the only candidate who pledged Supreme Court appointees that would believe in the protection of the unborn, HE was behind. THE LAST thing I needed was to be sitting on a blasted mountain with 150 women who were devastated because their candidate had lost and Hillary was our president. THAT was the last thing I needed. I knew God was God. I get it. But I also knew that the fivethirtyeight.com folks had supposedly figured this polling thing out, and they were saying Donald was down by ten.

So I argued with God while Mount Le Conte looked on as a witness. I gave God a list of reasons why this was a bad idea.

1) People don't want to travel during election week.
2) They need to stay at home and vote.
3) We're PROBABLY going to lose.
4) I will look like a blooming idiot.
5) I want to be at home with my husband.
6) I want to suffer the loss in private.

I had a little Kathy know-it-all moment as I rebutted with my list. I remember thinking, "Well, shooey. Me and God had just been getting along great, and then He does this." What a limb this was. So . . . if I have a retreat on election eve and Election Day, that means I need women to come. Which means I need to populate this info, market it, if you will. Ugh. I was a Trump supporter, an avid one. God knew that. I took my last swipe at this argument and said, "God, that means this event becomes quasi political. (I may not have said quasi, but you know what I mean) and God, is that your plan for these retreats? I'm so confused."

He spoke to my spirit. The message was clear. Work while it's day. Work while you can. The future of your grandchildren is in the balance. I want to heal America. I want to be your God again. I am commissioning many warriors to help bring God back to the White House.

Wow.

And He finished with, "You will do it or I will find someone else who is willing." Now I ain't stupid. I know what it feels like to do the ridiculous and stand back and watch God rain blessings down like a Tennessee thunderstorm. I've been there and done that. I am the most imperfect person I know. Period. My opinion of me gets "iffy" at times. But my strong point is this. I don't shut the voice of God down when He speaks. This was that. HE spoke. And now . . . what was I going to do? Remember, I'm still in the car looking at mountains and talking to God, while Steve, on the other hand, is fixing toilets and doing icky work. It takes both. Know your place. I know I'm the mountain listener, got the T-shirt and the crazy button, and Steve's the consistent toilet fixer. We're quite the team.

So I called Hidden Mountain Resort, asked for my friend Kay, and in my most convincing voice I said, "Kay, I think a retreat the week of the election may be what I need to do." She said, "We have plenty of availability." I was biting my tongue, thinking, "Yes, I bet so. NO ONE wants to leave on election eve . . . NO ONE." But I knew that God had to be the boss. I've tried to do things alone before, and the result was major fail. I wasn't sure how I was going to fake it until I could make it . . . but I knew I must.

I rented the cabins. I gave her my American Express number quickly, told her to run it . . . all the while knowing if I paid the deposit I wouldn't change my mind or be talked out of it by a reasonable person, like my husband or children. I could hear their comments, "What? HAVE you lost your mind?" I was committed. I did a video immediately and announced that we were doing about a hundred women. That's what I felt.

I realized this wasn't going to be a Pentecostal throw down. It wasn't to be a music concert or a preaching service. In my spirit I felt like this would be somewhat like a threshing floor. Let me explain.

I had a professor who made me read a book when I was in college. I will leave this writer nameless. His name doesn't matter. What matters is the story. The writer, who was no longer a believer, so he said, described his upbringing in depth. HE described a Pentecostal granny who took him to a church where he was molested. That's where the devil got a claw in this brilliant man. He described the services that lasted six or seven hours. He described the perverted molesters and saints alike that ended up facedown, ashamed, weeping and praying for God to have mercy on their plight in life. He described hot muggy nights, wrestling with God and trying to deal with the pain he was struggling with in silence. And all of this took place on what he termed a "threshing floor" in an old tabernacle somewhere in the South. He was an articulate African American who lived in Manhattan and did the college speaking circuit—very distinguished. I was from Beaver Dam and I was impressed with his arsenal of words. He captured me in that auditorium in Bowling Green, Kentucky. I too like words and stories and remembering. I didn't know it at the time, but this story was to be logged in the "keep" part of my memory. I went to hear him speak for extra credit in my writing class—of course I did.

He somehow conveyed in that speech that the threshing floor was the symbol of complete repentance for "this" people and "their" God. I was a twenty-five-year-old and didn't know much. But I knew this man was wounded from the abuse inside the church, and I knew he knew in his heart that God wasn't responsible. No matter what he said, no matter what he believed, I knew. HE had divorced that tabernacle and that group of folks. But when a man tears up as he speaks, listen. You will glean from it.

He shed a tear as he spoke of a grandmother and mother who continued to frequent the threshing floor for his sins. He was condescending on the surface, but I remember how he described being on that floor with his nose in the dirt, being filled with a "spirit" and speaking in an unknown dialect. In my world, we call that tongues. This university crowd awkwardly giggled. I didn't. I felt his vulnerability. He had lost his way. The struggle of the abuse had taken him hostage. I was a spiritual novice. But I remember this story like it was yesterday, and it was in 1982 or 1983. What does this have to do with the election and the retreat on election eve?

Let me tell you. I hadn't thought of this author in years, actually decades. But there it was, tucked back there in that gray matter just waiting for this moment. I knew. We were called to the threshing floor for this hour. I hadn't really heard this phrase used except by this author. It was so random, but the LORD brought it to me. We were to plead for mercy for the molester and the molested. We were to plead forgiveness for the sixty million babies who have been slaughtered since *Roe v. Wade*. We were to plead forgiveness for the judges who normalized it, the doctors who excused away murder, and the girls and women who selfishly decided that women's rights include murdering their own seed. We were to ask Him to grant corporate forgiveness to America. The cabin would be a threshing floor, a tabernacle of praise, a house of hope, for that thirty hours leading up to the election results.

I had a picture in my mind. I couldn't have described it if my life had depended on it. I knew the attendees would be a core group of people who were vying for the very soul of America. It was to be different. It wasn't Stronger, where we battle addiction and the devil, holding up the frail and rebuking the spirit of suicide, addiction, and self-loathing. I knew this wasn't that. I couldn't have imagined having a retreat without Amanda, Terah, and Kelly, for we started on this journey together. Krystal had a day job in 2015 when we had our first meetings, and it made me sad that she had never attended a retreat. However, this time, she was coming. She would be strength for us. I was tickled pink.

Then Amanda had a conflict and couldn't come. I told her it was fine. Terah had a conflict. Same. Weirdly, I knew it was fine. My scheduling habits without checking schedules can lead to conflicts. But as I've told you, this one is on God, not me. So I pulled in Karen Harding, who agreed to be there, but she had to leave on the second night. I knew that my daughter Kelly and her girls could help carry the praise and worship if Karen could play piano and help sing. And seriously, in a bind, I can pull it off, but that's a last resort. I had a friend named Sharon who decided last minute to come, and so did Marcia Henry. They're both gifted song girls and musicians. We had this thing covered! God knew I didn't need to play! Ha! We filled the available rooms. Some were new gals. I loved that, for I knew God had a plan. He knew who needed to be there.

The election looked possible back in June, before Comey told us Hillary was basically stupid, but innocent. Ugh! But the media and the George Soros machine were revving up every possible Trump crime one could imagine. From lawsuits to unwanted sexual advances, there was a plethora of damage against this man. And then came October 7. The *Access Hollywood* Billy Bush tape came out. It was a few days before the final and crucial debate. And yes, nineteen women came forward and accused Donald Trump of some sort of sexual offense. Most of them weren't believable, but nevertheless, they lawyered up, hired a makeup artist and a stylist and looked for their fifteen minutes of fame on every news channel known to man.

113

This final debate was the only hope Mr. Trump had. And, yes, I had a cabin rented and had stood square on the fact that GOD said. But Lord have mercy, I was losing sleep. I was out on this big limb and I could hear the chainsaws being started. My faith was nervous. HE dropped as much as 26 percent in some polls in the days after the *Access Hollywood* tape. And remember, I had rented the cabins. Holy cow. Jesus take the wheel was about all I could get out.

So on October 7 the *Washington Post*, a Trump-hating rag owned by Trump nemesis Jeff Bezos, who happens to also be the founder of a little company called Amazon. He broke the story. He purchased the paper to have a voice against the likes of Trump, it was reported. It appeared from what I was reading that Jeff feared that the Donald would go after him for an antitrust issue with Amazon, as well as make changes to sales tax laws. They hated each other. So Jeff jumped the gun in front of NBC, who planned to release the tape. As you probably remember, by October 8, the entire world knew about Donald, the "P" word, and his shenanigans from eleven years before. Lord help us.

I personally don't look at the history of ANYONE from eleven years ago. If they have a tattoo, I may be forced to read their thoughts and stupid slogans. But except for tattoo screw-ups, most of us can pretend our words of choice on a bad day, eleven years ago, twenty years ago, forty years ago, or sometimes yesterday . . . didn't happen. Right? Believers are pretty generous with grace for people who speak loud and carry a big stick. Within the Jesus movement, murderers can pastor megachurches, ex-adulterers (we always hope it's ex) can build a complete brand on their testimony, recovered drug addicts can manage ministry street teams, ex-prostitutes can be evangelists. You get it. Evangelicals are ALL about some grace. But holy cow, Donald, you're killing us. The troops covered their eyes as they watched on their flat screens; they wanted to cry, scream, or in my case, eat a Twinkie. The fact that there was so much film, audio, and transcribed comments out there floating was unnerving.

I mean, if you're a Bush, a Clinton, or even a Kennedy, you walk around with talking points; you never find a true level of candor for the world to video, because you're painfully aware that you may go into the family biz of politics. And there ain't nobody in political office who's ever won that spoke to the press or the world, if you will, without sanitizing their words completely into the safe zone. No one has ever shot straight from the hip. Well, until now. Sometimes with forethought, sometimes not. Similar to the way REAL people REALLY talk. In our homes, when faced with a problem, we don't bring in analysts and attorneys to deal with a sudden "right now" family crisis. We don't rehearse talking points before speaking to our spouse. Trump had successfully run hundreds of businesses, successfully parented children, and maintained a core group of friends with his gift of transparent candor. His intelligence is conveniently his number one asset. But make no mistake, the thing that eventually landed this crude guy from the Bronx a crib at 1600 Pennsylvania Avenue was his candid "I'm one of you guys" unscripted straight talk.

He was the master of it. Why? It was genuine. HE loves America. HE knows how to get the economy moving. He was appalled by the same things that appall most evangelicals: loss of liberty, abortion, social dysfunction, disrespecting our history, and the list goes on.

So on Sunday night, October 10, Donald and Hillary paraded into Washington University in St. Louis, a scant thirty hours after most of us learned about the *Access Hollywood* tapes. Trump supporters were coping, but oh so worried. But in true Trump fashion, he unnerved his opponent. There's no doubt that the Hillary supporters that were going through all of the Donald videos, audios, transcripts, photos, trying to find dirt; these same dudes and dudettes were popping champagne in a $3,000 hotel suite on the strip. I would bet a slice of carrot cake that the Democratic National Committee had paid for that room. As the debate was ready to square off, they thought he was buried alive. They had managed to bury this guy in a short seventy-two hours. Well, so they thought.

I doubt there's ever been a candidate who would parade in the accusers of a former president to unsettle his wife, the heir apparent, to this "throne" called the presidency. Gutsiest thing I've ever seen. But think about it. The pious accusers who were popping champagne, along with entire Democratic Party had no problem with the accusations against Bill Clinton, nor did they seem to have a problem with his wife who made the victims the villain. He was accused of lying, rape, and everything in between. Find me three people who believe that Bill or Hillary are innocent as it relates to Bill's abuse of women, and I will bake you a cake. She was a HYPOCRITE in every sense. Donald knew it. As with most things, a visual is truly worth a thousand words. The close-up shot of Bill Clinton's horrifically awkward face as Paula Jones, Kathleen Willey, and Juanita Broaddrick paraded in to that debate hall was worth five points in the next poll for the Donald. For, you see, America had never seen a candidate who would put on gloves and engage in a street fight, just like he would engage at a board meeting. Crude and rude? Maybe. But scrappy as heck. And America was paying attention to the fight in this crude New Yorker. We were forgiving of his distasteful ways for the most part. We knew WE were in trouble, and we knew it would take a president unlike any we had ever seen to walk us out of this mess. We had never seen the downright dirty jabs that were leveled by the likes of the Clintons absorbed by a candidate. Not only did he absorb, he punched back. Tonight? The punch would hit old Billy Boy square in the face. Ouch. And voila, it's showtime.

Trump's breathing scared me. His pursed lips saying the "P" word had been the most played five seconds of footage in the history of cable news. Over and over it ran. He had to be the most humiliated man on the planet. Well, I guess he and Bill were tied. As the debate started, as the world watched, I said to Steve, "If he can face those cameras, if he can find the deep resolve to stay on message and not let the humiliation reroute his brain tonight, he can be the president. To function under that kind of pressure will take a special kind of strong."

He survived to see another day. The polls punched him hard, but they were never correct when it came to measuring this candidate. He made it through the debate, and in my opinion won the debate. So Donald was still alive and I still had those East Tennessee cabins rented, and 100 women were coming to pray down the fire on election eve. Wow. Jesus! I'm hanging off this limb over here. This old gal was now officially worried. I didn't speak it, but oh boy. I was so in tune with polling, and WHO knew it would prove to be SO wrong? I watched Trump crisscross the country in Trump Force One, state after state: he went to Wisconsin six times while Hillary didn't darken a Wisconsin door, Ohio twenty-six times to her seventeen, Pennsylvania, Florida, North Carolina, all of the battleground states. The cable networks broke in with a Trump rally about every time I needed to pee, which is a lot. My countrified common sense told me that 28,000 people don't stand in long lines, rain, and what have you unless they're planning to go to the polls and vote. My brain also told me that that same person who was filling arenas for a man that we saw say the "P" word a few days earlier was also reasoning out the difference in the circumstances and the sin, extending grace, and moving on. Boom.

October nineteenth arrived. Last debate. This time the stage was set in Vegas. The dust had settled and we were in the home stretch. He was still VERY much the underdog. She was smug. She was also dressed in a pantsuit that was a cross between Benny Hinn and Kim Jong-un fashion. Ewww. I personally hated it. Twitter and Facebook blew up with opinions about it. WHY? Hillary: bad choice for common folks in swing states who don't relate to your rhetoric on the best of days. I think clothes can matter. This was one of those times, in my opinion. Seventy-two million people were watching. Seventy million of them were making fun of the Benny Hinn suit. Geez.

We wondered how Chris Wallace would handle them. After all of the other debates had been moderated by the most biased journalists in the history of the world. And I use the word journalist VERY lightly in this case. I felt that Chris was going to be fair. He asked the first question. It covered abortion. Hillary said, and I quote, "I have major disagreements with my opponent about these issues and others that will be before the Supreme Court. But I feel that at this point in our country's history, it is important that we not reverse marriage equality, that we not reverse *Roe v. Wade.*"

Boom! The evangelical Democrats had that front and center to deal with. First question. They weren't eating chips and queso yet, no Little Debbies yet, no Facebook stalking yet, just them and the answer from the white pantsuit. I embrace abortion. Period. She made it clear that she didn't want a conservative judge who may protect her unborn grandchild, my unborn grandchild, or yours. SHE clarified that for ALL of us. I didn't have any doubts about her position. I read. I know the Democratic Party that my grandfather, who was in the coal miner's union, voted for. This ain't it, folks. But some people, including church folks, just don't deal with these social and moral issues the Dems have embraced. Ignorance is bliss. They go to church, love Jesus, and vote for baby killers. Oxymoron a little bit? Some of you will burn this book. You will hate this part, but it's true. So swallow it, repent, and let's be friends. You don't have to like Donald, but you have to defend life. If you're a Christian and don't defend the most vulnerable of all, a baby? No words. Nothing is perfect, no one is perfect, and LORDY HAVE MERCY, these candidates were riddled with mess. But when you spotlight "I AM FOR KILLING babies" and compare to "I am opposed to killing babies" with seventy-two million people watching, it resonates with anyone who values life. Trump stated his pro-life position and we intently listened. We gained millions of swing voters that night, but the pollsters sure weren't talking to them.

Time marched on. He campaigned, she stayed out of sight on many days. Anthony Weiner had his mess brewing again in the background, unbeknownst to the media and the common folks. On October 28, eleven days before the election, ten days before we were to gather at the mountain and pray, it happened.

We were on our way home from the beach. We had attended a ladies retreat in Panama City. I was driving and my phone rang. It was Amanda, my daughter-in-law, and she said, "Are you listening to the news?" I told her no. We had been talking and listening to music. She said, "Turn on Fox News! NOW!" I did. Holy mother of all things good, the Lord had done went and messed up the Hillary throne.

Somewhere in Alabama I heard something like this: Breaking news. James Comey has sent a letter to Capitol Hill today that relates to the Hillary Clinton charges. He stated, "We, the bureau has learned of the existence of more emails that appear to be pertinent to the investigation." The messages were found "in connection with an unrelated case." Well, well, well. What have we here? Within an hour the *New York Times* was touting that Weiner was involved, and Huma of course. Woohoo! I stopped and got a cheeseburger and Diet Coke to celebrate, and if I told the truth? I also got a 3 Musketeers bar before I got back on the road! This was officially a party. I was about to break out in a Pentecostal helicopter move right there in that Alabama McDonald's.

The independent voters all had one thing in common. They didn't trust Huma, and they despised this man named Weiner who was clearly the lowest of low. He had used his political power to prey on women—some were actually children, not women. Slime. A slimy politician with a name that was befitting his sexting addiction. Yuck. No Weiner fans were to be found. The Comey letter restarted the Weiner posts on Facebook, viral pictures that were too telling and completely gross, and once again set the stage for a decades-old assumption that the Clinton playbook was full of acceptance of perverted behavior as long as it benefited the greater good, as in the power trip of the wife. Huma was Hillary. I already knew it, but now, thanks to the Comey letter, like the abortion answer at the last debate, it had to be dealt with in the conscience of an undecided voter in Middle America. As they read their daily devotion, the news kept saying "Weiner" and the stark contrast from Comey in the eleventh hour was telling, so we thought. It must be real bad for him to put himself in this pivotal position, so we thought. Now I could write a book on my opinion of James Comey but it will have to wait. We must get back to the Donald and Hillary.

The meat-and-potatoes families were coming home to the party of conservatism. Most vegans weren't. Ha! Starbucks snobs were rolling their eyes at Trump bumper stickers, F-150 owners were proudly plastering them on. The divide was increasing daily. But at least, finally, the conservative crew felt they had a voice. We prayed and posted. Rinsed and repeated. Daily. We, a couple hundred thousand people and me, were on a mission. We felt called for such a time as this. He was an unlikely candidate to say the least, but he thrived when the Jesus peddlers surrounded him. In my opinion, he didn't fully understand the power of prayer; there's no way that this Presbyterian from Queens could fully understand the mannerisms and complete absorption of these ministers as they ushered in a move of the Holy Ghost. It happened. And HE welcomed it. The stories circulated. I heard them and they encouraged me. He knew that God was his only hope to govern, he knew. The story of Trump should teach us so much as believers. God's not looking for perfection, ever. He's looking for a man or woman who would be willing to walk through fire to save a nation. He had His man.

The polls still looked terrible. There was bounce. However, Comey letter or no Comey letter, she was still in the lead and favored to win in every poll, except the *LA Times*. Seriously? No Rasmussen, Fox, but a California poll? I was addicted to www.fivethirtyeight.com. It updated in real time. There were changes every few minutes. But let me tell you, they sure enough got it wrong. In early November when I was packing my car to go to the mountain, it looked grim. The reality of the week was daunting. I was hosting a three-day party to pray for an election that wasn't going to go my way. Day one, we would pray. Day two was Election Day. I pictured looking at their faces. Excuse the dramatic description please, but I pictured them looking at me with eyes that said, "What happened? I thought God told you to gather us here." I was already reading everything I could on subjects like "When God has another plan" and "Jesus is still Lord no matter who is president" and the old faithful, "Well, it's just the fulfillment of scripture."

I was a wreck! A TOTAL wreck. In order to be able to cope, I had offered to cook a full-blown Thanksgiving meal on Election Day. I wanted to make it with my own hands for these strong-willed sisters. These women who took vacation days, sick days, left husbands and children behind, and went to the mountain with that crazy woman who said God told her to go. I looked at this in an abstract way, and I laughed. I thought, who would do this? Why would they do this? But here's the truth. God's ALWAYS going to have a people. A people who march to the beat of a different drum, a people who won't allow the vision to be erased, a people who are willing to fight when necessary. We had them coming. One-hundred-plus Jesus mommas packing a punch. They were battling on their knees. They were fasting and speaking life to their children's future. They were believing that the soul of America was worth a few sweaty nights on the threshing floor. They were girl power personified. Some of them had been walking this road for six decades, and they hadn't turned around. They knew Him. They knew who THEY were in Him, and they were there to get the job done.

We settled into our rooms. I love to stay at Hidden Mountain. I've been going there for many, many years. I was in the big River Lodge, with its upright piano, chef's kitchen, and room to sleep forty. The huge fireplace with the television over it was positioned in the main living room. The dining room seated fifty or sixty I think, and we spilled over into the living room for our meeting. I went down the day before and stayed with my friends Melinda B., Donna, Melinda C., and Susan. They were all Stronger Sisters and had encouraged me to come stay with them on the eve of election eve. My cabins were rented so Kelly and I went and stayed with these precious friends. This group of girls had met at Stronger and now exemplified the movement. They held each up through texts, calls, and an occasional long weekend. They were separated by miles but that didn't stop these sisters. They stayed actively involved, as friends should. I busied myself with the chore of making vegetable soup, enough to feed 115 or so. Kelly brought her girls and we had a few late deciders, so we were now closer to 115 for a final count. So on election eve eve, the polls were still telling us that doomsday was near. Hillary had been in the lead for ninety-eight weeks. The Comey letter pulled Trump closer, but the *Access Hollywood* tape, along with the "fake news" that seemed to be bolder than ever about this candidate, was enough to keep the polls tipped for Hillary.

I knew what God could do. But I also know that sometimes we get in the flesh and clearly I must have been in MY flesh when I planned this election week mountain retreat. And sometimes when we mess up? We gotta take the medicine. So I felt like an old constipated woman who was facing a dose of castor oil. I was ready to take it and get it over with, pray I didn't vomit, and prepare the bathroom for what was coming. It's that simple. I was going to have to participate in the drive of shame back to Nashville after encouraging these women to come and pray down the fire. Were we doomed to watch Hillary wear some god-awful pantsuit and flash us that condescending smile?

Jesus. HELP me. That pretty well summed up 90 percent of my prayer life. By now, election eve eve, I was praying even when I was sleeping. If I was on the toilet? Praying. Cooking? Praying. Facebooking? Praying.

It was time for the service, prayer meeting, hen-gathering, whatever you want to call it. It was time. I didn't have clarity on what we were to do. This was different. Good grief, I didn't have clarity on anything. God has asked me to follow Him with a blindfold on. So here I am, we've eaten our soup and buttery grilled cheese—only the best for my sisters—and now what? I hadn't asked anyone to speak. I don't roll that way. I usually know exactly what I want. I know what I want them to sing, when to sing it, who is going to speak, and what the result needs to be. And of course, it's ALWAYS subject to a move of the Holy Ghost, always. But my motto with the kids was always have a plan in case God makes you prove you went to the trouble. So now. I panicked. I didn't have a plan. And this was obviously a different animal. We weren't here to be Billy Graham. Sure, salvation is always the GREAT message. But this meeting was geared toward strong gals, women of serious faith, women who displayed serious concerns about America. This was the A team. The get 'er done mommas. They were proactive about God and country.

We proceeded. After a dozen or more years of friendship, I've learned something about Karen Harding. She's an incredible singer, yes, that's a given. But don't let the talent fool you. She's a lot more than a studio singer. I've never felt it was a mistake to hand her a microphone and say, "Sing for me, Karen." For, you see, the day that God told me this mountain meeting was to be, He also told me that Karen was to be there. I opened this meeting up with a slight bit of candor about the reason we were there. I wasn't totally candid, because if I had been everyone would have gone home. Instead, I rallied the troops. I believe that we ALWAYS have to "fake it until we make it" and sometimes speak it until it becomes reality. I did my best and then handed Karen the mic.

If memory serves me, she opened with "Holy Ground." The talented Sharon Walker, a friend and pastor's wife, accompanied her on keys. The spirit fell immediately. It was like a light switch was flipped. These women sang, and praised, and cried, and testified, and prayed . . . for hours and hours. About fifteen minutes into the night I stood and assessed. I was amazed. These gals had traveled from all over the United States to this little mountain in East Tennessee. They were the modern-day picture of unity. They knew each other how? Most were acquainted through Facebook. Most had walked through some stuff. Most knew how to get down to business – with God. Maybe it WAS going to be okay.

The night grew long and the spirit grew thick. My friend Marcia Henry was praying for the needs of these girls. We had a makeshift prayer line by now. The music was still heavenly. Kelly, my dear friend Heather (Ruppe Bennett) alongside my granddaughters Hope, Gracie, and Katelanne kept the flow of worship. By 11:30 one thing was apparent to me. These women had the faith to believe that their prayer and dedication to this mission was working. They thought Donald J. Trump would be our next president. These women were the best of the best. After midnight we split into groups. Some went to bed and promised to pray in their pajamas. I was one of those. My body was exhausted. I had a physical struggle that hadn't been diagnosed yet, and I was struggling. I went to my room and begged God to wake the nation, admonish them to get up, stand in lines as long as necessary, and vote. It was a requirement that these ladies had to early vote if they were coming to "Fire on the Mountain." I early voted weeks before and had to stand in line, so I feared that long lines would discourage folks who had to get to work. I prayed for rain in urban areas and for sunshine in the South. Judge me if you want—I'm just being honest.

I slept for an hour or two. I felt like the soul of America was on the auction block. And it was strangely, weirdly, my job to stay on the "threshing floor" all night for her. I did my best. My sister friends were amazing. I got text after text: 3:00 a.m., "Praying still." Another at 4:19 a.m., "We're over here still praying. The Holy Ghost is moving." And I'm fully aware that we weren't the only ones. Millions upon millions went to bed praying for this election. Was this sleeping giant finally awake? We would know in twelve hours.

Nothing is much prettier than a mountain sunrise; that is, unless you've had almost no sleep. The chatter was brisk, the coffee smell was drifting to the basement where I was sleeping, and I could hear someone singing. I resisted as long as I could, but it was time for my hiney to be up. I had put my turkeys in to cook at about 4:00 a.m. and I needed to check on them as well as start my day as Chef Kathy. For on this day I was the cook and chief bottle washer. It was by design and it was what the doctor ordered. By 11:00 a.m. I was so busy working and preparing, and occasionally a sister would come hang out and help. I hadn't watched anything on television. Now, granted, I had checked the polls. Clinton had an 85 percent chance of winning, so they said. "Just make the dressing, Kathy. You've got deviled eggs to do, green beans to do, pies to make, potatoes to get on, hams to glaze, sweet potatoes to peel. Just stick to the plan," I told myself. Yes, I talk to myself. There, I said it. So do you—you just won't admit it because you've been told only crazy people do that. Not true. Everyone does it. On November 8, 2016, I mastered the art of having conversations with myself.

I cooked three turkeys with three pans of cornbread dressing, four brown-sugar-glazed hams, thirty pounds of mashed potatoes whipped with eight sticks of butter and a quart of heavy whipping cream, three gallons of green beans laden with ham chunks, three sweet potato casseroles, two gallons of cream corn with butter, three broccoli casseroles, two gallons of creamy mac and cheese, two quarts of cranberry sauce, dozens of amazing desserts that the ladies brought, 120 glasses of sweet tea (yes, we had picked up another visitor or two, we were up to 120) and two hundred yeast rolls and creamy butter, delivered straight from Heaven. I saw the label on the rolls: it said "Made in Heaven."

The girls helped me decorate that huge forty-foot-long dining table with everything that screamed fall. We grabbed items from the house and then went into the yard. Within minutes it was perfect. We were ready for some Pinterest, let me tell you!

That table was camera-worthy, and I hate to brag, but Granny cooked a great meal for her sister friends. They gathered in for dinner around 5:30. We ate. It felt a bit like the Last Supper to me. Sort of. My faith wasn't completely dead, but it was weak. I was blaming me, as I said. I was wanting to sucker-punch myself for missing God. As I watched these wonderful girls and realized that they trusted me with such a big piece of them, I felt such a responsibility to be who they perceived me to be. Most of us live our lives trying, and most of us never feel like we make the mark. Tonight was one of those nights that I would give a week's wage to turn the clock back and rethink a choice.

Well, pass the dressing and the bread, my nerves were in control of my willpower that day, November 8, 2016. We ate the feast and laughed a lot. There's something about food that soothes us for a moment. We ate the amazing cakes the ladies had baked, topped off our drinks, and we began to switch gears. We filled the living room to capacity with a standing-room only crowd. It WAS ELECTION DAY. The polls were closing in the East. My heart was in my throat. I prayed that valve that had been repaired was doing the job, because my pulse was off the chain. We began to sing, praise, testify, and that night I was heavy on the "God is in control" theme! I was preparing these girls, so I thought, for the letdown. Momma Kathy was trying to cushion the face punch that Hillary was set to deliver, according to every news outlet. I knew God had been in the house. I knew He had delivered a couple of girls from some junk, and I told myself that good things happened, so all wasn't lost.

The returns were as expected between 7:00 and 9:00 p.m. Red states were red and blue states were blue. No surprises for the most part. The partiers were gathering at the Javits Center in New York City, the chosen spot for Hillary's coronation. Hillary's friends were smug, confident, and oh so appalled that hateful Trump was allowed to run. After all, shouldn't this be a coronation of sorts? As Al Sharpton, Melanie Griffith, Debbie Wasserman Schultz, Mayor de Blasio, Katy Perry, Governor Cuomo, Chuck Schumer, and many of their elitist friends drank their wine, smirked at the "ignorance" of the flyover states, and confidently watched the returns come in. The donor lounge was packed and alcohol was flowing. The Madam President buttons were ready for the vendors to sell, the speech was written, and the party was in place. The media was already in place, and boy were they slobbering. They had rehearsed their lines while looking in the mirror. "Clinton wins in a landslide!" They were SO ready to start the party and would as SOON as they had those dad-gum projections. They had this.

Meanwhile on the mountain: by 9:00 p.m. the mountain sisters were truly in a state of travail. Some of these women had fasted for months for this election. They didn't believe the media and they had persisted with their fasts for months. On this night, we praised, stopped, and did long prayer intervals; occasionally someone had a word, and when a state would fall for Trump, we turned up the television and cheered. It was mostly a spiritual experience, but the patriotism was as evident as the love of family. They loved America.

Along about 10:20 I think, the swing state of Ohio was called for Trump. WHAT? And we all know that as Ohio goes, the election goes. The room erupted. I was giddy. Suddenly. From needing a nerve pill to giddy in five minutes flat. How human we are. The girls screamed and erupted in song. "Oh Victory In Jesus, My Savior . . . Forever!" Shew!! They sang it. Facebook live was watching these gals as they journeyed into the land of "put your money where your mouth is and go to an election retreat and proclaim that you're going to pray the fire down."

And back in New York, Katy Perry decided to address the Clinton crowd. She knew. You see, Katy is the child of Pentecostal ministers. She knew Mom and Dad were praying. She had been out campaigning with Hillary, alongside a dozen other heavyweight stars, but about 10:14 p.m., a few minutes ahead of the big bomb of

Ohio, she began to ramble about her parents voting for Trump, and the audience gasped. They were strangely confused. But me? I say that little missy knew that her parents and all of their Jesus crowd were just getting it . . . praying the fire down. I think Katy is smart enough to know what she's dealing with. Her choice to speak up way ahead of the data on that night supports my theory.

It was enough to make an atheist rethink their choice. But it occurred to me that a few Hillary supporters were going straight for the Jack and Coke. My mountain women had some brass—brave souls they were. They ain't scared to climb trees or go out on limbs. But that night? They sang and prayed. About 10:50 my phone rang. My friend Brian Hudson called and said, "God told me to call you. You need to get all your women to pray. You need to pray for ten minutes starting now." First of all, Brian's not terribly political. And second of all, he said he didn't know we were on the mountain praying already. But we stopped and dropped. We made an altar and prayed. Someone set a timer. We prayed ten minutes as instructed. When the ten-minute prayer was declared over, you could hear a hundred women saying, "In the name of Jesus! We claim it." I had chills. Much was going on in the spirit realm.

Within forty-five seconds we heard Fox News project, "Donald Trump wins Florida and North Carolina." We shouted like freed prisoners! The spirit of celebration was in the house. We ate cake, we hugged, cried, praised, and ate some more cake. I knew enough about the demographics of America to know that Ohio, Florida, and North Carolina had decided.

Back at the Javits Center the math skills of the Clinton camp seemed to fail. They told supporters and media alike that the West Coast would save them in the electoral college. I was screaming, "It WILL not! Are you smoking crack? Did the math change?" They were in sheer panic. Anxiety was a real thing to those folks at the Javits Center that night. No one . . . and I mean NO one, from the top to the most menial staffers . . . had prepared for this. After all, that very morning, some of their folks were spouting that her chances of a win were sitting at 99 percent. So the Hollywood moguls along with every film star living couldn't save her. Every singer that had ever wailed a note, with about three exceptions . . . posted and touted "I'm with Her" and it didn't sway us, the working class. Good grief, many FAMOUS pastors and Christian singers promoted her . . .and it wasn't enough.

The Clinton supporters were clearly devastated as midnight approached. The night had been long; so were the faces. Tears started to flow. The question was asked by so many in that weirdly insulated crowd: "How could 'they' be so stupid?" They despised our clinging to our religion and our guns so VERY much on this night. They despised us for going to the polls. They spoke of low turnout and popular vote. They spoke of racism and moving to Canada. They spoke of the world ending. Yes. As the "Hillary" documentaries looped and the lyrics to "Ain't No Mountain High Enough" were audible, CNN, MSNBC, and dozens of news outlets frantic, the on-air personalities were losing their ever-loving minds. The difference in their countenance was astonishing. The assured liberals were perky and smirky at 7:00

p.m. By 11:00 p.m.? They looked like they had been caught in a hotel romp . . . a bit disheveled, distracted, and overall . . . they just didn't want to be there. They continued to say the world just couldn't continue. We were a financial and moral wasteland, NOW that TRUMP was going to be our president. HA! Forty-five!

Back at the Trump residence in Trump Tower, it was becoming clearer that Donald J. Trump would become the forty-fifth president of the United States. When he realized that Pennsylvania was going to fall for him, he started writing an acceptance speech. No alcohol to curb the disappointment, no Xanax to mellow the Donald, for he wasn't a fan of mellow or alcohol. He'd never had a drop in his life. Something about that made me incredibly proud, of him, and for me. I bragged about it, touting that a man who's never had a drink SHOULD be nominated. HE wrote and we partied. No one seems to be clear on what Hillary was doing.

She didn't come to her failed party at the Javits Center, and no one heard a word from her. Along about 2:00 a.m., she sent John Podesta, her campaign chair, over to give a pathetic speech.

Meanwhile at Trump Tower the Trumps were giving the Kennedys a run for their money. Camelot 2.0 maybe? The family is tall and angular and wear clothes like only the tall and rich can wear them. They take family pictures to a whole new level. And tonight was the pinnacle of family gatherings for this famous clan. It was STRIKING that this man had garnered the respect of all of his in-law children in the truest sense. Jared Kushner was a died-in-the wool Democrat, yet he ran the online portion of this campaign, lending immense strategic knowledge and Facebook training that he received from the Facebook developers. He asked for a brief tutorial on how to target states, demographics, and voters in general. Mark Zuckerberg's folks accommodated Jared. So this lifelong Democrat had just managed to pull off the biggest upset in the history of elections for his father-in-law. Clearly, he loved and respected him, his heart, and his patriotism. The daughters-in-law seemed equally committed to this man. With two ex-wives, five children, a passel of grandchildren, and approximately 23,000 employees, Donald Trump still found the energy, finances, and time to run against seventeen candidates in the primary, Hillary in the general, and pull off the defeat of our lifetime. And I have a special kind of respect for men who keep their families together after the mess. I'm confident that his divorces were probably a result of his failure—well, most likely. But here's my point. He didn't walk away from the family. SO often . . . men will avoid the reality of their choices, their sin, by avoiding the reminders. The children. The grandchildren. They find a new family, a new normal, and their children are crushed. It changes the outcome of generations when abandonment is this cruel and abrupt. I've seen men who claimed high standards and completely abandon children that they raised, grandchildren too.

So Donald J. Trump didn't drink, didn't divorce his family to get rid of the personal guilt, and he agreed with many of my opinions. Additionally, he hadn't allowed failure to define him. Divorce, bankruptcy, public disagreements didn't deter him or shame him into silence. We are surely related in some way!

He gave a beautiful speech about 2:40 a.m., surrounded by sleepy children, proud adult children, and a beautiful wife. He was humble. He didn't divide; he invited his enemies to be his friends. It was good. I think the Lord was pleased.

And so I shall never forget. Election Day 2016. The mountain. The faith that was deposited into each of us that night? No words. It will make us rethink that response to our children. Instead of saying, "That's impossible" we will be more inclined to say, "Hard work and God can clear the path for that to happen!" We left changed. EVERY SINGLE one of us. We packed the cars, gave our hugs, cried a bit, and said our parting prayer. I felt like we had lived out an Old Testament story. God had delivered again.

This chubby chick drove back to Nashville in disbelief. I kept saying, "What just happened?"

I expect to be a little old lady in a nursing home, eating lemon Jell-O delight, playing the piano in the recreation room for the "old" people of which I will be a ringtail leader, and I expect to be telling the story of the mountain, the election, and the day He spoke to me and said, "I want you to get your girls, go to the mountain on election eve and pray!"

I was blessed to snag some tickets for the inauguration from Diane Black's office— she's my U.S. Congresswoman. I took my granddaughter Cameron with me. She's the most political eighteen-year-old I know, and this granny loves it! Aaron and Amanda (my son and daughter-in-law) were invited to sing at the Faith, Freedom & Future Inaugural Ball. What a bucket list thing that was for me. I told God that if he won, I wanted to witness the swearing in. Diane Black's office gave me little to no hope regarding tickets when I requested them. They were scarce, I was told. They followed up with an email that said I would not be given tickets. I was disappointed. I considered trying to find an alternative source, possibly through a pastor or speaker who was to speak. But in my spirit I knew that God had this. He would provide without my help. HE would honor me. I knew it.

My original request was on November 11, by way of email. The response was speedy. On November 18 the representative responded with an unconditional no. About seven weeks later, on January 4, I got an email that said:

Good evening—I hope you are well!

Since my last correspondence, our office has had tickets become available.

With that, I am thrilled to inform you that our office is able to provide you two tickets to the ceremony.

Each office received less than 200 tickets to offer to constituents, and unfortunately not all requests can be honored. So congratulations!

First, we need you to confirm your acceptance of these tickets by Monday, January 9 by 5:00 p.m. EST time via email. This is because we would like to make these tickets available to other Tennesseans if you are no longer able to attend.

So you are aware, Inauguration tickets cannot be mailed and must be picked up in our Washington DC office (1131 Longworth House Office Building, Washington DC, 20515) between Tuesday, January 17 and Thursday, January 19 by 4:00 p.m. (EST). The best entrance for our office is on Independence Avenue, SE, between South Capitol Street, SE and New Jersey Avenue, SE.

Won't He do it! He gives us the desires of our heart.

And so I watched as Donald J. Trump was sworn in. I was cold and wore duck boots. It wasn't perfect, but it was good. Nothing is perfect, but it can be good. Perfect is reserved for Jesus and Heaven, in case you hadn't noticed. Earth and Trump ain't never going to be perfection. Ever.

He didn't look to the left or the right. He kept his eyes on the prize. And, yes, he persisted. And listen up, folks. HE honors God, the word of God, life, and he likes jobs and people who like jobs. It's enough for me.

I'm thankful for the mountain miracle. And I would advise you to never tell those women that they didn't change the course of history. I'm fairly positive that they would disagree. Sometimes it takes a mountain prayer meeting to get the job done. This was one of those times.

As I type this last paragraph, our president is embroiled in multiple investigations that are completely ridiculous. Nevertheless, the economy is booming, people are talking about God in public again, and the polls tell us that we are an optimistic people again. It's morning in America! And once again, Donald J. Trump has proven that he knows the "art of the deal" and he's going to use those skills to fight for everyday Americans, not illegals. As long as he allows the men and women of God to speak into his life, he's going to continue to slay. I believe it's God's plan and he's God's man.

Liberals. Get over it. Soon. You're getting on my nerves.

Fire on the Mountain FOR REAL

On the morning of Saturday, November 26, 2016, Steve and I packed up his trusty green (who buys green?) extended-cab Ford F-150 pickup with our must-haves. Admittedly the list of must-haves has changed considerably over the years. The cute pajamas, size five jeans, and hiking boots of my youth have given way to the flannel gown, a travel bag full of daily medicines, and a warm pair of stretchy leggings. Now, mind you, I was sure to bring long shirts to cover the sin that's so easily visible in those leggings. Yes, I got the memo that leggings ain't pants. I know. But when one is headed to the mountains with the crew of best friends, and when one anticipates pancakes, catfish, loaves of hot bread and apple butter, this stretchy leggings thing is on point. So on this particular Saturday we were happy to be headed east on I-40, and we were trying to continue our thankfulness past turkey day.

The election was beginning to sink in, and Steve and I were very happy to see the end of socialistic ideology and liberal leadership on social issues that crossed the line with us, as it related to morals. We knew that the media and the opposing party were losing their minds, and we knew there would be consequences directed at we the people. These folks thought the Bible Belt, the evangelicals, were a nonissue. They thought the blue-collar vote was a given for Hillary. And I knew they would stop at nothing to disrupt the transition. I knew the media would feed us nothing more than salacious Trump stories from unnamed sources until the cows came home. After all, every person at CNN, MSNBC, and ALL of the liberal media was in hysterics. Doomsday, they said. On Election Day when it was evident that a Trump win was happening, Rachel Maddow said, "You're awake by the way, you're not having a terrible dream either, and you haven't gone to hell."

And when Chris Wallace at Fox News said, "I think Donald Trump has a path to the presidency" you could hear the haters moan in disbelief. It was depressing, to say the least. The bias among the media and the rich and famous was so thick. And suddenly, these folks seemed to hate the common man. For we had thrown a wrench into their liberal agenda. But I knew, and you probably knew as well, that God had stirred His people, as we stood on the jagged ledge ready to fall. For AMERICA was on the ledge, socially and economically. Change had to come. We were standing on the cliff and Barack and Hillary were standing there with hands raised to push.

The day after the election we had a letter in our mailbox from our good friends at the IRS. Talk about timing. Targeted? Maybe. But nevertheless, it was real and relevant. Yep, we were facing an intense IRS audit. The nagging torment of a lawsuit or an audit marks your psyche with its own special kind of crazy. Life is good, the world is sunny and bright, your kids are amazing, your grandkids more amazing, Jesus is still on the throne, He's still healing and delivering, the house is clean, the husband is all smiles . . . and then you remember. UGH! That audit. Jesus! PLEASE let there be an immediate shutdown of the IRS. After all, you're able to do anything! Do it Jesus, do it. You know that kind of prayer that you pray after a breakup or divorce.

The prayer where you say, "God, you know what a rotten piece of dirt he is! And you know WHAT he did. And you know HE deserves to be fat, bald, or I could even go for dead. But now, God . . . I would never kill him, I'm just saying that he deserves it." And then you have to repent for the prayer? You know what I'm saying? Well, that was a bit like my IRS prayer. I wanted them shut down! I was praying that the flat tax that a gazillion presidential candidates have peddled . . . would suddenly be the day's headline and be the law. I said, "God, you can do this!" But He hadn't done it. And I am not ignorant concerning these things. It's not possible to pray the IRS away, nor is it possible for God to hear prayers of vengeance toward wicked people. He's God. I'm not. And that's good news for lots of folks.

So, thanks to the beautiful people at the IRS, this chick had scheduled the next two weeks, after this little mountain getaway, to work on reconciling information for the CPA who was representing us in this nightmare. Well, at least that was my plan.

But today, on this beautiful Saturday in Tennessee, I was thankful. My enormous family was healthy, Donald Trump was the president-elect, and I was going to the mountains for a few days with my Stevie Ray. I made a deal with myself. I do that a lot. I convince myself to compartmentalize struggles. It's a form of picking and choosing which battle to fight. The only way to win the battle of the day is to be focused. The enemy can win with very little effort when we are scattered and sloppy with our defense. This audit would take intense effort on my part and I knew I would have to hibernate, turn off the peripheral components of my life, and focus. I had put the worry of the dreaded ordeal in a little box, at least for this day, and tucked it away. I was ready for mountain air, friends, and some amazing food, and NOTHING was going to ruin my mountain time. Nothing.

We were meeting Linda and Gale Warren. Linda has been my friend since I was about eleven years old. We've weathered the storms of life together. She's one of the few people on planet earth who is brutally honest with me. We're as close as family. Her husband Gale has been there with me as well . . . through the good, the bad, and the ugly. I love him like a brother. The good news? Steve loves them too.

When Steve and I got married in 2006, I was ecstatic to get my friends back. I had lost the closeness of the friendship during the fifteen Crabb Family years. For reasons I won't discuss, it didn't work out to have close friends. It was a loss, a huge loss for me. I had been friends with these folks for most of my life. We had played together, cried together, been pregnant together, raised kids together. So losing them during those years killed me. We weren't estranged as in an argument; the dynamic was just different. It didn't work.

Linda and Gale were bringing Donald and Debbie King with them. They too had been friends for decades, but there was a gap of about fifteen years with very little interaction. But, hey, this was 2016, and Steve liked my Kentucky friends for life, and we were going to the cabin for a fun weekend. Linda and Gale, as well as Donald and Debbie, were deeply rooted in faith, family, and friendships. They brought me calm.

Unintentionally they reminded me of who I was, where I had come from, and how good God was. For, you see, they remembered when I was seventeen and got my throat cut. They remember the struggles of my life. They were there. Old friends validate our truths as we sit on a balcony, look at the stars, and reminisce about the "but God" moments. The fact that others remember is a tool that we can use against the devil, who has been known to whisper in my ear when trying to tell MY story, "That didn't really happen. You're confused, you're don't remember that story correctly."

Why? He wants me to back it up. Zip it. Shut it. Our testimonies of LIVING through it are truly our weapons. And then when you couple that lying devil with a hater or two . . . it's easy to be silenced. So easy. But I've been blessed to have friends who encouraged me and prophecy here and there that declared . . . that I would pour it out for the encouragement of the broken, the voiceless, the forgotten. So on this night we were laughing and eating, remembering, and as always, I shed a few tears. I cry. I cry when I hear about struggle, always. Why? I identify in such a deep place. The tears must come or I could explode. So as the girls told me stories of friends that had been diagnosed with cancer, I cried a bucket of tears.

So, on this long Saturday, November 26, I wiped my tears and we finally went to sleep in our little mountain home, with full bellies and an extra blanket. I was thankful for a much-needed break.

Sunday was uneventful—well . . . except for the "prosperity steak" at Cherokee Grill. The acorn squash and steak were to die for and were truly eventful for a foodie. While we were enjoying our meal in town, the worshippers at Roaring Fork Baptist Church on the edge of Gatlinburg sang and prayed. Unbeknownst to them it would be their last time to sing "Amazing Grace" in that beautiful mountainside church that had stood as a beacon of hope for nearly seventy years. Those mountain people had no clue what was coming. Neither did I.

The next morning we awoke to a smoky view. At first, I thought it was just low-lying fog. But we soon realized it smelled like a fire, and there was a thick ashy residue on our cars. Weird. It was snowing ash. I knew there had been fires in the Carolinas, Georgia, and throughout a region in the South. We had seen smoke when we were driving in from Nashville the day before. It was beginning to worry the entire region. Prayers had been going up for those in the path. This was the driest, hottest, summer and fall on record for Gatlinburg and the surrounding area. In a normal year, Gatlinburg averages fifty-six inches of rain, so it doesn't take much time for a drought to hit this normally moist landscape. These mountains are the wettest area in the Southeast, and the drought had made everything mountainous a tender box. I had been researching and reading for several days, and I was beginning to wonder when this dry spell would end.

The smell was permeating the interior of the cabin. We made the mistake of going out on the deck early that morning. That was a mistake. Our clothes stunk immediately. Nothing smells worse than the stench of fire. We decided to stay in for a while and keep the doors closed. But it was to no avail. The smell was traveling through the heat and air ducts. It was bad.

We looked at each other and said, "Should we leave?" I was coughing and my breathing was starting to be impacted. But in my head I was thinking, "What do I know? If this was imminent danger it would be on the news." We watched the local news and searched online, and it seemed that the locals felt sure that all was well. The news reported that there was a fire on the opposite side of Gatlinburg near Chimney Tops in the national park. They were working to contain it and it had been there for several days, they reported. Okay. Fine. We discussed it and of course I said, "It's all fine. Let's go enjoy our day."

We went and shopped a bit and ended up having lunch at the Chop House. When we came out of the restaurant, people were starting to congregate and discuss. A couple told us that they had decided to go home. Linda and Debbie were worried, I could tell. Suddenly the wind changed directions and the smoke seemed to worsen. The ash increased and we began to see people wearing flu masks. The ash looked like snow as we made our way up Dollywood Lane to the cabin. I had never seen anything like it. The wind was picking up as well.

When we got to the cabin, my Kentucky guests all decided it was time to get out of Dodge. They kept telling us to leave. Within ten minutes the wind had whipped up speed to the point the porch swing was banging on the windows, the rocking chairs were turning over, and the howling was unbelievable. I live north of Nashville in an area that's plagued with deadly tornadoes; I've seen them up close, I've witnessed winds and destruction, but I had never seen wind like this before. So think about this. We had desertlike dryness in an area that is normally the wettest in the Southeast, a fire boiling over on the other side of these mountains, and now these horrific winds.

I'm oblivious to weather until I'm wet, cold, or hot. I rarely look at the forecast. I'm not scared of storms, and I sleep though tornado warnings. My kids gather in a basement and pray. They call me to come to the basement? I tell them I'm sleepy and I'm not afraid. If you read *Stronger* you know how I roll. I'm scared of people, not weather. So my built-in radar that measures weather danger, or in this case weather and fire, is missing a chip or two. I'm deficient in that department. I'm not brave, just completely oblivious and possibly a bit stupid as it relates to weather. I would not be one bit afraid to ride out a hurricane at the beach. There, I said it. Don't judge me. I suppose I like watching the big hand of God show us that we have no control.

On November 28, 2016, I was in that place mentally. No fear. As my friends tried to convince Steve that we needed to leave, I was dissing their every word. They were persistent, but I knew we had a tile installer coming on Wednesday and it was only Monday, and I said it: "WE can't leave." After all, Kathy the impatient control freak had to get that tile replaced, fire or no fire. And I said so. They said, "Okay, we're out of here." As they left, I started videoing on Facebook live. I had no CLUE that the video would prove to be surreal a few hours later. They drove out of the driveway and I remember flipping on the television and scanning the Internet, Googling "fire in the Smoky mountains" and "fire in Gatlinburg." I found a story that said they had evacuated a school in Gatlinburg before the normal dismissal time. However, nothing seemed immediate or imminent. The school thing seemed pretty relaxed. No one was telling us to leave, so I assumed we weren't in danger. I assumed if we were, the city officials, parks department, mayor, governor, fire chief, dog catcher . . . someone would be doing a press conference. They weren't, so I stood on the "let's stay" opinion. Mind you, minutes, not hours had passed. Linda and Gale had been gone less than ten minutes. My phone rang. She said, "Get out of there. We've just met fire trucks and they're turning at the next road, right beyond your road." Our turn was Stinnett Road. I knew the next road was very close. It was another log cabin community.

We jumped up and ran to Steve's truck. We were headed down the mountain to see what was on fire. The smoke was thick enough to choke us. We covered our mouths and ran for the truck, the wind stronger than I had ever seen in my sixty years. The trip down the mountain is exactly one mile by way of roads, about six-tenths as a crow flies. By the time we got in the truck and started down the hill, trees were falling. We're talking three minutes, not twenty. I realized these roads could be impassible in minutes. The wind was starting to concern me. When we rounded the curve at the bottom of Stinnett, we saw what looked like a thousand lights flashing. And then, I saw it. The mountain next to us was on fire. I'm not saying a house was on fire; a mountain was on fire. These mountain resorts meld together. One ends and another begins. It's difficult to tell what was on fire. I was fairly certain that the cabins were not only in Fox Ridge, our neighboring resort, but the intense orange was wrapping back around to our area. In minutes it had made a ring that closely resembled what I envisioned Armageddon would look like. I screamed, "Jesus! PLEASE help us."

We immediately realized we had to leave. We had nothing . . . no clothes, no medicines. And then I realized! I said, "OH MY God, Steve. We have a guest that just got to our other cabin. WE must go back. WE must. She has her daughter and there's no way she will know to leave. There's no one telling people to evacuate. She and her daughter can't die on my watch." She had just arrived and I was concerned when she came to check in on a day like that, but she was local and I let it be. We rushed back up the hill and I realized I had her number. I called her and told her she must leave! By this time the electricity had gone off for as far as the eye could see. With the smoke and the lack of visibility, that may not have been far. But I felt like it was out for miles and miles. We were almost to the cabin and decided to risk getting our meds. I've had open heart to repair a valve and medicine is a pretty big deal now. With only the light of a cell phone, we frantically navigated a narrow spiral staircase and grabbed our medicine and a computer. That was truly a risk. That staircase was scary for me with lights, but with no lights and Ugg boots on? It was more like a death trap. We both nearly fell. By now, we knew every second counted. I am almost ashamed of the level of panic I was feeling. It was a self-imposed situation, with me being the hard head that was determined. I told Steve that I was sorry we didn't leave when Linda and Gale did and that I took full responsibility. We got in the truck and I glanced at both of these cabins that I dearly loved. I burst into tears. The sky was red and it was nothing less than a full ring around us. I'm lost for words when trying to describe. We headed up the hill from our cul-de-sac; it's about four hundred feet. When we topped the hill, it was as if we had a view from a Panavision movie camera on the set for *The Day the World Ended*. I screamed, "JESUS help."

The ring of fire was completely around us, on all sides. It was difficult to know how close it was or if there was a clear path out, but we knew we were in trouble. The horizon was a hot red with flashes and hot spots that would send flames shooting hundreds of feet into the air. Every few seconds a hot spot would manifest. I looked down our street on our way down the mountain and I could see the silhouette of cabins, on fire. I watched as a roof caved in and the entire structure fell at once, completely imploding. The only thing in my wheelhouse that I could equate it to was the Twin Towers. The implosion was so fast, and when a cabin fell, the entire thing burned. The appliances, metal roofs, everything was liquefied. The average house fire is about 1,100 degrees. They estimated this fire to be as hot as 2,000 degrees. My beloved mountain community had become a living, breathing hell. And we were trying to get out of hell.

We navigated down the hill and made it around trees that had fallen and blocked the road. We saw flying debris. The nightmare had surely begun. As we rounded a curve and got a clear view, I knew. We approached the exit of the neighborhood and there was nothing but taillights. Everyone was leaving. Traffic was at a complete standstill. So now, here we are, surrounded by fire, a ditch on the left, a ravine on the right, and a completely blocked road. I felt like I was going to smother. As we inched toward Upper Middle Creek Road, I could see the mountains between me and Gatlinburg that God created to provide that beautiful landscape; not only were they burning, but the headlights of cars headed out of Gatlinburg were bumper to bumper, as far as the eye could see. Cars. Trapped with fire all around them. As we finally pulled out onto Upper Middle Creek, now remember, we are moving a few feet at a time. Everyone was panicking. The volunteer fireman who was trying to direct traffic as it crept onto Middle Creek Road told us that hundreds of fires had erupted within minutes. That was a no-brainer. He told us that the spur that connected Gatlinburg to everything was on fire. Westgate, a large resort, was burning and the fire had jumped the road and shut down the spur. He said that people were calling 911 and there was no one to respond. No one.

Jesus! So that's why the headlights were scattered across those fiery mountains like ribbons of light. EVERYTHING was on fire and these people were trapped. The spur moved 90 percent of the traffic that was going to I-40. We turned right onto Middle Creek Road and Steve passed on the shoulder. I was sobbing. I knew people were dying. I also knew that it was ride or die. We moved a short distance down Middle

Creek and realized that the road was on fire. The fire on the left side and the right side had jumped the road and was lapping up under vehicles. We got turned around. I'm not sure how, but I know it was a miracle that we did. Steve was driving with a lot of aggression; a shrieking woman in a green truck will do that to a driver. So as we headed away from town, at less than one mile per hour, I digested what I knew. Dollywood Lane was on fire. The spur was on fire. Everything around us was on fire, and there were reports that the fire was on property at Dollywood. Based on what I could see, it had to be there by now. I knew that people were burning, at that very moment. It was impossible to see what we saw, to see the Gatlinburg traffic trying to escape only to be stalled on the side of the mountain . . . sitting in traffic . . . I knew what I knew. The folks who were backed up on the top of the mountain where the fires were so incredibly hot? They had absolutely no way out. Jesus!!!

I was overwhelmed with emotion. Fear was sitting on my shoulder. I've had several "dark of the night" encounters with fear, but this was a doozy. It occurred to me that thousands could perish. Traffic was crawling on the route that we were being sent on, but that mountain traffic seemed to be completely stalled. From out of nowhere zoomed a white BMW coupe, passing in the wrong lane, driving seventy-five or eighty miles per hour on a blind curve. I suppose he couldn't take it anymore. He wasn't going to burn; he would risk a head-on collision. There was no oncoming traffic on that stretch of road, but I knew when he got out to the next turn toward Newport Highway, if he made it that far, he would be in trouble. Steve said, "He's an idiot."

He was. But in a weird way I understood. The desire to flee was the most overwhelming thing I've ever felt. To be trapped is indescribable; until you're trapped, you don't get it. Social media was alive with videos of those who were trapped. Many of you saw the live videos on the news. I was seeing it in real time.

I had been texting the kids, but I don't think they truly understood the severity at first. Who would? Two hours ago there was no mention of struggles in these mountains. The national media hadn't picked up the story either, and my goodness, I don't think the local media had either. Facebook live was the news. I posted the "pray for us, we're trapped" post and people prayed, but I didn't post live videos of the fires. I just couldn't.

I knew I had to call the kids. I couldn't reach them all, but I sent a group text and said, "I love you all very much. You've been the delight of my life. PLEASE pray that we can get out of here soon." Jason called immediately asking for our exact location, our plan to get out, etc. Within a few minutes they all started calling. My voice was shaking. They knew I was scared. I told them that I was confident we would lose the cabins and that people were going to burn alive. They seemed shocked that we weren't warned. How could this have happened was the recurring question. It was a good one.

Steve kept saying, "We're going to make it out."

A trip that felt like it took five hours was actually about an hour and forty-five minutes. The turtle pace finally gave way to twenty miles per hour, then twenty-five miles per hour, and then a sign that we were almost to I-40. The smoke was thick, and ash was still falling, the entire sky was on fire, but we could take I-40 toward Knoxville until we felt safe. Then what? I realized how bad we smelled. We had no clothes, no toiletries, nothing. We went straight to Knoxville and got a room. We knew they would be full within a few hours. No food, no stops, straight to an exit with hotels. Steve got a room. I can't remember if it was a Hampton or a Holiday Inn or what it was. I just remember there was an Applebee's next door. He got a room key and we went to Applebee's to grab a glass of tea and a bite of something. We hadn't eaten dinner. And there's one thing Steve and I have in common. Stress doesn't stop our food intake. We like food. When we're sad, we eat. When we're mad, we eat. When we're happy, we eat. You get the picture. Food is typically my reward to myself when I have a day full of coping. So you see why I'm fluffy. I have lots of those days. Today was an award winner. We wanted a snack, both of us!

We sat down. I immediately did what I do. When I looked across the table at him I immediately puckered up and started my routine. It occurred to me what we had just escaped. I was overcome with grief for those unknown families. I told him so. I cried as I imagined the funerals of these nameless people. I'm dramatic like that. I can't help it. There's a place in me that's so tender for those who are grieving. It's truly embarrassing at times. Transparent emotions are often confused with weakness. I'm not weak. Actually, I'm anything but weak. But those tears falling are a by-product of my ability to see the pain that's here, or coming, or that was. People who have been extremely wounded . . . and they made it, they figured out how to convert the pain into the gain . . . those people allow themselves to cry. They hurt for others. It's called empathy. I was full of empathy as I sat in a booth with torn upholstery eating disgusting chicken fingers. Disgusting, but I was still eating them, and crying a river . . . dipping in honey mustard and wiping snot. My mind was numb and I smelled like I had been on a party bus through hell. Steve looked like he had seen a ghost. We ate and barely spoke.

At the next table was an unseemly little couple. I was confident they had voted for Hillary based on their appearance. They looked like they probably had degrees in conservation, or maybe they had studied pottery making and bead stringing. It was one or the other. They either drove an electric car or a vintage VW van with a mattress in the back. I couldn't be sure. But clearly they were decades and a world apart from my current ideology. They stared at me as I cried. His tattoos and unkempt hair were hard to miss. His girl was equally attention-seeking with dreadlocks and piercings in everything that could be pierced. He got up and came to our table. I was a bit embarrassed about the snot tissues and the disheveled state of our general appearance. I said, "We just came from our cabins in the mountains. The mountains are on fire." He hadn't heard. He offered sincere concern for us. Where would we stay? Did we have a plan? We told him we lived outside Nashville and had another home there. He was kind and said he wanted to help us. I knew he was sleeping on someone's couch. He didn't own a home. He probably didn't even have a rented room. It was easy to know that. We thanked him for the concern and asked for his prayers. He promised we would have them.

We walked out. He stopped us. He said, "I must give you what I have. I must." He pressed a bill into Steve's hand. I looked at him and said, "Only if God told you to." He shook his head as if to acknowledge. I said, "Steve, take it. God's got a blessing for him." We walked outside and in true evangelistic fashion, Steve snuck a peek to see if it was a five, ten, or twenty. HE should have been an evangelist. Ha! It was a hundred-dollar bill. Steve said, "I can't keep this! This is a fortune to those kids." I told him, "Yes you can. That boy just sowed into his own destiny. He just created an atmosphere of blessings for his own life. He may not know it yet, but he did it. He listened to the voice of God."

Let me be crystal clear. We didn't need his money. His giving didn't change my life, change my day, or change my hour. But only God knows what it unleashed for him. He listened. It's very possible that this was all he had or nearly all he had. Trust me on that. When's the last time you did that? Ever?

I absorbed that small incident. I allowed it to be a nod from God. He hadn't forgotten me or any of those in harm's way. He was God. He was still healing the sick, making it rain, telling the ocean how far it could come, and speaking to a little hippie boy at Applebee's, convincing him to give the smelly couple in the booth behind him his money. He didn't question why; he did it. That's fertile ground for God to work in his life. It was also the ultimate wink for an old woman who thought her beloved cabins were burning to the ground. I was on His mind. Don't ever hesitate to do a good thing if you feel led. The old excuse "Well, I'm not sure it's God" won't cut it. If it's a good thing, do it. If it's costing you money and you're a stingy something? It's God. Do it. It's a win-win.

We went into the room and I stripped down to a towel. Steve kept his jeans on and took all our clothes to a washer and dryer down the hall. We had clean clothes, except his jeans, and it felt good. I slept in my shirt and was just happy to be alive. We slept in separate beds but talked most of the night. We were back and forth. Were they burned? Were they spared? The not knowing was killing us. I had pulled up my insurance agent's info, tried to find the policies in my email, and we had a plan to call and start the claim process. And then one of us would say . . . "But what if the fire stopped short of us? What if?" We were back and forth all night. But as always, when one deeply believes that God is in control, I knew that it was okay either way. This wasn't my first rodeo. After all, this was just wood and stone. It didn't matter really. I finally slept. The next morning before we awoke, the phone started blowing up. A friend called from Nashville and he had seen an image from the air. He told us that he THOUGHT our cabins were still there. He wasn't positive, though. Another friend, J. P. Miller, who lives in Pigeon Forge, called and said, "I've driven to your neighborhood. There are guards and it's a struggle to get in, but I did, and the cabins are there! BOTH of them."

So when the morning sun came up, we not only had rain, but we also had two intact cabins, but otherwise the numbers were devastating. Fourteen people were dead, 138 were injured, and approximately 2,700 structures had burned. We had escaped, our cabins had been spared, but not everyone had. I was sad to the bone.

The images were shocking. Cars were liquified; families had been burned alive in their homes with no warning. This fire was so hot and the wind was so strong, it truly was a perfect storm. There are no words. The stories were heart-wrenching. The burn lines came so close to our property line, but the fire veered when it got to our street. God doesn't love us more. Hear me. He doesn't CARE more for us than them. But someone prayed the right prayer of protection, someone. I believe that with everything in me. The hedge was intact. Whoever did that? Thank you. I believe the Facebook army was on it. Yep. I believe that our ability to populate information and bombard Heaven is often a game changer. I wish I could say that it always is, but that's not the truth.

We drove back to the neighborhood. The charred foundations were smoldering with rubble, hundreds of them. It looked like a war zone. But with the exception of a few shingles and a lot of smoke and ash to remediate, we were good. Three days later you couldn't tell there had ever been a fire in our little cabins.

The point of this story? It rains on the just and the unjust alike. Fire, rain, all about the same. We win some, we lose some. The naysayers made comments like "Where was God for those people who died? Where was God for those people who had houses that burned?"

Thanks for asking. I will tell you. For those who went to Heaven? He was waiting. He was their Savior, their Redeemer.

For those who lost a family member? He was their peace that passeth all understanding. Still is.

For those who were injured? He's their healer.

For those who lost property? He was their insurance check when it was $50,000 more than expected.

For those who were spared? He is their faith builder.

For HE is "I am that I am." He's whatever you need Him to be. He's God. He's God on the mountain, through the fire, through the flood, and always will be.

Sorry to oversimplify, but it ain't rocket science. I promise you if you don't know Him, you need to. You have everything to gain and nothing to lose.

And my last thought on this story: I pray for the little Applebee's hippie. I hope I see him again someday.

The Tough Business of Marriage

It was early November 2017, and this old chick was tired. The beach retreat that I had hosted in October had been good, but oh my, so eventful. One person who decides to let the devil use them can destroy the peace of hundreds. God moved, but we fought devils. And I'm TALKING DEMONS in people. Spirits of all kinds being manifested, and women who were not interested in being free, they were simply there on a mission: to destroy. Not many people know what I know, but holy smokes. It was very difficult to bring that retreat to an end. The devil called all his minions to help, and we fought. Now I will tell you. WE WON all rounds with him. But it was still a fight. I was dog-tired. I came home from the beach and jumped right into the last-minute preparations for the fall mountain women's retreat, "Miracle on the Mountain."

We had also hosted a couples retreat in September called "Mountain of Mercy," once again in the mountains, once again sold out, and once again, life changing. Dr. Dominic Herbst was a guest speaker at the couples retreat. I can't explain the depth of understanding that Dominic brought to these couples of all ages, all demographics, all social statuses, for clearly, not one corner of the population had the marriage thing figured out. We all kind of stink at marriage at times. The church AND the world, the statistics are sadly the same. Fifty percent of us are the children of divorce, and 60 percent of us have cheated, are cheating, or will cheat. We're all broken people, marrying broken people. Oh my, I had NO idea until I started researching. And the pornography statistics for the church mirrored the world's statistics. We clearly aren't faring any better than the world on marrying, staying true, and staying married.

I felt like an idiot. I have been married several times and I openly made fun of my own ability to get it right. I decided to take that embarrassment and shame away from the devil. You don't have to whisper about my multiple marriages. I will tell it on myself. Therefore, the gossips have no power over me. I take away their whispers. Try it—it works! When Aaron felt led to do this conference, I quickly said, "I feel really weird being involved, but I will organize and help you." He was so quick to tell me, "Don't kid yourself, you have much to share." Hmmm, did I? I sure never thought so. I had married for all the wrong reasons. I was a lost teen looking to belong, I was a "fixer" looking to fix a backslidden preacher, and so on. Another day, another book, I suppose. But on this day, when Aaron was believing that couples everywhere needed a mountain experience, together, I concurred. We would give it a whirl.

The couples who could commit to help were Mike and Kelly, Krystal and Brian, and of course Aaron and Amanda. Steve and I went as well and offered support, of course. Chrystal Cassetty had agreed to oversee the food service in the kitchen and help with all decorating details. We needed her support.

I was so incredibly sad that Jason and Shellye couldn't be there. They have an incredible testimony of God's faithfulness and have those beautiful girls to prove it. God has been good to them, oh so good! And to hear them tell it in that setting would have been nothing short of amazing. I also wished that Terah and Jon could have made it. Jon's schedule of touring is erratic, and they hesitated to commit, for fear of a last-minute conflict. And such is the story of Jon. That boy travels more than any of us. He is the best bus driver in Nashville and spends over half of the year on the road. He's driven every star you can name and provided well for his little family by doing so. Their story will encourage you. It wasn't easy, but they made it. It's their story to tell, and I'm sure they will some day. Adam and Kaitlyn couldn't make it work with scheduling, and they were newlyweds. Most newlyweds, especially who are blending families, need as much time at home as they can muster. They were there.

So Mike, Kelly, Amanda, Aaron, Brian, and Krystal forged ahead. They took the concepts of Dominic and created an event that transformed these couples, which in turn transformed homes, churches, etc. It clearly worked. Amanda and Aaron were ministering at night. It was like having a mini version of a Restoring Hope revival in a mountain setting. Actually, it was amazing in every way. There's not another couple on the planet that sacrifices like these two. I am lost when trying to describe how much they give, how much they travail, for the people, those that they feel God placed in their world. They are called to the highest calling one can fathom. They shared from the depths of their humanity, complete truth, the rawest truth I've ever witnessed. These couples saw hope. Some of them were in trouble, living in private hell in a parsonage, living in varying degrees of struggle. But the tears streamed, the altars filled, and I watched Amanda and Aaron as they surveyed what God had done. Their vulnerabilities had been uncovered, their truths told, but the Lord had honored their truth. Marriages were saved. God won. The devil lost.

Krystal and Brian did an intense daytime session on Tuesday that included financial knowledge that they had learned and subsequently used to get out of debt and saved tens of thousands of dollars in a few short years. They shared. They also shared personal testimonies. Krystal and I had been through so much in her lifetime. And the truth is this: she didn't figure it out until she pulled completely away from my nest. Everything about the forty-three-year-old Krystal was completely different from the thirty-year-old Krystal. Her discipline was unmatched, her steadfast loyalty to the word, to let it be more than a catch phrase to use as a comeback in an argument, was on point. She rightly divided the word and read everything she could get her hands on. She studied, read, and chased God in the shadows of a stage. She still resisted this uncomfortable world that most of her family lived in, the world of interviews, microphones, and stage lights. She solidly rejected the spotlight for so many years. But this was 2017, and she and Brian had been nursing an idea to build or buy a property near Nashville, use it as a haven for married couples who were ready to turn a sinking ship around. They had built a curriculum, and he had prodded her to open up and let the world see who "she" was when there was no glare of the Crabb Family. So this was his dream and clearly God was in it.

In reality, Krystal had grown into this full-blown sacrificial Christian. Brian had stepped in and helped her raise Cameron and Edie, and then they had Sophie in 2007. Brian had no clue what he had signed up for. Statistically, they were doomed to fail. Brian grew up fast, and Krystal attempted, once again, to grow up. And somewhere between frustration and restoration, the family thing happened. Trust grew and the family would live. I almost didn't include this paragraph. But it's for some of you mommas and daddies. Listen to me. That hard head that you raised, the one that is turning your hair gray and draining your bank account, yes, that one. Not only will they figure it out and turn it around, they will also surpass your dreams for them, spiritually and personally. It's going to happen.

So I was allowed to sit in the lodge at Hidden Mountain, on a Tuesday in September 2017, and see the fruit of Krystal and Brian's efforts as it related to staying married, staying out of the poor house, and staying sane. Brian was brutally honest. It was refreshing. And, yes, when the bright lights of the stage were dimmed and Krystal was in her element, this nonsinging sibling dealt a pretty impressive hand to those who were intently listening. She was a natural. The devil fought her. Why? She's bright. She's a people magnet. She's a world changer. He whipped her butt in several rounds back in the day. But on this September morning it was clear that she had won the war. Her candid vulnerability completely sucked us all in. She was raw and unafraid, and the listener related to her truth. Satan no longer owned her; she was now free. And holy cow, I bawled my eyes out. This momma wondered how I could be this blessed.

And if you haven't read *Stronger*, you need to. The unedited version of her story is there. It's truly one of the most beautiful stories I've ever written. She's a picture of grace and works. Sometimes we understand faith and grace all too well, but we slack on works. It takes too much discipline. When the Lord turned Krystal around, when she got her feet planted, she became a bit like James; she was the "I will show you my faith with my deeds" girl. No butt-sitting for her. She plowed straight and didn't understand fear. God can certainly use that.

Mike and Kelly took the session on the last morning of the marriage retreat. If you know Mike, you know what I'm going to tell you already. He complained about speaking; he grumbled and sweated bullets. His comfort zone is centered around a melody and a song. He doesn't like environments that are unscripted and personal, especially since the bus wreck and the brain injury. But I really didn't care what he wanted. They were there and I knew they needed to share more than a song. We know what Kelly's capable of when it comes to speaking, teaching, or preaching. She's got the goods, and for a quiet girl? She can carry the mail. There's no limitations on her when she's in the preach mode—she strips herself of "her" and takes you to the truth, every SINGLE time. I hate to brag, but Kelly hits 100 percent of the time as a speaker. She's a great singer, but her gifts are completely used when she can do both. So I knew that the Mike and Kelly portion of this day may be heavy on Mike singing and Kelly speaking, but it was fine. Whatever they had, the people wanted to hear.

But, oh my, that Mike Bowling, shuffling his feet, awkwardly wiping tears, began to share their truth. The story of a crumbling marriage, a trip to a lawyer's office back in 2005, a home that was so completely fractured that they doubted that it could be healed. He sobbed as he told their story. He pulled back the covering to show the truth and scars, like so many ministry families possess. Busy ministry lives with exhausting travel and schedules becomes a perfect playing field for the devil's games. Mike told us their version of such a common story, and he cried. I had never heard him do this. It shook me to my core.

His scars were in full view; so were his tears.

Through her tears, Kelly said, "We would come home from the road. We were on different buses and doing different tours. But when my head hit my pillow at night, I could hear Mike praying for God to soften my heart. I heard him pray every single night that we were in that house together. The road was tough. I was gone, and he was gone a lot. But he kept asking Jesus to fix it. The thing that smacked me and made me stop in my tracks was this: I went into Hope's room one night to tuck her in. She was clutching a picture of me and her dad. She knew. She was only six, but she knew. The reality that she was in line to be a child of divorce, as I had been, made me fall on my face. I didn't want that for her. I wanted that generational curse to end, and somehow I hadn't grasped this completely. That night I asked God to help me, make me appreciate Mike for everything he was, and forgive him for everything he wasn't. I realized that he was already praying that prayer. I knew that my babies were worth more than being right or being selfish." Mike and Kelly stood unashamed before God and those couples as they wept. They had totally exposed their humanity and their personal failure, and no one judged. NO one. There wasn't a dry eye in the building. The men cried, the women heaved, for we've all been there. We're so human at times.

Aaron stood and said, "And think about it: there wouldn't be a Gracie. If you had signed those divorce papers, how different would it be for those girls?" For those of you that aren't familiar, Kelly and Mike's girls are incredibly gifted vocally. The sky is the limit. They are veteran ministers/performers at ages eighteen, fourteen, and eleven. Gracie is the third part, the soprano. As Aaron painted the picture of a world without Gracie, as he raised his hands in praise that Mike and Kelly saw fit to crucify their pride, and save their home, my tears erupted. For God certainly had a plan, but the devil feared the weapons these girls were armed with, their voices! On this day, in the mountains of East Tennessee, this lodge full of people cried and praised God for mercy, grace, and Gracie.

I looked over at my husband, the man who signed up for a wife and ended up with a village, the man who doesn't have a single child with his DNA, yet he's "Poppa" to the masses. And of course, that big lug was bawling. He loves his family, including his ridiculously pushy wife.

My heart was full. Marriage was alive and well on that mountain on that day. Aaron's vision had been fulfilled, and I believe that God was pleased. The truth is this. Marriage ain't easy. We must keep Jesus in the mix, learn the difference between love and lust, and learn to forgive. I used to ask my kids this question when they would fall freshly in love with a young man or woman, whichever the case may be.

I would ask them if they thought they could endure a life of pushing "said" lovely in a wheelchair every time they left the house, and could they endure the daily bed-pan and catheter routine, should they have a terrible accident that paralyzed your love the day after your wedding? They always said, "Oh yes!!!"

Then I would ask the bigger question. I would ask if they thought their love would do the same for them. Man, what a wake-up call Negative Nellie mom can be. But the truth is the truth. Often, we don't understand commitment until it's too late. The "for better or for worse" portion of life always defines our character and commitment. They're sort of one and the same in my book. People stay as long as it's all fun and games, but when the storm comes the bad ones start packing the bag. Many a person walked when the suffering started. Their "forever" didn't last too long. However, if we're to be the parents we're supposed to be, if we're to be the leaders we're supposed to be, we must clean up our homes first. And yes, that includes staying faithful and staying married. On this day, on that mountain, we resolved to do better. Including me. Unless Steve Hannah beats the daylights out of me or decides to commit adultery with no remorse, we will die together. I'm in it to win it this time. Granted, I can't make him stay or live right, but I have a feeling that with Steve, that won't be a problem.

Truly, it's never too late to get it right. We're living proof!!!

A Bucket of Oil

So back to November 2017. My girls had been to the mountains in September for the marriage retreat, the beach in October to minister, and now it was early November, and they were heading back to the mountains with me. We were headed there for "Miracle on the Mountain." The name sort of says it all. The fruit from of the first mountain retreat, that first batch of miracles . . . was still manifesting. The mountain seemed to remain a favorite place for the broken to come to have their wounds bound and their tears wiped.

As I write this chapter, I'm keenly aware that after a mountain meeting we always lose one or two to death. The illnesses that drove these girls to chase God occasionally won. They left their families, their friends, new and old alike, and went to their eternal homes. Some made it to Heaven because of the mountain. Of this I'm sure. Also, the girls that reluctantly came, those who needed the chain cutter, those who needed to be freed from addictions of all kinds, sometimes lost the war. The demons that tormented their minds didn't always give up. This ain't kids play—it's truly warfare. And I'm not writing a nursery rhyme, I'm telling it like it is. Many addicts left and transformed their life, but of course there are some who don't, won't, because . . . that big bag of junk that they brought to leave at the altar? They're unsure how to live without it, and they don't.

The outcome isn't on us. We're just responsible to present the opportunity as we've been instructed. That was all I had to see to, the opportunity. So once again, we were headed east down I-40. I was so tired. My Ya-Yas had agreed to go and help me cook. Sister Connie, a Stronger sister, was also bringing a crew. I had this overzealous need to cook for these people! That's the southern woman in me, I suppose. We're always trying to comfort with food, and let me tell you, some of these gals needed to be comforted. We arrived on Sunday night and started preparing food. At 2:00 a.m. on Monday, we were just returning from carting humongous pots of homemade vegetable soup, in scalding hot pots, pots that looked like they came from an army mess hall, up to the lodge. This wasn't only dangerous—it was almost impossible. Friends who will stay up until all hours of the night participating in shenanigans like this, well those friends are keepers. I had some keepers, that's for sure.

These girls (my Ya-Yas) are all Baptist. We are like blood sisters, all being from the same place in Kentucky, all having been bonded by friendship or blood, for more than five decades. We are surely a tribe of gypsy girls who didn't make it to gypsy land. We got detoured by the time we were eighteen or so. We married young and started families before we were old enough to buy alcohol. We didn't buy alcohol, but we couldn't have if we had wanted to—we were still teenagers. Babies having babies. But we came from a place in time, and a place on the big United States map, where this was the norm. It's what our moms, our grandmothers, and great-grandmothers had done before us. They got married, had babies, loved Jesus, and fried chickens and potatoes. As I think back on a lifetime of friendships with these girls, I realize how deep the roots are, how much we've walked through together. Four of seven of us have been married and divorced, some multiple times. The rough spots in the road have caused us all to stumble at times. But here comes the tribe, ready to pull the wounded out of the pothole. I've walked through hell and back a few times myself. The details are private and THEY will never tell, not in this lifetime anyway. What happens in Ya-Ya Land stays in Ya-Ya Land. So on this Sunday night, the first Sunday in November 2017, some of my girls were innocently walking into a "Kathy" moment that they wouldn't soon forget: the all-night soup prep, the ridiculously hard work of cooking and serving 250 women, and a move of the Holy Ghost.

Here we go. Monday morning I realized that four hours sleep wasn't enough. With the help of my squad and a bunch of patient folks at Hidden Mountain Resort, we got everyone checked into the cabins. These women were pretty happy campers, for the most part. I mean, how do you beat a week of mountain air, beautiful leaves, friends, hugs, and the anticipation of what was going to happen. You could feel it in the atmosphere. As usual, they came expecting. The event was sold out and we had some new girls. I love new girls. They are so unsuspecting. God moved. Terah, Kelly, and Karen Harding sang the paint off the walls. I had three granddaughters there and they jumped in and hosted, sang, and did what they know, ministry.

Let me divert for a minute if I may. If you want to give your child a gift that will last a lifetime, teach them to make others comfortable in any situation. For the Maya Angelou quote will forever be a truth: "People will forget what you said, people will forget what you did, but people will never forget how you made them feel." Teach this early and teach it often. Push your kids, stretch them: it will serve them.

So on this night, I was stretching the granddaughters. It was a God night, but to tell you the truth, this old sister was so tired she was numb. Amanda asked me if I was okay. I told her that I was, but she raised an eyebrow. I was tired, burned, and needed a dose of Jesus about as bad as anyone there. There were many awesome moments that first night, but my bed was what I was obsessing on, and when the service was over and I had eaten a piece or two of cake with the sisters, I headed up the mountain to my little cabin home. I crashed. We all did.

The Ya-Yas were in the cabin with me. Tuesday was supposed to be a day of shopping, rest, porch rocking, or anything these girls wanted to do. It was a free day. But me? I had to tend to a gazillion little details. I spent most of the day alone. Exhaustion owned me. I questioned God. Don't act like you don't do that—you know you do. I asked myself over and over, "What in the heck are YOU doing?" You're an old woman. Why aren't you at home resting, playing with grandbabies, or better yet, cleaning your house? I had left my house in complete disarray. My personal time had been nonexistent, and Steve hadn't bothered to call the domestic help that I used occasionally. Ask me why. Thanks for asking. Because Steve doesn't care! Ha! As long as the fridge works, the television works, and there's a path to the bed, he's ALL good.

Me? I believe that the dirt is easier to tolerate than clutter. I am one of those people who wants the house to look worthy of a *Better Homes and Gardens* photo shoot at any given time. And, yes, the closets may be a train wreck, every item in the fridge may be out of date, and the pantry may look like the toddlers arranged the shelves, but hey . . . if those pillows are fluffed on the sofa, the shoes and socks are picked up, the counters are shiny and decluttered, I'm all good. But when I left my Hendersonville, Tennessee, one-level ranch that I share with Mr. Hannah, it resembled a frat house. It unnerved me. I told myself AND God that I was finished. This was no way for an OLD woman to live. Geez Louise.

I reflected on the personal devastation of the year. My sister Linda had died unexpectedly earlier in the year, and I hadn't completely processed it. Sad didn't begin to describe the details and I had tucked my grief away, telling myself that it would need to wait. I was in such a weird place emotionally, trying to find my peace with being the one that's left. My mom, my dad, my brother, my sister . . . were all gone. I had one sibling left, and that was Anneta. And then, in late October, just a few days prior, she decided to climb up on a nightstand and hang a curtain rod. The impatient nature of our gene pool is deadly at times. She lost her footing and landed in a rocking chair, still standing, but of course a rocking chair doesn't make a very good ladder. It threw her. So now Anneta, the only sibling I had left, the sister that had survived three open-heart surgeries, three valve replacements, a near-death car accident that left her on life support for seventy-three days, six strokes, and a few partridges in pear trees, had just added brain surgery to the list!

She had loved me unconditionally, and I loved her in the same way. I was so afraid she was going to die. But as always, the show must go on. Anneta had instilled in me, above all things, we must persevere. She wanted me to go to the mountain, have the retreat, and see what kind of class of 2017 we would have. I wondered. Who would avoid hell and make Heaven their home as a result of this week? But, oh my, my brain hurt, my feet hurt, and I was spending a lot of time absorbed in arguments with myself. I'm pretty sure that's a bad sign.

The Ya-Ya girls had intentionally left me alone. They knew I was toast. So here I sat . . . in my cat gown, looking at the ragged pink fabric, thinking about Anneta and her outcome—it didn't look good. The reason my house was a trashed mess? I had been burning up the road from Tennessee to the Kentucky hospital where she had been a patient since her surgery. She fell while I was at the beach retreat, and as soon as my feet hit Tennessee dirt, I packed a bag and went to see her.

These retreats were just a few days apart. And the night she fell we were headed out to our first service on the beach, when I got the call. My nephew Ryan called me and gave me all the details. The bottom line was that she had a brain bleed and was headed to emergency surgery. I couldn't believe it. I began to cry. There was no way for me to get a flight out of Panama City that night, and there was no way to get there in time for the surgery—they were rushing her out right then. Transport was there and Ryan said, "I'm going to have to go." Amanda said, "Put the phone up to her ear while they wheel her to surgery." He did. My girls, Terah, Krystal, Kelly, and Amanda, began to plead the blood. They began to rebuke the enemy that had come to disrupt her life and that retreat. They prayed loud and proud, and they prayed with as much authority as I've ever heard. They told her, "You shall live and not die and declare the works of the Lord!" They prayed for the surgeon's hands, the anesthesiologists, they prayed for peace to cover her, and then they prayed for me! Remember, they were on speaker on Ryan's phone. He's a valued hospital employee and he hung with her and us as long as he could. After about six or seven minutes of all-out spiritual intercession by this mighty army of girls, we felt it break. And about that time Ryan said, "I gotta go. Love you all." And he was gone.

Amanda said, "Come on. Get up. She's going to be okay. Let's go to church." We did and she was. And now I was sitting here looking at these mountains, still wearing the exhaustion of a busy life, lack of sleep, and a curtain-rod-hanging sister. Only Anneta. My kids call her a cat, and she was on life number eleven or twelve. The three trips to Kentucky in four days, and then to this mountain, that dad-gum all-night soup cooking episode, and this sinus headache. It was too much. I was too old and too eager to save the world. I asked myself, "Who is going to save me?"

I stared at Mount Le Conte and, as always, found some strength and the will to get up. I slapped on some lipstick and decided to try it again. I needed to go see what God was up to. I needed to persist like never before. I headed back to the lodge.

They sang and I watched my friends as they praised. These women praise like only THEY can. They're on a mission. Most are there to get a tankful of Jesus; some are there as a last resort. Some are there because they know where they came from, and like me, they promised God when HE so generously strengthened them, that they would be the hands and feet of JESUS and lead someone else out of the dark world of victimhood. It was a calling, and many of my Stronger girls realize that this is a God plan, and they're a strong link in the chain. I surveyed the room full of women, and I thanked God for the strong—we would need them tonight. I felt it.

When we are weak, He is strong. I was weak. I knew the strong MAN was SURELY in the house. Terah and crew sang. Amanda, Kelly, and Krystal joined her. Kelly brought a word; the power was in the house. That's pretty normal in these services. But then I saw it. A bowl of oil. Not a bottle, a bowl. The girls instructed these women to form a line. They did. Terah and Kelly prayed for their hands, Amanda and Krystal knelt, anointed with oil, and prayed for their feet. One at a time, all 250 of them. I am so lost for words that can adequately describe what happened that night on the mountain. I almost didn't write about this because I knew that words would fail me. I know that every possible struggle was represented in that prayer line. EVERY struggle. Sexual addiction, alcoholism, cancer, demon possession, gluttony, jealousy, rebellion, diabetes, disappointment, rape, abandonment, abortion, self-destructive behavior, kidney disease, heart disease, the heartbreak that was the result of children who were addicted, the heartbreak that only a momma who has a child in federal prison knows about, abusive relationships, affairs, and on and on and on.

Truth. I wanted to say to these girls: I will never betray you, but I know you. And "you" is a mess sometimes. The line started, the girls sang. It was good. I was in the floor more than not. God was ministering to me in the deepest parts of my soul. I watched: God was doing some stuff. It was amazing, to say the least. EVERY SINGLE woman was being anointed, and it wasn't a "pat" sprinkling and move it on out. They were pouring into these women. Praying for healing like they would pray for their own family members, rebuking the generational curses. It was thick. I could write a complete book on this night, and someday I may.

But as I remember my exhaustion and my "I can't do this anymore" that I had told God repeatedly that day, as I remember the "nothing can be worth this" moment I had at the cabin prior to this service, I have to summarize for you. This book wouldn't be complete without it.

We were playing music instead of singing. Terah was anointing hands with Kelly, and Karen Harding was praying with people. That left Katelanne and Gracie, Kelly's daughters. They're eleven and fourteen. They grew tired after an hour or two. Derrick Casteel, a friend of ours, had brought sound equipment and supported in many ways that week. It's always good to have a guy or two around. Derrick is a friend of my boys, and one of those people who is eager to help. I like people like that and I always take them at their word when they say, "Call me if you need help." So Derrick, realizing his little singers were tired, decided to DJ and cranked up some worship music to the PA from his iPhone. I don't remember what the first song was. But, oh my, I sure do remember what the second or third one was. I heard the intro to "Alabaster Box" start, and I felt chills from the top of my head to my toes. For that song is not JUST a song. It's the anthem of EVERY woman who's been with Jesus. It's the go-to on the bad days, the reminder on the good days, and the song that best depicts my heart. Period. I've told my kids many times that they're to play it at my funeral. 'Cause truly, NO ONE knows the price of my praise . . . NO ONE knows the cost of your shout . . . and as I type this, tears are falling, they always do when I repeat the lyrics in my head.

Tears are automatic. I don't care where I am or who I'm with, I'm gonna cry and get a little praise on when this song brings the anointing into the atmosphere.

The room came unglued. The spirit of the Lord blew through like a wave. Baptist women were in the floor. Derrick was catching them as they fell. Not one, not two, but dozens. My granddaughters were in the floor, under the power of God. It was an unbelievable sight. For those who are scared about now, don't be. I'm simply telling you what happened. I have 250 witnesses.

Miracles started flowing like water. It was indescribable. But about the third time Derrick played "Alabaster Box," it hit me. This picture. OH MY! The picture of my

Krystal pouring oil on the feet of these women, rebuking Satan, storming the gates of hell and fighting for their freedom, could this be true? This girl who had run through eight lanes of heavy traffic in nothing but a pair of panties after she took bad drugs that were laced with a hallucinogen. Twenty year ago that was my Krystal story. Hell, pure unadulterated hell. The emergency personnel told me, "She should have been hit by a car, but somehow she wasn't. It's a miracle." My mind flooded: she, like me, could have been in hell on this night; the escape was narrow and I remembered. But instead, she was HERE, on a mountain in Tennessee, ANOINTING the feet of others. I don't remember much—I too went down. The Lord took me to a mountain in a vision. In my vision I saw a sea of people . . . as far as the eye could see. They were clearly in unity and they were waiting for someone to take a stage. There's more, but it's not time for me to share.

When I awoke and got up from the floor, I realized that Terah was now washing Amanda's feet with her hair. I couldn't take it. AS I heaved and cried, as I watched Terah honor Amanda, her pastor and sister-in-law, as Mary had honored Jesus, I fell on my face again. I told you I stayed in the floor more than anyone that night. I've got the sweetest picture of my Baptists Ya-Yas sitting all around me on the floor, and I'm slain in the spirit. I think they were unsure what to do, so they rubbed my arms and my hair.

My girls prayed for women for five hours. They were exhausted! But happy, so happy. To be in your calling brings that kind of fulfillment. I've never seen them more fulfilled than that Tuesday night in November.

Also, Katelanne got a touch from God that night that she will remember until she's an old lady. GOD did a thing. It was one of those nights. Everyone got a touch, a much-needed one. So when the Wednesday morning ending service came to a close, as we surveyed what God had done, we all agreed: you had to be there to get it. But this much I will explain: they filled a bowl and used two bottles of olive oil on those women's feet. I believe in anointing, but I had never seen 250 women take their shoes off and have their feet slathered with oil and the glory fall . . . on EVERY . . . SINGLE . . . ONE.

Obedience is better than sacrifice. The girls said the Lord told them to anoint the hands and feet of every single person there. They were EXHAUSTED, but nevertheless, they persisted. They didn't stop until EVERYONE had been with Jesus. And as I type this last sentence I can't help wonder, who will make it to the end because of the obedience. This night will be one of those nights that we haul that sorry devil to, when he torments us. You can take him to the place . . . for the LORD surely touched us there, ALL of us.

I was nearly raptured! What a day. And to think earlier I had asked, "Who will take care of me?" I had my answer. Jesus was my ticket. For the most part, OUR family was blessed with revival.

The Bonus Room Meeting

By November 12, 2017, as I said, most of the family found themselves in a full-blown revival. We went to the beach for a retreat, we girls did, and the power of God was so strong that girls were being filled with the spirit on the beach, in their bathing suits. God doesn't care. He didn't get your memo that He couldn't do that. They were slain in the spirit in the pictures that were coming to my phone. Ding, ding, another picture, another one got it. I was at my condo, crying like a two-month-old baby. How amazing was this?

They were sending pictures to me, all the girls who had strolled down to get a little vitamin D. And, lo and behold, some got what most of them really came for. Water. LIVING water. The struggles of their REAL lives, back home away from this beautiful beach, were heavy. Some of them came with little more than a tank of gas and a bag of chips. While some came with enough money to shop and eat lobster, most were living in a season of lack, pain, or rejection. The beach was a treat. The services were a treat. The friendships made were a treat. Economic circumstances weren't a litmus test for this event.

That's the beauty of the Holy Ghost: there's no credit check, no background check. All you need is a desire. Some of these girls had watched and realized they too wanted to wade deeper. So as the waves rolled in, they fell out. Some were speaking in tongues and some praising, but all were clearly in new waters. The beer drinkers and party-hearty onlookers were probably videoing and posting. My girls didn't care. They were over it.

And truly these retreats PROVE, over and over, that God isn't restricted to our little boxes. Your church may teach that God can't do this or that. But let me tell you, sweet friends. Your church is wrong. God doesn't need your permission to move on the beach. He doesn't need my permission. Aren't you tired of the ordinary? The world is over us and our lack of passion about this walk called Christianity. We CLAIM that without the experience of Christ one will find him- or herself living in an eternal state of burning and pain. Yet we mention Christianity with a backward glance, a muffled comment, and an occasional post or bumper sticker. When's the last time you had a radical conversation with a nonbeliever about what God has done for you? When is the last time you rolled up your sleeves and showed someone your scars, the scars of abuse, abandonment, grief, and personal disappointment? Candor and passion are a sure-footed formula for drawing "all" men, women too. Candidly tell them what your experiences have been, be honest, and then walk them through the faith part, where God did what God does . . . and allow your passion to run wild. Describe this God with your hands, your face, your voice, your tears, your laughter, your body language, your choice of music, your actions . . . allow your testimony to be alive and in you! PEOPLE will pay attention. Promise.

Well, on this day, on a beach, some girls were alive and had their testimony living and breathing in them. And other girls were paying attention. It's the perfect kind of collision. When need encounters provision, watch out. It's a perfect storm. So this was our life in late October. Daily moves of God. The beach, the mountains, our church . . . were all serving as opportunities for people who wanted to come and experience the fire.

The fire had truly been flamed back in July 2017, at Overflow. Overflow is Restoring Hope's annual conference. I call it revival. It is difficult to explain and truly must be experienced. In 2017 I witnessed the chains of pride fall off of entire congregations. I have no reason to believe that Heaven will be more tangible or the mansion will be bigger for people who are shouters, dancers, or those who are completely willing to give in to God and let the spirit take over their body movements during a service. As a matter of fact I've known people who came straight from the motel room where they had committed adultery, walk on stage, shout the glory down, and I watched as people would fall out in the spirit when touched, and boom. Rinse and repeat, again the next night.

It's been one of the greatest struggles of my life to deal with. I've asked God for years to explain this one to me. I'm sure you have too. We've ALL watched ministries that we loved fall. The best I got was this: singing, preaching, writing, evangelizing, praying, most of what we see when someone takes the stage is simply their gifts in action. When my children make me angry, I don't go to their house, beat on their door, and load up their favorite chair or blanket that I gave them. I don't grab their Kate Spade purse, dump it out, and say, "I gave you this for a gift. You made me angry yesterday. I came to get it." You don't either. Well, there are extreme cases, I suppose, but for the most part, a gift is a gift.

Adulterers write songs that make you cry and make sinners repent. Drug addicts pastor churches. Homosexual men preach tirelessly about the immoral sin of "Adam and Steve" versus "Adam and Eve." Hypocrisy is alive and well in the Pentecostal Church, more so than those churches who don't profess the fullness of the book of Acts, at least in my opinion. Hypocrites do the unthinkable, yet God doesn't always take their gifts . . . their ability to communicate the message in word and song, their ability to charm and make your granny swoon; He leaves it intact, usually. It doesn't mean they're okay. It doesn't mean they're anointed. They're typically not, but they are GIFTED. I preach daily, "EXAMINE fruit. Today's fruit. Grace is enough, and we're not hired to be God, but we are fruit inspectors."

Back to my point about uncensored, radical worship; the men and women who find themselves immersed in Jesus, with total abandon, exemplify a life where pride has moved to the back seat. Sometimes these hypocrites that I described earlier will find true worship, for a minute. In that moment they decide that they will NEVER do "it" again. They will stop before they're busted. They live in the moment completely— that's what charismatic people often do. They live in the now, because they can; it's always worked for them. Charm and harm, it's how they roll. But then the service ends, the impulses start, and they're back in the hypocrite line, waiting their turn with a whore or a drug hookup.

But those people aren't normal, and they're probably not reading this book. Uhm, if so I doubt they've made it this far. To the rest of us there's a lesson here. Complete surrender to Jesus involves a bit more than our money, time, and resources. It also involves our pride, the way people view us, the fear of being outside OUR comfort zone. I think it's safe to say that God can rarely use us to our maximum when we're living in our area of comfort. The folks who are stretching, reaching, pushing, those who are health challenged, financially challenged, relationship challenged, they easily lose their pride.

People often send me letters and say that they admire my ability to be unashamed. Sometimes it's my political stand. Other times it's involved with my post of someone buck-shouting, speaking in tongues, a child that's slain in the spirit, something unusual, and potentially controversial. MANY times a social media post will prompt a private message that goes something like this: "I'm Pentecostal too, but I don't know how my friends would feel if I posted the things you post." Once again. Pride is the enemy. So you're Pentecostal, but you're a closet Pentecostal? You believe in the Holy Ghost but you don't want your Catholic coworker to know? You love God a lot but you don't want cool people to know because they may think you're uncool? That's pride, pride, and pride. It won't work. Lose it.

If your tears shame you, if you don't talk about the spirit of the Lord as frequently as you talk about the Voice, or the View, you've got some work to do. It's impossible to see that deep, raw, transforming move of God when pride is in full possession of our psyche. When we check to see if anyone is videoing us before we lose ourselves in worship, when we try to remember if we have on our jeans that make our butts look smaller before we kneel and pray, when we do a mental roll call of those in attendance before we lose ourselves in God . . . because if "SHE" is here I just ain't feeling it? Trouble. God won't be our entertainment, our substitute for a movie at the Cinema 16. He won't. When you get this far into the water, you shouldn't be playing church. He's not.

Pride isn't always about pretending to be richer, better, or holier. Sometimes it's about being cooler. There's an entire generation of selfie-taking, Snapchatting kids who are absorbed with the pride that so easily besets our kids in 2018. No one is more aware of this pride factor than I am. Not because I'm young but because I have grandchildren. Many of them. They have great spiritual direction and great parents. But they're kids. And they're not immune to the struggles of the world around them. So I watch, I make mental notes. I ask them how they enjoyed church when I want to get a read on one of them.

All kids are different. Eva is only eleven, but she worships as if she's in the presence of Jesus. No concern about who is watching, no concern about being judged. She's Amanda's daughter. She does exactly what Amanda does. Without fully recognizing it, she's led the others into comfortable worship, unabashed worship, boundary-free worship. Again, she's Aaron and Amanda's daughter. They've made their kids so completely comfortable with corporate worship, it's like breathing to them. That's what happens when your parents are worship leaders, singers, ministers. Kelly's girls are pretty much the same; they're road kids who have been in church more nights than not.

However, Hope is a poised eighteen-year-old. She worships, but I can see the wheels turning. I can see her trying to reason out the rational answers of an adult mind. I watched her as she went through a phase of cautious examination. That comes from the road, seeing so many things that jade your ideology, and it also comes with being eighteen. She is living on the bridge between childhood and a mortgage payment. She's feeling this adulthood thing out. She thinks for herself these days.

And so it was on Sunday, November 12, 2017. I had been out of town for several weeks and the kids weren't sure how to feel about that. So on this particular Sunday afternoon Edie said, "If we're going to see you, we're going to have to come to your house and just stay the night." And they did. Edie loaded up her babies and headed over (at the time one was sixteen months old and the other was five months old). Then Cameron and Hope trickled in; Gracie, Emma and Sophie came too. I'm not sure how this mix of granddaughters happened, but it did. They were high on Jesus and loving the cousin/sister time.

Edie moved back to Tennessee in July of 2017, and she and Cameron had developed a VERY close sister network. They are six years apart in age, Edie being the older at twenty-three, and Cameron also being a newbie to the world of adulthood. She celebrated eighteen last September. So these sisters were learning to be adult and Edie was learning to raise Irish twins. Their baby sister Sophie was there as well. So all three of Krystal's girls, two of Kelly's, and Emma, Jason's youngest, were there. And Granny was having a sleepover. Well, Granny is old and had to go to bed about midnight. Edie is adjusted to sleep loss—she has two very young babies—and the other girls are very accustomed to late nights, or ALL-night living.

I told them goodnight, headed to my old people mattress and went to sleep. Steve beat me to the punch. He's an old man with old man habits. He leaves the living room sometimes and doesn't say a word. I turn around to tell him something and he's gone. I yell for him, no answer. Many nights I find him already asleep, socks strewn on the floor by the bed (it's a rule for him, they MUST be on the floor). Tonight was the norm.

About 2:00 a.m. I woke and wondered if we had locked the front door. The kids had come in that door and we rarely use it. I jumped up to check it and, of course, go to the bathroom. I'm also old. So the potty happened and then I walked into the living room and stopped in my tracks, it was so weird. I heard singing. Now, remember, it's 2:00 a.m. at Ma and Pa's house. The normal sounds would be snoring or a toilet flushing, possibly a Fox News reair of Hannity, but never singing.

I listened and followed the sound. It led me to the bonus room. We never use that room. I often say it's a waste of money to heat it and cool it. But it wasn't wasted on this Sunday night that had stretched into a Monday morning. Lord help me tell this. I feel a shout. I quietly tiptoed through the kitchen, careful not to turn on lights to warn them I was there. For, you see, I didn't know what these girls were up to, but I knew I wanted to capture it. That's what I do. I capture things. I'm a grandmother. I realize that I annoy them, but I don't care. That's my job.

So I crept quietly up the steps. It was dark and they didn't have lights on. I could hear lyrics and beautiful harmony. They were singing, "Sing, my soul will sing, my soul will make this place an altar, make this place an altar, make this place an altar."

I stopped when I realized that this was sacred. I slipped out quietly; they didn't see me and I didn't see them clearly. But I realized what was going on. They were having a worship service. I returned to my bedroom and had a little praise service by myself. I watched the video I had just taken before realizing it filmed a bit better than my eyes could see. I could see that their hands were raised and full-on corporate worship was happening. Emma was in the floor, slain in the spirit. I had never seen anything quite like it. I cried for an hour. What had I done to deserve this kind of blessing? What? To see complete, unashamed surrender to God is possibly the most beautiful thing we will ever see.

The choices were clear. They were going to stray from the norm, these girls had decided. They weren't just singing, "I will enter His gates." They were actually entering His gates. Lord have mercy, when I remember what they sounded like, I can't even. There was no congregation, no ushers, no pulpit. They were in a dark bonus room at their granny's house. But they were spending time with Him. My, my: They will remember that night when their hair is gray and their sight is dim.

Nights like that are the markers along the road of this Christian walk. I knew God was pouring into them, just them. I knew that this night would be one of those places that they would take the devil to when he came to destroy their faith. I innately knew. It will be a boulder in the foundation of their God moments. It was one of those nights. The next day Edie told me that Hope shouted and knocked over a lamp. Hope doesn't shout. As I said, she's a thinker, maybe an overthinker. But on November 12, 2017, along about 2:00 a.m., Hope Bowling shouted in my bonus room. She may never shout again. That's okay. But I promise you she won't forget that night.

I also promise you that Sophie, Cameron, Emma, Gracie, and Edie won't forget it either, not soon anyway.

So some of you are reading this and thinking, "This would never happen in my family. My children aren't serving God, my grandchildren certainly aren't." Take it from someone who knows. Keep standing. Keep telling them the truth. THEY ARE coming back to GOD! Remember, these experiences are free for all. We don't become eligible when we earn our certificate of perfection. These God moments aren't reserved for those who have served Him for a gazillion years. They come when we lose our pride. Period. End of subject.

Teach those youngins to be candid and raw. If they learn to be transparent with us, they will feel comfortable being transparent with God. Teach them that lifetime friendships matter and petty jealousy doesn't. If they value REAL relationships with people, they will value their relationship with God. Teach them that their cousins and sisters will always be there. Treasure them, prioritize them.

Teach them that it's okay to cry in restaurants, scream at ballgames, and laugh at their dad's corny jokes! But ABOVE all, teach them to be comfortable talking about JESUS. Anytime. Anywhere. In any room. The result will be adult Christians who reject ugly pride.

That's the ticket, my friends. No one has failed more than I have. I've done it wrong most of the time. But like my momma, who didn't get everything right either, we got the Jesus thing right. Even in my most flawed seasons, I've never had a day that I was ashamed of Him. I'm often ashamed of me, but not Him.

Folks, I've known some VERY flawed individuals who weren't ashamed of Jesus. They lived in personal shame and hypocrisy. However, they understood who HE was, they understood that He had paid the price, and they openly acknowledged Him in any situation. In my opinion, God's grace has been exceedingly plentiful on these people. They have walked in a measure of favor that is unmerited by their actions, but their "David-like" unabashed worship appears to reward them with a bit of extra patience on God's part. In the end? We shall see. I'm not the judge and they should be pretty glad.

In my opinion, this is the key. Lose the pride. If you're guilty? Rebuke it. Scrub it off if you must. Go to Walmart and witness to someone in the frozen food section—that'll break some pride off of you. It will blow your mind how free you will be without the chains! I've seen it change families, churches, entire communities.

The loss of pride will start revivals, lower the divorce rate, settle lawsuits, bring estranged children back home, and pretty much every other good thing you can think of. When I give in and lose my pride in a tough situation, I feel like I've had a good ol' bath! If you want God's favor? Lose your pride and talk about Him without hesitation. Let His spirit move as you walk through this life. STOP restricting Him to Sunday morning between 10:00 a.m. and noon. How insulted He must be!!!

Realize, finally, that nothing else matters except pleasing Him. He's the BIG boss. Try it for a week. Allow your spiritual man to breathe 24/7; you're choking him. It will change your life. Don't let your tears shame you. Open your mouth and tell how good HE'S been to you!!

Modern-Day Miracle

The winter of 2013–2014 brought an end to a season of incompletion for me and mine. The Texas years would soon be coming to an end for Aaron, Amanda, and the kiddos. As you may know, they spent several years working for Pastor John Hagee in San Antonio. When they left, I cried my eyes out. Sometimes when I would talk to them on the phone, I would hang up, pull my car into a parking lot, listen to their music . . . and just blubber. I've done it more than once in the Kroger parking lot. It was as if part of my heart was missing. I know that sounds sappy and so grannyish but it's still true.

I asked often, "Ready to come home? We have a house you can live in." They would say, "Not yet, but it's not going to be long." Well, in the fall of 2013 I met them for breakfast downtown. They had been gone for four years and it felt like forty to me. They were in town for a day on business with the Hagees and we were excited to sit down and have a meal. Somehow when I know they're next door, it's fine if we don't see each other every day. But when your family leaves and moves across the country, it's then you crave those random meals and visits.

I was so ready for them to come home, and on this morning, I knew. In my gut I knew that they were about to tell me they had news. I ate eggs Benedict and was wearing a leopard shirt. It's amazing how we can remember the little things on such days. I remember what I was wearing when JFK was assassinated even though I was only seven. Those life-changing days come with distinct memories of where we were, what the walls looked like, the carpet, clothes, and sometimes the food, smells, and smiles.

This life-changing breakfast was hurried and to the point, but, oh my, did it change everything. THEY were COMING HOME! We needed a building, a house, and a lot of prayer! Their plan was set, their minds made up. Aaron had heard from God through a vision about a tree. It's his story, not mine. You will have to wait for his book to get the full details, I suppose. But I don't have words to describe the sheer glee that my spirit was feeling as I listened to the details of the "tree" vision.

The road had jaded them in many ways. They had gone to the Hagees to find stability, so they thought. The truth is this. They had to go there to become who they are now. The discipline that Aaron learned prepared him. The struggles of life would be OH so real in San Antonio, but they would pass the test. The hardships nearly broke them and their marriage. Again, it's their story. One of them will write it some day. But here's the important part for this book. They HEARD from God, and they listened. They stopped in their tracks, caught God's vision for their lives, and started making the proper steps to execute the plan. Like giving Pastor Hagee a long notice, reaching out to find housing in Tennessee as well as a meeting place, and gathering the family and casting the vision.

It was a few days after Christmas 2013 when they gathered the family. We were all there. They simply said, "We're coming home at the end of the school year to start a church. We would love your support, but if you feel that God has planted you elsewhere, stay until He tells you to leave." A few opinions floated around the room, and the joy for their return was intoxicating. The kids were so excited. I barely knew Ean. Eva left before she started kindergarten. They had missed birthdays, Christmases, and lots of pool parties. This granny did nothing but smile, and, yes, cry. I always cry.

We made arrangements to buy them a house to live in for a minute while they worked a deal to start the services on Wednesday nights at TBN. The TBN property was nearly next door to our home and it was large, beautiful, and VERY expensive. It was rumored to be for sale, but the price wasn't realistic for us. I know God's able to do anything, I do. But the auditorium was ill-suited for church use. The alternate spaces were there, but the fact that the property had been built by Conway Twitty as a tourist attraction was obvious to me. The functionality wasn't there for OUR purpose. There were several residential houses on the track, plus a separate unattached recording studio, and all in all, it wasn't good use of dollars, especially if it was out of our price range by millions.

God had this. I knew HE did . . . but I wanted to know WHAT He had. I am a control freak by nature, but I'm in a recovery program. The recovery program involves telling myself every hour or so that God knew this day would start with the rising of the sun, and He knew that it would end with the setting of that same sun, and He knew exactly what would come my way between the sunrise and sunset, and HE knew all of this before I was created. He isn't a God that throws paint on the wall and just lets it dry. He creates things, paints pictures, orders our steps, makes the job of sustaining the universe look like it's a piece of cake. He doesn't operate in disarray; He's clearly a God of order. If this was His will, it would be His deal. And I tried to chill. Tried. HE had a plan and it was in order, not frantic panic. I was waiting, but tirelessly thinking. My wheels turn 24/7. It's a curse and a gift. Most gifts can be our curse if we allow them to be.

A few years earlier I had shown a church property to my friends, but the deal didn't work out. The seller wasn't extremely motivated. They bought a different property and moved on. The seller wasn't negotiable on price and refused to consider a lease. A couple of years had passed and the building was still empty. The property had once housed a thriving congregation and was a respected spirit-filled church. I knew the pastor's sister-in-law and several of the church members. When the end came, it was ugly. The entire congregation was devastated. The pastor and his wife divorced. Her story is very similar to mine. I will leave it there. But in the end, the 26,000 square feet that had been built by God's people, with God's money, sat there on Center Point Road as a daily reminder of what happens when the devil wins. The place felt like death when you drove onto the parking lot. I had been in the building a few times and it was like a time capsule. The remnants of Holy Ghost services remained, but the stench of death was in the air.

So about April or May of 2014, we were anticipating the arrival of our Texas kids, and, man, was I ever excited! As God would have it, the house they were moving into was at the same exit as the "death" church was. I was going to Aaron and Amanda's new house to meet a painter on this particular day. I was out driving like most realtors do, and, yes, I was trying to get the house up to speed with fresh paint, tile, and carpet. That's the "Kathy" in me. I sure love a paint color wheel and a carload of tile and fabric samples. But on this day, as I turned onto the Center Point Road exit, I slowed down at the church property. I traveled this road every day, but that day I pulled into the parking lot.

At this point Amanda and Aaron had a glimmer of hope for the TBN property, but I didn't see it. It wasn't right for their needs. As I stared at these empty buildings on Center Point, as my mind wandered back over the mess that had caused the death of this ministry, I asked God, "Can these walls live again? Can we see Holy Ghost revival on this property?" Of course the answer was yes, but I needed to have that God moment, just God and me in the parking lot, I suppose. I'm dramatic like that. I will work like a maniac on achieving a goal, but only if I know it's right, and only after God and I talk about it. If my passion isn't squarely in place, I don't have the savvy to be effective. But when I believe in something or someone, clear the runway, I'm coming through.

Ultimately, I knew this wasn't my decision; it was Aaron and Amanda's. I called them. I was still in the parking lot. They answered. I said something like, "I think we need to rethink the Center Point Property." They agreed. I called the agent who had it listed. It had been on the market for years, but no one could make a deal work . . . no one. I think they had turned down seven or eight offers. The market was still a bit soft, and selling a commercial building that's been purposed as a church isn't always the easiest thing in the world. This building needed a bit of work, but we could move in and have the doors open in weeks, not years.

The agent called me back. It was the same guy I had worked with before. At least the pleasantries were easy and I went straight to the point. I told him about Aaron and Amanda's vision. I spent a good hour telling him that God had made a way out of no way for our family, over and over. He was familiar. I told him about our Kentucky beginnings, working for $300 a night, three hundred nights a year, and raising a passel of kids on a bus.

I don't know much, but I know this. This agent would be the voice that would have the ear of the seller. He needed to see our heart, our passion for souls, for that would be the ticket to getting in this building. They wanted to sell it, not lease it. They had turned down all those other offers; one of them was mine—remember I was the agent for another church. Thankfully God took care of that church and all is well. They bought another property and they're in a great place. But they were an established ten-year-old congregation, with giving records and the ability to do the diligence to obtain a bank loan, and still no dice. It didn't work. So . . . we were a

LONG shot. On this day I was working on my selling skills. Ha! I needed this listing agent on my side.

Restoring Hope Church wasn't tangible yet. This church was little more than a logo of a trickling water drop on white stationery, and a vision about a tree. And about now, I'm feeling this chapter! But God. He doesn't lie. If he said, "Go to Tennessee and start a church," then He had a place already prepared for that church. The stench of death ain't no big deal for God. Lazarus proved that. My life proves it too, and so does yours.

So in early June, they loaded the cars and a U-Haul, and they headed toward Tennessee! The picture that they texted the family was surreal. I still have it. For, you see, I know what I know. I knew our lives were going to change. I knew this was God, and I knew it was big. I understand that music is ministry, and I cherish our musical roots, truly. I am not dissing it. Many won't come to church, but they will flock to a concert. But times were different for our family. We had been fractured, knocked out for a minute, but everyone had found the oxygen again and decided to get up for another round. Mistakes were made, careers had been difficult, and the changes had left scars. I had walls AND the rest of the family had walls. Walls come when we're trying to protect our heart from another blow.

We were still a very close tribe, but the years spent apart couldn't rival the decade spent on a bus 24/7, with complete accountability—well, for most of us. The couples were close, the daughters-in-law and the sisters were close, and of course the guys were as well. When you cram fourteen or fifteen people on a forty-five-foot bus, there's not much room for secrets. All the kids, and myself, we walked in a season of transparency and complete dependence on the anointing during the road years, the Crabb Family years. They needed it to have effectiveness on stage; I needed it to make good business decisions. It was a rolling music factory, and a very sweet season. Yes, there were struggles, and, yes, the end of this season completely crushed our hearts. So we sometimes struggle to look back with clarity. But that day, February 2, 2018, while sitting on a sea-glass green sofa in a beach home that we all own collectively, I'm trying to see those years through eyes that no longer cry EVERY single time I hear them sing "Please Come Down to Me," and with a heart that's been nurtured by Jesus and Steve Hannah. On the other side of heartbreak, I think I see clearly.

So on a pretty June day in 2013, Amanda, Aaron, and those sweet kids moved into a house in Hendersonville, Tennessee. They were home! WE partied. During the course of the summer we had Wednesday night services at TBN; Aaron and Amanda busied themselves with the nuts and bolts and busy work of starting a church. They were adamant that this church would reach out to all. They had lofty ideas about giving to the needy in our community. Sometimes I would think, "Do they really get it?" I knew they had no money, no building, no assets except a couple of worn-out cars, and they spoke constantly about giving away to the community, and we had no money to buy anything to give away. Not yet anyway. And to their credit and mine too, that's how we had ALWAYS lived. Go big or go home. God's will? God's bill. It never makes me nervous for me, but it was making me raise an eyebrow every now and then when it was their name on the dotted line.

I suppose I didn't get the memo that they were grown. I suppose I thought it was my job to protect them from bad decisions. Clearly, it's not, but we never stop being "that" parent, and I'm a classic case.

I began to dialogue with the real estate agent who had the Center Point church. Summer was wearing thin and we were going to start Sunday services in September, somewhere. We didn't have a home yet. We were at TBN, and they were gracious and accommodating, but we needed a permanent home. They loved us, and we loved them. Still do. I will forever be thankful for Paul and Jan Crouch, and oh how God used them to spread the gospel. Their vision is unmatched and as a result TBN is the largest Christian network in the world. Paul believed in the story of a crucified Jesus who arose on the third day, ascended, and now sits at the right hand of the Father. Paul didn't get into the weeds on doctrine. As with most folks who have power and stature, there were rumors. I get it. But here's the truth. Paul Crouch WAS Christian television. The son of Assemblies of God missionaries, his brilliant mind and his love for evangelism helped him to own or control over 18,000 TV and cable affiliates. Paul and Jan had trudged through demons and devils up to their eyeballs to build the largest television network in the world. Of course, they're controversial figures, even after their deaths. But guess what? Most people say the same thing about me. So what. Here's what I know. They were good to my family, and they were responsible for more people hearing the gospel than anyone in the history of the world, and they were generous. When Mike and Kelly had their bus wreck, they gave us their staff for a benefit event, and their facility. They came and supported, they wrote a check, they single-handedly provided a financial solution for Mike, Kelly, and family. Period. The event raised enough money to make the Bowling's payroll and sustain them for a year. So once again, the TBN folks were accommodating us. This time it was Aaron and Amanda and their vision for a church.

The month of August was busy, and part of that busy was an offer on the Center Point property. I felt we had done our homework, and I knew God was in this. Favor rested on the offer in so many ways. I struggle when telling someone else's story, and this is truly Aaron and Amanda's story, so I will stick with the real estate angle. I was the agent. We made an offer that included a three-year lease, a solid yearly reduction in the purchase price, and a contract to purchase within a three-year period, with a nice juicy carrot if we purchased the first year. But at that moment, we had to worry about the large up-front money we needed to secure year number one of the lease. The building needed so much work, and we had agreed to pay $40,000 plus the first month's lease payment, which was closer to $10,000 than to $5,000, and then there was insurance, large utility deposits, and only the good Lord knows what else we had to buy. The list was long. But to summarize, we had committed to a thirty-six-month lease, a million-dollar plus purchase within three years, and about $70,000 out of pocket, RIGHT now, within a month or so, and we hadn't had a Sunday service yet. Yikes!

Yep. That's pretty much how I live my life. And Aaron and Amanda certainly had paid attention all of those Crabb Family years when we moved out of the comfort zone, strictly on faith. Amanda is like me. Go. Let's do this. But Aaron is a bit more measured, typically. We've always called him Papaw, because he has an old, gentle soul. But in this season of "living out the tree vision"? He had dumped his reservations. He had become so much like me in his mind-set. He didn't have it in him to doubt. He knew that God had pointed His finger toward Hendersonville, Tennessee, and that was all she wrote. No fear.

So like a couple of kids at a "buy here, pay here" lot, these two signed a lease on a building that they had no idea how they were going to pay for. They just knew they would. Now to raise the $70,000. Family offering time. We started texting. I started Facebooking. Actually, I think we all did. To the best of my recollection we had that money pledged within thirty-six hours. It took it a day or two to trickle in, but the Lord provided. Impressive, but not surprising.

I've lived out many ministry dreams that the Lord planted squarely in my spirit, His idea, not mine. And where He points, He always provides. But notice, his plan always involves a tremendous amount of faith, sacrifice, and discipline. That's our to-do list. And they were faring pretty well with all three. They scrubbed, worked, poured hours upon hours into the manual labor of preparation. I always say, "If it was easy, everyone would be doing it." And take my word, it wasn't easy.

However, they had great help early on; the folks were coming and working. For, you see, on September 14, 2014, the first Sunday service EVER for Restoring Hope, we announced that we already HAD a building. The large crowd at TBN was jubilant. I was jubilant and praying for a PEOPLE that would boldly embrace the need—not only the financial need but the hard work, prayer, and commitment that was going to be necessary to build this thing! It happened. Restoring Hope was building a church family. Wow, that was fast!

As I said, Aaron and Amanda had lofty ideas. They had a vision. The time spent in San Antonio had been a dose of discipline and a crash course in church protocol. I'm not saying Restoring Hope is patterned after John Hagee's church. No, not at all. But I am saying that Aaron learned to chew up the meat and spit out the bones. He learned discipline in Texas. I saw it as it was happening, and I knew it would serve him. He learned, they both gleaned, and they came home with an understanding of leadership that they didn't possess when they left. For that I'm thankful. John Hagee probably didn't know that he was teaching Aaron what to do and what not to do, but he was, to a certain degree. Restoring Hope is the most Pentecostal church I've ever been in. When you comingle the structure that they learned with the freedom they craved? Oh my.

So here we are just over here praising Jesus, desperately trying to build a stable congregation. The looming date of September, 2017 was tattooed on my brain. At times I would wake up in the night and the devil would say, "What if you can't get a bank to loan them the money to buy that church, what then?" I have quoted this to the devil hundreds of times, "God's will, God's bill. I know it's God's will so shut it, devil."

So we made our lease payments, loved the community, watched the Lord move in ways I can't describe, and we kept giving. The ten-year-olds were getting filled with the Holy Ghost at Restoring Hope. The freedom was unlike any church I had ever attended, and the leadership that Aaron and Amanda brought to the pulpit is incredibly rare. They have two gears. High and off. I've seen them anoint with oil, lay hands on, and PRAY for EVERY single person in the congregation. One night it took five-plus hours. Aaron's clothes were soaked, Amanda's hair was a mess, her makeup was gone, and they were so exhausted I was concerned.

They often fast and push themselves physically to the outer edge of exhaustion. This was one of those nights. I stood in the family section and cried like a baby. This kind of dedication is so rare these days. Churches have become big business. We're polling and asking people what they want when we should be telling them what GOD said. So many pastors are gifted speakers, but they don't have a clue what to do if something goes off script. Sorry to brag, but these kids are triple threats, both of them. They know how to pray, preach, and sing. The pulpit is as comfortable to them as their kitchen table, and Hendersonville was paying attention.

We sang, shouted a little, walked a little straighter, praised a little more often, and came back and did it again next week. We had a church. And what a beautiful thing it was to watch. The tithes were always more than enough, the giving increased each quarter, and our attendance was building as well. A year passed and we were still shouting. We discussed trying to get a loan and save that $100,000 on the purchase price, but it was a bridge too far. I discussed it with a bank in June, about three months ahead of the September one-year deadline. As I expected, they told me that we would need at least two years of giving records as well as many other things. We didn't have it.

The banker also asked if we planned to join an organization such as the Southern Baptist Association, the Church of God, the Assemblies of God, or the Nazarenes? I quickly said, "Nope." We texted back and forth a few times over the next year. This question always cropped back up. Organization? My response was always, "Nope."

I have a circle of people who are "must-haves" in my life. They are people who have been fiercely loyal to me and my family. In return we reciprocate. We are loyal to them. That's how my life churns: loyalty first. My circle is a bit closed off with a few CLOSE friends who have mustered the guts to be candid and truthful with me when no one else would. I hold these people close. I detest yes men and pandering. Ironically, I have a handful of bankers in my life who are candid with me. They have been loyal friends for many, many years. They shoot it straight, but they also hear me out. They've financed buses for me, for my friends, and for my kids. Bus loans aren't easy to come by, but they heard me out and realized it made sense. For decades, they've patiently listened to me as I shared my wild ideas and painted my "end of the idea" picture for them. Most of the time they got it. I've sent texts from the mall that said, "Buying a house on an online auction. I need a loan" only to receive a response saying, "Let me know what you need."

This is a privilege that I protect. How do you protect a relationship with a banker? Pay. It's pretty simple. How do you make these relationships last? Work. Listen. They are smarter than I am. Also, to have friends you must be friendly, so the Bible says. Relationships ALWAYS take work, but if you want those long-term multiple decades kind of friends, you learn to be a friend, not just when YOU need something, but in good and bad times. It's a two-way street.

I prioritize TRUST and that undying loyalty. So back to my point: I had long-term banker friends whom I was bouncing church financing ideas back and forth with. I remember calling one of them while standing in line to ride "It's a Small World" with grandkids. I had an idea about the church loan, and of course it couldn't wait. Ha! But by this time, it was spring of 2017. Time was my enemy. My fear was creeping back in. By this time we had been through the rigorous process of gathering the mountain of documents that is expected when applying for a church loan.

Unlike your mortgage or my mortgage, the underwriting process is very different. They must analyze the health of your giving and givers. Where does the giving come from? What is the giving unit count, the average giving, and total giving units? In other words, is the church supported by a dozen BIG givers who could get mad at Sister So-and-So, choose to walk out, and destroy the churches finances? Or is it made up of many small givers, which would indicate a level of poverty among the members. In the real world we need both. WE felt we had both. But there was one little caveat. Our out-of-town and online giving numbers were through the roof.

The frequent visitors who drop off on a Sunday or Wednesday, on their way to Florida, or to the Smokies, or anywhere for that matter, that number was high. We have weekly out-of-town guests. We wanted to be that convenient "lighthouse" that was a hop, skip, and a jump from I-65, I-24, and I-40. But as the loan processor was combing through the information, it confused her. It clearly wasn't the norm for the "First Baptist" down the street, or any church that had been established in a more traditional manner. We weren't traditional. Our out-of-town giving and our online giving was glaring at these folks. In my mind I'm thinking, "Ain't that a good thing?" I wrote letters explaining, they sounded good to me, but no enchilada.

My personal banker was frustrated. She's a very close friend and this was a matter of the heart for her. Like me, she thought the online giving was a great piece of the future of Restoring Hope. She realized that we were ahead of the curve, and she realized that 10,000 extra viewers each week meant souls for the Kingdom. But she couldn't quite make the decision makers catch the vision with her. People reject that which they don't understand. Period. Trying to understand creates too much work. It's easier to reject.

After a month or two she called me for a meeting. She brought another bank employee, and we congregated and hatched a plan. The loan was presented. They agreed that the numbers looked strong and the property value was good, our loan to value was NOT a problem, but here we go again. The same question kept cropping up: Why aren't these people in an organization and what is this online giving thing? What happens if . . . ? Ultimately, they wanted personal guarantees or an organization to back us. Both presented a problem. Aaron and Amanda didn't want anyone personally guaranteeing, nor did they want to hook up with an organization JUST to get a bank loan. The deal was a big fat no. Nevertheless, we persisted. We moved on. My banker friend was heartbroken. She bats a thousand typically. But God had a plan. She agreed to pray with me, and let me tell you, she's spirit filled and the girl can pray. I thank God daily for her. What a gift. A Holy Ghost–filled banker! She encouraged me and I encouraged her.

The bank had relayed these thoughts; we have organizations for a reason: to be oversight and guidance when change occurs. That sounded reasonable, I concurred. But the answer was still no. Aaron and Amanda didn't want anyone dictating the direction of Restoring Hope. It was never about money, nor will it ever be. They're blessed in the fact that money doesn't own them. They don't love it. It's a means to an end—that's about it. It's necessary to move ministry, nothing more. They knew that God had called them to lead a people, and they knew that the vision couldn't be circumvented by organizations with their OWN agenda. Those people didn't have the tree vision, nor did they sign the lease, move their kids 1,800 miles with very little money and no promises. I often say, "No one cares about your business like YOU do." Sounds simple, right? But if you will remember this every day of your life, it will change your life. They clearly remembered it.

We would often powwow about the progress of the church financing; it was down to months, not years, and their calm countenance amazed me. They would say, "God's got it." For years, my big comeback to many folks was "You trust Him or you don't. You decide." Well, during this season of my life I had to repeat that to myself about 789,340 times a day! But I also knew that God wasn't likely to bring a shower of hundred-dollar bills to the stage the next Sunday. That just isn't how it works, typically. We needed precisely ten thousand hundred-dollar bills. Yes, a million dollars. And the clock was ticking, and I was starting to lose sleep. My "friend" bankers had to have board approval for a loan this size. All of them. Bottom line? Those board members were scared. We were a new church. They loved the family but wanted us to hook up with an organization.

Two of the banks were out of state; that didn't help. They didn't completely understand commercial property in my area, and the third bank was a large Tennessee bank, but they simply didn't get it. The fourth was a broker who simply looks for the loan. He called me to say, "Good luck with this."

The decision makers did NOT want this loan. Okay. So one more out-of-state bank was in my arsenal. I called. The answer was "I think we can make it work." Okay, praise Jesus. I sent the mountain of documents once again and started into the "begging" phase that desperate people find themselves in. We no longer have our head up, shoulders back, and our BOLD voice as we go before the throne. We enter like, "JESUS, please, oh please. God, you know we won't have a church if you don't do something. You know the things that you were going to do in that body of believers will be much more difficult if we don't have a home . . . I mean, God, we're close to being homeless! God! Where ARE you?"

Yeah. I'm dramatic like that. Even with God. I think He probably laughs at me. But He doesn't laugh when tears run down these wrinkled cheeks. He bottles them, and He takes me back, reminds me of ALL the times I thought it was over, but it was just beginning. He takes me back to those roadside markers where He firmly planted reminders and I journeyed . . . the reminders serve me on days when I fear and doubt.

So my normal day in late spring of 2017 involved frequent chats with Him about Center Point Road. The church that had been the final piece of the healing of our family. The church that had open arms for the addicted, the prostitute, the haves, and the have-nots. That was Restoring Hope. And the members loved their church with a fierce kind of love. Passion is an understatement. I felt we could take it to the people, be honest with them about the serious nature of this deadline, but I certainly didn't want to. MY motto has always been, "Fake it till you make it and NEVER let 'em see you sweat." Amanda is a student of that philosophy. She continued to tell me, "God's going to do this. Let's just stay on course." Agreed. But what was that? Where was the road that would lead us to a closing table, a deed, and a permanent home for this "soul" hospital that we so fondly refer to as our church?

One morning in early June I was driving on Vietnam Veterans Parkway. I was between exit 7 and exit 8. Yes, I remember the weirdest things. I think it was on Tuesday, the week after our annual family vacation. My panic was in full-blown mode. We had three and a half months. As I said, I knew God was able, but I also knew that solutions typically come through God's people. What had I missed? What stone had I left unturned? Steve randomly called. He usually does that about twenty-five times a day. He said, "What's wrong? You don't sound good." I had been in one of my begging sessions with God and had been ugly crying and listening to Donnie McClurkin sing, "I Call You Faithful." But Steve heard the tears in my voice. He said, "You're worrying about the church loan? Hey, call my old friend Bill." I said, "He's your friend, you call him! I don't know him." Steve said, "No, you need to call him. Set up a meeting. Get him out to meet Aaron and Amanda."

I called his cell. He answered. I exchanged pleasantries and got straight to the point. Bill was a no-nonsense kind of guy. I had sent him a commercial loan or two in my real estate career, but I wasn't sure I had ever met him in person; I couldn't remember. But this was a good day! Bill said, "I would love to meet your kids. Would in the morning be okay? I drive by that church every day. I see that there's a lot going on there! Ten in the morning? I can meet you at the church?" I said, "I will be there!"

He came. He met Amanda and Aaron. It was clear that he liked them. Steve came as well. When Bill the banker was walking across the parking lot to his truck, after a short thirty-minute meeting, Steve Hannah knew. He looked at me and said, "God just took care of this. Bill is going to do this loan."

After four bank turn-downs, years of anxiety, and many fights with the devil in the middle of the night, I felt that Steve was right. Finally, this 40,000 pounds might be unloaded off my back. Realize that no one placed it there but me. I self-impose my stress. I pick a battle, load it up in a bag, and throw it over my back to carry. Don't waste your time lecturing me, just pray for me. It's how I roll. You can't fix me. Maybe God doesn't want me to be fixed, right? I get many lectures about overdoing it and slowing down. I can't. I will never. Sometimes it's purposeful to feel responsible for a big task. I don't pick up those big bags unless there's ministry attached. So don't you be worrying about me. God's got me.

Anyway, by June 23, I emailed this letter to myself. I am weird like that. I want to remember in detail.

From: Kathy Crabb Hannah <kathyjhannah@aol.com>
To: Kathy Hannah <kathyjhannah@aol.com>
Sent: Fri, Jun 23, 2017 12:21 pm
Subject: June 23rd

Today, we got the final approval from _____. I'm porch sitting, listening to the rain . . . and trying to comprehend that God really has a plan . . . and that somehow He allows us to have a small glimpse of the plan . . . so that we can put on our walking shoes . . . and know which way to walk.

He so generously allows us to have the mountaintop experience when the path is cleared . . . and we know our destination is in sight.

Today was that. A mountaintop for me . . . for sure. Now I can take my "worry" hat off that I've worn for three years.

Why do I do that?

Praising Him in the rain today. Praising Him for the faith of Aaron and Amanda. The missing piece to our family puzzle has been solved.

We have a church.

Nothing but tears . . . and the sound of a bird . . . as I sit on my porch and feel the Lord, the rain, and that satisfying feeling that only comes when the Holy Ghost is sitting with you.

Sent from my iPhone

Now, on to closing. No guarantors, no organizations, just a letter to summarize an exit plan in the event of a "life" event, GOD forbid, for Aaron and Amanda. They wanted an exit plan in the event of divorce or death. That was a reasonable request. We organized the answer and satisfied the request in writing.

We needed to bring a balance to closing that would put us in line with the agreement we had made three years earlier. We needed a "giving" offering. Brian Lawing, my son-in-law, had a suggestion. Brian and Krystal had been attending a megachurch in Nashville for twelve years. Krystal had been on staff for about five years. They could write the book on church growth. They also know that to move ministry it takes money. They have a healthy outlook on these megachurch takeaways . . . and truly they have utilized the knowledge. In early 2017, they decided to transition from their positions at Cornerstone and join the rest of the family at Restoring Hope. By June 2017, they were solidly there, assisting and sowing with the rest of us.

I was personally elated because this was my heart's desire for so many years. Like all clannish, southern women, Momma wants all her babies in a roost . . . clucking and pecking together. I am a textbook southern granny. I wanted them there, but I said little and prayed. God had answered and Restoring Hope was ready for their expertise. So all of this was transpiring at the same time. Brian and Krystal had actually stepped up and offered to sign the bank note personally, as I had, but it wasn't necessary. Banker Bill had caught the vision, realized the health of our finances, and did what a bank should do. He approved a solid loan. Boom. I'm thankful for the experience of this, but not so thankful for the gray hair that came with it.

So we were brainstorming through text messages—we do that a lot—and Brian had a suggestion that seemed simple enough. Next Sunday, let's pass out envelopes to everyone! Let's have envelopes prepared with $1, $20, $100, $250, $500, $1,000, $5,000, and so on. Let's ask everyone to take one, young and old alike. If you didn't have anything to give, he suggested we pass out money to those folks. We wanted every single person to have an offering. It was the ritualistic approach to unity, Brian thought. I'm not much on rituals at times, but the Bible is full of them. They marched seven times around Jericho. Why seven? Because God said. Naaman dipped himself seven times in the river of Jordon. Why? Because the man of God had instructed. Brian felt led; therefore he was the current man of God. Amanda and Aaron listened. The corporate effort was key. God wanted everyone to feel invested.

I was suggesting a dinner, a get-on-my-own-nerves kind of fundraising effort that would have worn me out physically and mentally. Insert eye roll about now. Sometimes we suggest what we are familiar with. It was a bit lame and we were too busy to do it, thank GOD!

So on a Sunday morning in July, our pastor humbly stepped up to the pulpit and explained in the simple terms what Brian's idea had been for this offering that would go for our long-awaited closing. He presented the need. This was above and beyond tithing. We hadn't had a months-long building campaign with overhead slides and color-coded pie charts or renderings of things to come. Nope. Just an unpretentious little guy from Kentucky with no real interest in loans and such. His interest is clearly people. Results. Heaven. Hell. Truth.

But on this day he was the vision caster; after all, it was his vision. He boldly stood and did his least favorite thing in the world. He asked us to give. The envelopes were passed out. It was quiet for a minute. I wasn't sure for about thirty seconds. But then, like popcorn, they started standing. I will give $1,000; so will I; I will give $5,000; a dozen or more stood to give $500, and on and on.

I had projected that the offering would be ten to fifteen thousand dollars, based on past experiences. We could build on that. We would have to do another event to fund-raise, but as I said, that's what I know. We would have done it. But it wasn't to be.

In less than ten minutes that congregation had given $40,000. The lender had allowed Steve and I to give our $36,000 real estate commission as down payment as well, so that $70,000 amount that we needed? Done. Just like that.

The favor of God can do more in ten minutes than a year of our personal labor. This was that. Unmerited favor, from beginning to end.

So with the simple moving of a number on a HUD closing settlement statement from a commission column to a down-payment column and a ten-minute offering, we were finished. On that day I was thankful I still had a real estate license. It allowed me to be a blessing.

And that Sunday after that offering? My lands a mercy, a few of us cut a rug, some cried, some shouted, and a few fell to their knees. What a time we had. I went to the side of the church, as I often do, and surveyed EXACTLY what God had done right before my eyes. I rewound the scenes in my mind. I remembered an eleven-year-old who was unsure of SO much, bruised by the pain of divorce, cautious about his heart and his words. But now? He was a grown man and was boldly building a church, a soul hospital of sorts, squarely in the middle of a town that the devil had marked for sin and pleasure. For the enemy had put a death grip on Nashville. The town that was famous for "country" and Jesus was a far cry from the early days. The Ryman Auditorium, the original home of the Grand Ole Opry, is commonly referred to as the mother church. In 1885 a wealthy, rough-hewn riverboat captain named Thomas Ryman, heard an evangelist named Sam Jones preach. He was preaching a tent revival in downtown Nashville. It changed Thomas Ryman's life. He decided to allow God to control him, not money. He built the Ryman as a church for the city, a hospital for the soul. That's why that building feels different—there's a reason. So here was my boy: he had risked it all, about 130 years later, for the same reason. We were a few miles from that old Ryman Auditorium, and like then, Nashville stands in need of revival.

I cried and remembered all the highs and lows, the good the bad, but in all of it, there was always the knowledge that Aaron would be the pastor. I cried. The years of struggle had been worth the trouble. I remembered August of 2003 when Amanda was so radically filled with the Holy Ghost in Central City. I had watched God transform her from miserable to purposeful, from bitter to better. She had successfully managed to shake off the role of victim and become a victor . . . in a world where most don't. Most wallow in it, for decades . . . Our rehabs and cemeteries are full of the victims of molestation.

Not Amanda. She shook it off and put on her boxing gloves and went to find that devil that tried to kill her. She basically made him wish he had left THIS one alone. The enemy that robbed that little girl oh so many years ago with an inappropriate touch of someone she trusted, she turned that mess into a testimony. That girl needed that big dose of Jesus back there in Central City, Kentucky, in a right-now kind of way, and she clearly got it.

She chose to radically follow Him, and it changed the trajectory of both of their lives, the lives of those four children, their children, and their children's children will be forevermore changed because of a crying girl on the steps of a building that was fed up. She had had enough.

We all have a moment that could have gone the other way: the door could have been shut and the world would have been oh so different. On this Sunday morning my mind wandered through the years like a time traveler. I knew that her decision on that fateful night to let God heal her pain of abuse was a cornerstone in this ministry. I knew that Aaron's faith to follow the "tree" vision when it didn't make sense was another cornerstone. I knew their struggles and their ability to be honest and open before God was another cornerstone. I knew their desire to knit the family together, always, and provide this environment for the cousins to gather and worship in truth was paramount as well. I watched my grandchildren with their hands raised, singing and worshipping, and I realized exactly how blessed I truly am. No words. I have everything I ever dreamed of.

So on Monday, July 31, 2017, we went to an attorney's office in Hendersonville. Not for a bad reason but for a good reason. With two strokes of a pen by Aaron and Amanda, we had a church. Our days of leasing were over!

He did it. His will, His bill. I left the closing and drove by the property. And again, I remembered my question to God back in 2014: "Can this place live again?"

I think you know the answer. Restoring Hope is experiencing tremendous growth. Aaron and Amanda are committed to Kingdom work, God's Kingdom, not their own. If you're ever in the area, you must come. You will never be the same! Promise.

And I have a confession. The day we closed, I bought myself a cake and celebrated. God was in it. For I had truly watched a miracle unfold. If you're not into financial kinds of things, you may be bored about now. But trust me when I say God did this. He gave us a miracle.

Don't limit God. He's not just over there handing out healing and salvation; He's also moving on bankers, the board of directors, judges, juries.

He's able kids, more than able. Dig deep, find your faith, be that persistent girl that never gives up. He's got this.

Finish Well

In May of 2015 our family reverted back to BIG family vacations, just like we did in the early days. As a matter of fact, our 2017 beach vacation included a beautiful beach wedding. Adam had been coming to this beach house as a single guy. In 2017 he had actually been single for about three years. He would come to that beach house in May, always the last to get there because he had to do road dates for Gaither, and always a bit sadder than I wanted him to be. The divorce had been oh so hard for him. I got it. I had been where he was. I often said to him, "I totally get it. It will hurt like someone hit you in the stomach, and then, one day . . . someone will grab your attention first, your smile second, and your heart soon follows."

So our 2017 beach trip included a little surprise! OUR Adam was smiling, for he had met Kaitlyn Howard back in the fall and he was smitten. She was beautiful and funny, and most importantly, he looked alive again. So with our family as witnesses, the beautiful Panama City sunset provided the perfect backdrop to this happy couple to pledge their "forever" and their right now as well. Hannah and Charlee watched their dad light up like a Christmas tree as Kaitlyn walked out of the whitewashed beach house. We cried, we loved, and we realized that we had done what families must do. We bind up the wounded, we love the offended, and we hold them until their beautiful beach day comes. His day had come and his smile was worth a million dollars to me.

I was used to the days of togetherness. This was that. Jason played and the nieces sang to the couple, Shellye cried and Krystal readied the cake, Terah was FaceTiming her mom in Kentucky, and we were all hands-on. That's how we roll. MY friend told me yesterday that she thought it would be intimidating to marry into a family like ours. She said the independent nature of so many, coupled with the immense talent, had to be daunting to be compared to. I thought about her comment. I digested it, and there may be some validity to it. But in the end, the time spent tears down the walls. Unity is the great equalizer. When there's unity, a corporate effort, there's no need for intimidation. We're all equal. No Big and no LITTLE, just us, one tribe, one goal, and one voice. And truly, that's been the key to having a close family. Unity.

When all of the kids first married, we lived next door to each other, ate together, played together, shopped together, mopped floors together; we did everything as a family—well, almost everything. These girls kept getting pregnant. I suppose there were a few things that they did independently of the family. Ha!

During the Crabb Family era, before my divorce, we operated as a communist village. All for one and one for all. Everyone had the same salary, the same perks, and the same goal. If one person won, everyone won. I used to say that Crabbville was a bit like Communist China. Hey, don't knock it. I was told by many that I would never keep these kids together once they started getting married. Well, we lasted about a decade after they started having babies. And the truth of the matter is this: the end of the Crabb Family wasn't a result of in-law/outlaw issues. It was simply my response to a bitter divorce. I didn't want to do it anymore. I didn't want to bear the responsibility of the "what ifs" that I knew would transpire. The divorce and subsequent criticism of my "management style" made me stop and realize several things. One was this: I was the only person who had the debt and responsibility of two buses and a couple dozen employees. I was also the only person who wasn't guaranteed a paycheck. So with that in mind I started doing some thinking.

I was almost too bitter to pray. I had watched the character of so many people as the truth unfolded. They didn't care about truth. They didn't care about morality or agendas. They only cared about self-advancement. Period. So as my circle became smaller and smaller, as I watched so many back up and see where the golden egg would land after the divorce, I made a decision to crack the golden egg and scramble it. You can't unscramble eggs, you know.

So the reality of my demise set in. Kelly was going with Mike to be a Bowling. Well, she was already a Bowling, but she was having her third little Bowling girl, and they wanted to raise them together on one bus. I knew she wanted to leave the Crabb Family. Aaron was openly interested in ministering with Amanda. Amanda had a transforming GOD experience and she was starting to minister with Aaron and occasionally on her own. I knew she was called. I knew they needed to be together as well. This was certainly a transition season. Jason would be fine; Adam and Terah would too. Krystal was about as bitter as I was. She ran the Crabb Family office and she had seen too much and knew too much. The decade preceding had been tough for her. She had one too many backstories and harbored the disappointment of the hypocrisy. She was ready to move on away from the trappings of knowing too much. She said a "retail job sounded pretty good." The kids were not the offenders; let me make that clear. My innuendo is not directed at my family.

The judge awarded me complete control of the business, better known as the Crabb Family. He awarded me the exclusive right to "do business as" the Crabb Family. The Lord had protected me and ALL of these kids. As I said repeatedly in *Stronger*, they were the innocent victims. They didn't create the firestorm; neither did I. But we still smelled like smoke and had to rebuild the house.

The kids had worked day and night, for more than a decade to be able to enjoy the success they were enjoying. Actually, they were at the pinnacle of their career when all hell broke loose. The judge's decision regarding my divorce allowed the family to continue to minister, make a living, and further increase the kingdom work that we had been called to.

So here we are, through the worst of it, but I just wasn't feeling it. The criticism was SO harsh, and I was so damaged. I wanted to run away and be in the circus or sell ice cream cones on the beach or be an acrobat. Yeah, go on and picture that one. Ha! I know some of you will understand this, but some won't. Abandonment is the cruelest thing I've ever dealt with.

We had a three-million dollar-a-year touring business and we owned the largest music festival in Kentucky, called Crabbfest, that had an economic impact of $2,700,000 on the city of Owensboro. We had a couple dozen employees, which included our kids.

I was in a pickle. Divorce is a nasty business. Especially when there's complete abandonment from one party, absenteeism at its finest. The death trappings are real, it's LIKE a death, but there's no body, no funeral, no one to honor. NO one. I lived my life with an icky knot in my stomach. The memories become impossible to process. Was it all a lie? Apparently.

I've watched those around me suffer similarly. I've watched as they cried, patiently waiting for an entire decade, hoping for a Hosea ending, pretending not to know what they knew. I've watched as the reality was painted over with a pretty paint that was meant to cover ugly lies, but the paint wasn't enough. The soul that lives a lie becomes addicted to the thrill of the lie. The end is sad. No one wins except the devil.

But what do we do? We get up. Sometimes it takes a minute, or a year, or three, or five . . . but we eventually do it. On a random Tuesday, we decide we're tired of the snot and tears, we're tired of driving by to see WHO is at their apartment, we're tired of the anger that's imminent for those who care too much. Sometimes people mean it when they say forever, but then there are the ones whose forever didn't last long.

If you're reading this and identifying with the dumped, the forsaken, the abandoned, listen to me. This chapter is FOR you. If you've lost your job, your friend, your love, your house, your parents, your child, let's talk. I want to speak to all, but especially those of you who are past your childbearing, head-turning years. I want those of you who feel like so much of your life is in the rearview mirror. You are so deep into the fog of struggle, you just want someone to let you out of the car. You ain't interested in traveling anymore. This "life" trip has beaten you up pretty bad. Your heart can't take it, your feet can't take it, and you're done. You look forward to sleep because you HATE being awake. Reality is your enemy. You live in the anxiety of the "what ifs" and dread "that" call. You're waiting for the next shoe to drop. You can't even enjoy your cheeseburger and fries because of the anxiety that seems to hit at the most random but frequent times. You feel crazy on some days, brilliant on others. The pain has completely changed the way you sleep, think, eat, move, and in general . . . the way you live.

You're past starting over. You can't. Your child is in the cemetery. You can't get out of bed, much less go to work. You've served Jesus since you were seven; you dedicated her to the Lord, but she's gone. The overcorrection of that spoiled rich kid hit her little Kia. She didn't even get to wear her prom dress. The rich kid went to prom and college and the beach. But Leah didn't. She was unrecognizable. They wouldn't let you see her. You can't. You're not getting up. You're finished and you wish the Lord would get on with it. You tempt Him daily and ask Him to take you. But He doesn't.

Here's the truth. No one should have to bury a child. Ever. The most inhumane thing I've ever seen is a police officer knock on my neighbor's door and deliver the news to her that her twelve-year-old son was found in the bottom of the city swimming pool, in the afternoon, after the pool closed. Her bloodcurdling screams rang across those Kentucky hills; the sound was indescribable. The primitive sound came from so deep within her. I didn't know what had happened, but innately I knew what had happened. For, you see, I too was a mom. I can't remember her first name, but I remember her screams. Forty years later I remember that sound.

I don't think there's ever been a mom who lost a child who didn't want to be buried with them. And when I think of "strong" and honorable women? I have a list of moms and grandmas who have walked this walk, and they're still breathing, living, and giving. The ultimate challenge in life is clearly the ability to start over, without them. Period. Nothing else comes close. But Momma, Daddy, Granny, Poppa, listen to me. You don't get to choose. You must. You don't get to decide IF you will eat another meal, breathe another day. YOU will. It won't be easy, and you will be numb. You will struggle on certain days, for the rest of your life. But you must, for the SAKE of the living, you must. I don't understand some things. I have many questions when we get there, so many. I don't know why children have to die and rotten child molesters live to be old men. I know a couple who stood for God, preached healing, prayed for the sick, and watched God heal them, and yet they lost THEIR own child to cancer. I could go on and on, so could you. We all know someone, probably many someones. We live in a sin-cursed world. It's not always easy. But, friends, if you haven't heard another thing I've said thus far, listen: God is still good, and sometimes, just sometimes, we must dig deep and find that "Job" spirit down in our soul. We need to realize that God knows us in such an intimate way; He knows we're going to hurt. He knows how much we love. But like Job, he trusted us. When the enemy of your soul sought to destroy you, God said, "I know what's in there. I know what they will do. They will not give up-I trust you to persist, to fight for one more day."

So to all of you who have lived in seasons of grief, to those who have gone a week without bathing, eating, or talking, I will be the first one to tell you that I personally think that's okay. There's a time to mourn, a time to have greasy hair and eat peanut butter fudge, there's a time to scream at God and your friends. You have a pass. Do it. Take your time. Lie in it for a minute. But when you least expect it, somewhere in the most unexpected place, the overwhelming presence of God will embrace you. He will wrap you, hold you, and wipe your tears. He bottles those, you know. And when He does, you must allow Him to speak peace. It may not be as soon as we want it to be, but it will happen. I've talked to many parents who have walked this road. The ones who made it through to the other side are the ones who allowed Him to lift the two hundred pounds of grief off their backs. They gave themselves permission to smile and laugh again. They embraced the opportunity to honor their child by choosing to give back to humanity.

I had a cabin guest who came to my cabin to stay about three weeks after he and his wife buried their twenty-year-old son. He died unexpectedly in the middle of the night at his East Tennessee college dormitory. He was an honor student and a wonderful son, so they told me. Apparently he had a health issue that was undiagnosed. It was oh so tragic. This couple was devastated. They checked into my cabin and after check-in he sent me a private message on VRBO. He told me the story of the tragic loss and that they were drawn to my cabin. I didn't know these people, but I sat down and cried like a baby. And quite honestly, I hear stories like this often. I have been blessed to pray with and for hundreds of parents after a loss. But here's what sticks with me about this story. When they buried their son, the light of their lives, they stopped and reevaluated their lives, immediately. I don't know if they were church folks or not, but they certainly had Jesus habits.

When they checked out of the cabin they left a sweet note and told me they felt peace there. We all do. But the thing that I remember that's significant is this: they were planning to sell some assets and go to a third world country for a couple of years, simply to serve others. Why? To honor their son. They said, "We've had a role reversal in our family. He lived to make us proud, and he did. Now, we want to live in a way that makes him proud. This will do it." That grieving dad had already figured out that "stuff" wouldn't give him purpose or stop his nightmares. He realized that his portfolio of properties that he had worked feverishly to acquire for his heirs to inherit didn't make much difference now. This dad had caught on REAL fast. He realized that what we do for people is the only thing that will bring us purpose. Oh my, they caught on fast. And if we decipher this, we take it one step further. By doing for people we become the hands and feet of Jesus. I don't know where they are today. Probably in Africa. Are they all good and happy? They're probably as happy as they can be in this new normal.

We truly can never go home again. Some things change the landscape forever. And we needn't try to replace or repair what was. We must allow the magnetism of purpose and meaningful days to pull us to "that" place where we can pour out the love that otherwise would be wasted. Yeah. It's never the same, but it's certainly worthwhile.

Grieving comes in waves and it has its own schedule. Nothing is a cure-all or magic pill. But it's amazing to watch those who make it and those who don't. Those who stand tall and decide to LIVE among the living are ALWAYS walking in some kind of purpose that's bigger than they are.

There's a special reward in Heaven for those who have walked this road. God has rewards for you that your mind couldn't comprehend today. On the bad days, please remember: you can scream, you can cry, you can kick the door, throw your food at the wall, scream at the newscaster—it's fine. Do it. But you can't quit. We don't quit. It's not WHO we are. We must finish well.

And then there's this: your husband left you, your three children, six grandchildren, and you can't even deal. For heaven's sake, you can't make yourself get out of the house. The mirror hates you. Your hair is a bit grayer than hers, I suppose. She doesn't make a cherry pie like you do, she doesn't sleep with the grandbabies and rub their back all night like you do, she didn't have yard sales and work two jobs to raise his children like you did, but hey . . . she weighs 120 pounds. Things that matter, things that don't. Insert sarcasm here. His pot belly and bald head were part of the aging process, so you thought. But I suppose the grace that he was afforded to become a middle-aged man wasn't afforded to you in return. The grass was greener, and yes, it's soppy with septic water and sewer, but hey, it's greener. And his parting words to you were, "I'm just not happy! I deserve happiness."

Newsflash to all you people chasing "happiness" and walking out the door to chase it. You didn't sign up to be happy. You vowed to be faithful in good times and bad, in sickness and in health. Period. The church is as guilty as the world; actually, the statistics concerning affairs and divorce for church leaders is reprehensible. The word is clear on this subject. Your happiness doesn't depend on your marriage, folks; it depends on you. Life is typically what we make it, good or bad. Take it from someone who has been divorced multiple times.

Yes, it's nice when marriages are happy, but my happiness does NOT depend on my marriage—trust me. I've lived for decades in less than reasonable circumstances in the past. I was still happy, in spite of those circumstances. I loved my kids, my work, my goals, and of course my commitment to the Lord. We expect the carnality of the world to fester in the corrupt eyes of a sinner, and he/she will roam and prowl, always on the hunt for the forbidden room where the lust is welcomed. But the church? When our behavior and statistics are the same? It's a stench to God.

Grow up. Learn to tolerate and encourage. Husbands: she needs to lose weight? Encourage her. Is she healthy and living a life free of medical issues and YOU need her to lose weight for YOUR stinking pride so that your arm candy looks as good as the guy you work with? Jesus help us. Learn to appreciate the core of your spouse, and then make your way to the packaging. What would Jesus do? I just told you. Pretty ain't always pretty. Jesus looks within, and I'm thankful.

And once again; your man is a jerk and leaves you for the twenty-year-old? You're allowed to get mad. I'm personally thinking it might be okay to slap him silly, if he's not too big of a coward to be in a room with you. Do it. You can. You can cry, and you will. You can throw his clothes out in the yard, sell his tools in a yard sale; you can do whatever you need to do to process the anger. Well, short of breaking the law, that is. Be angry and sin not. The slapping may be questionable, but I say go for it! But here's the bottom line my friend.

You don't deserve to live with an unfaithful man. You deserve better. And you don't deserve to be lied to, cheated on, and used. I'm not talking about a marriage bump in the road. I'm talking about a man who has been unfaithful and walks away with no remorse. Cold, uncaring, while his children and grandchildren plead. Let him go.

Mourn the years that he stole—it's fine. Get in the floor, the closet, or wherever your safe place is. Cry and snot, but remember to pray. For here's the truth. God didn't do this. His heart is as broken as yours. He knows what that man was given. He knows how many times he begged God to work something out in his life. God feels used too. Let the anger wash over you, let the grief own you, for a season.

But get ready. For there will come a day when you will realize that you weren't born to die in a heap of mess in the closet floor. God didn't call you to be addicted to Oxycontin or Demerol. You weren't born to be a victim. You were born to prophesy and pray for the sick. In spite of the sin in your home, God has blessed you. And the word says that HE will set a table for you and let you eat in the presence of your enemies. And LORD knows you didn't get up one day and decide you wanted enemies—you ain't got time for that. But icky divorces and NEW wives of ex-husbands always create an environment of divisiveness. And Miss 120 Pounds clearly hates you, and she doesn't know you. She took YOUR husband, but she hates you. Funny how that happens.

Well, sister, from one sister to another, let me tell you. Go set the table with your finest china. Pull out that linen tablecloth your grandmother gave you and use it. Go wash up the Waterford crystal tea glasses, 'cause we ALL know you're going to have some sweet tea with this meal. Dress that table as if a king were coming to dine with you. He is.

Now go put on your little black dress and find those pearls you love. Actually, put on a couple of necklaces: layered necklaces prove that we are brave and don't follow fashion rules. And, yes, we're brave. Now find the red high heels you bought yourself last year. You know, the ones that make you cry because you don't have a clue when you will have an opportunity to wear them; yeah, those heels. Put them on. It's time.

There's no telling how much walking you're going to do in those heels. Dream of roads you're going to walk, people you're going to meet, places you are going to see. It's coming.

The word tells us so. Your best years are ahead of you. I don't care how old you are. Trust Him with a new trust, believe every promise in the book. Write them down on sticky notes and put them on the refrigerator; read them to yourself every night. Trade the tears for the truth. The chains are gone. It's just you and God and truth, and an occasional piece of strawberry cake. And actually, you are stronger than you knew, braver than anyone thought, and you my dear . . . will amaze the masses.

Now, kick back and relax. That meal is coming. I imagine this: you will be served a beautiful caprese salad with fat vine-ripe tomatoes and the freshest slices of mozzarella you've ever tasted. The soup is a fresh cream bisque loaded with shrimp and small diced potatoes; next is fresh seared lobster tail with drawn butter and dry-aged prime rib that's prepared perfectly and served au jus. The herb-infused yeast rolls are brushed with sweet cream butter and they are to die for! The pan-seared asparagus with parmesan cheese sprinkle is wonderful. And last is strawberry cake that's made with fresh crushed strawberries, whipping cream, creamed cheese. It's topped with a dozen strawberries that are hand-selected for their perfection. This meal will be perfection personified. God arranged it, remember that. The water will be sparkling, and the tea will be the best in the South. You will eat and you will truly TASTE every single bite. And with each new thing that delights your senses, you will remember the Lord's protection; you will remember His faithfulness, and you will be reminded of His words and promises. For this meal will be "that" moment that your enemies must surrender to a God who decides what is good and right and what is ugly and spiteful. The enemies who tried to destroy you? They must sit and watch. That's His word, not mine.

This meal may be an overdramatization, clearly. But you get the point. When God does things, He does it up right.

Victory. Persistence. We must get to the dinner, girls—we must get there. We must walk straight and walk with Him if we want our dinner.

Your load is heavy and you say I can't. Your child is a product of your life and the generational curses are clearly in overdrive. You tried to protect him from himself, you tried to be both Mom and Dad, you tried. But it didn't work like a charm, no. He's serving twelve years in federal prison. He couldn't stop once he started. The addiction of the man you loved at eighteen was the gift to that man's son. Actually, the gene pool of an addict was the only gift he ever gave him. And you? He didn't give you anything except a swollen belly and a hard bed to lie in. But you raised his son, you did your best at times, other times, not so much. But now? You are tired. You're close to retirement age and you're raising his three kids because he's in prison. Their momma is an addict, addicted to drugs, sin, and men. You work two jobs and the next generation of your flesh is unsupervised, ungrateful, and uneducated. Daddy is in federal prison and Momma is in an addict's prison. They go to school, but they don't learn much. Their teenage lives consist of Jay-Z, Queen B, profanity, alcohol, and sex. And the curse lives on. You love God, but you're so tired. You go to Bible study and cry. You wake in the mornings and dress yourself in guilt as you dread the day that will be spent stocking shelves. Excuses are handed out as liberally now as they were for your OWN son. For, you see, you, my dear, are an enabler. The common denominator isn't the deadbeat dad; it's the enabling mom/grandma.

You say a dozen times a day, "I just don't know WHAT to do!" Well Sister Sue, I have news for you. YES YOU DO know what to do. You just don't want to do it. Why?

You're scared. Of what? You're scared they won't love you anymore if you tell them the truth. You are an enabler of the very worst kind. You peddle your passivity to the world as "motherly love" and occasionally throw in a bit of WWJD when you're in a churchy crowd. So what would Jesus do?

Well, thank you for asking, because I'm fixing to tell you, sis. Jesus would tell them the truth. He wants us to teach our children to live responsibly. He wants us to teach them that there are consequences for sin, for irrational choices, and for rebellion. He wants us to be their leader, not their follower. He wants us to come to terms with the fact that love without truth isn't love at all.

Your kids and grandkids don't need a BFF. They need someone who will set boundaries and teach them to mop a floor and fry a chicken. They need to know that you will rescue them from an unfair world, but you won't rescue them from their OWN bad choices. They need to know that you love them unconditionally, but you won't allow them to disrespect you.

In my opinion, the laziness and disrespectful attitudes that are rampant among our kids today in epidemic proportions are a national crisis. They throw a fit and need a switch. Momma hands them an iPhone to play on and says, "They didn't have their nap." Then Daddy says, "Kids will be kids." The excuses start early. My philosophy is pretty simple. You teach them the ropes or the world will. When you teach them, the punishment system is fairly gentle. When the world teaches them, they may end up in prison.

Certainly there are men and women in jail who had parents who did 99 percent of the parenting correctly. And certainly there are heroin dealers who have children who are missionaries. I know there are exceptions to EVERY rule. However, this I also know: I read your messages. I read between the lines. And we have an overabundance of enabling from middle-aged women in our country. As the drug epidemic rises, so do the "momma" excuses. Stop. If there's to be change, you must stop. I love you and I am sorry if I sound harsh. But the truth has a home in this chapter.

It is never too late. Read books, talk to counselors, read every article you can get your hands on about enabling and codependency. The church is full of these folks, your family has that someone I've just described. If there's going to be a happy ending to these kinds of stories, there must be truth. And, granted, the best parents on the planet are suffering at times. It happens. They do everything right and STILL the drugs win the war and steal their child. The truth of the matter: addiction is stealing our babies.

If you're an enabler, the one that you've enabled will be angry when you stop. But you must do it anyway. They will scream, blame, and tell you they hate you. But you must persevere. For here's the deal: most people don't care enough to get in the middle of their mess. Messes ain't fun. But if you love that child like you say you do, you will find the courage to do what's right, so that both of you can finish well.

Truly, the only hope they have is that YOU and GOD intervene. Prayer and an intervention. And listen, you're strong enough to do this. God will walk through it with you. Be it fire or flood, it's all covered by the blood. The generational curses CAN be broken. Remember, he's got chain cutters. Let's lose the chains, girls . . . let's finish well.

Let's face it, starting well is usually easy. We're in love with him. We want to lose this weight. We want to live in this house. Beginnings are typically FUN because they are choices that WE make. But then . . . the policeman is at the door with the news, or he's packed his bags, you've gained back the forty plus twenty, the foreclosure sign is posted on the window for the world to see, and the finish doesn't look so well anymore.

And it's true that finishing well means different things to different people. But along about my fiftieth birthday I started to talk to God about my finish. I was two million dollars in debt and had a very broken heart; you know the story. My life's work was clearly ending and I was unsure of tomorrow, much less next year. The word says He's near the brokenhearted, and He is. It took me another seven or eight years to get to the end of this process. Don't be like me. Let this soak in.

Slowly but surely I started to realize that I had no choice but find His favor like never before. I was drowning in problems in EVERY single area of my life. If you haven't read *Stronger*, read it. It's all there. And, no, I wasn't ready to face a firing squad and be martyred, but the problems at hand were the problems that God had allowed me to bear. I read about martyrs, and occasionally I felt guilty for complaining about the lawsuits that I inherited from those who wanted to entrap my family. I prayed like a sniveling wuss. I would say things like, "God, please, please help me to survive this. Please, if it be your will, let me get to a better place."

Hogwash. One day I realized that there was life and death in my requests. My tongue was going to speak my future into existence, one way or another. Now I will admit, I have always spoken "dream it and you can do it" over others, my kids and grandchildren specifically. I would say, "God, YOU alone can do this," and He would. But me? When I asked for a dream for myself? Well, I didn't. Somehow I felt unworthy. I thought if it was for Kathy, she had to work for her blessings . . . work, work, work.

And yes, it's amazing what happens when we work, AMAZING!! But along about the time I turned fifty-eight-ish, I began to ask God to bless me. I never had. I told Him that I wanted to make Him proud, my kids proud, and my husband proud. I asked Him to give me the soundness of mind to wade into new waters.

I asked Him to give me the ability to do the work of three people and to bless it with a double portion, and that would be the work of six people. I realized that finishing well wasn't all about martyrdom. For me, it's about living, not dying. One minute of His favor is worth a lifetime of my labor, and I knew that. And one day, I realized that He WANTED me to ask. He didn't want me to come groveling like a starving dog lying under the table that was living off crumbs. The dog may not starve on crumbs, but it's living like a dog.

I didn't clearly understand the love of a man. I had no real reference. Steve tried, but I was not completely willing to be vulnerable enough to love. I had too much hurt. Therefore I struggled to understand the love of a Good Father or a good husband. I loved Him, I knew He loved me, but I was a crumb eater, an unworthy crumb eater. Oh my, what a vulnerable subject this is. Losing my dad and the circumstances that surrounded that season, coupled with the failed relationships, had molded me. I knew God was good, but I wasn't sure I was good enough. I knew He loved me, but I wasn't sure why.

I understood the cross, the blood, and salvation. I had fire insurance. I was Heaven bound. But I didn't understand living well, much less finishing well. I was STILL the dog living under the table. I hope I was at least a cute dog. Ha!

Sometimes people say to me, "I really didn't know you back in the Crabb Family days. I didn't know you had a testimony. I sure didn't know God had protected you from so much." Nope. Guess not. I was the puppy under that table. I didn't tell anything. I had accepted my fate and place in life. There's more to this story, but now ain't the time to tell it. I was surviving on those crumbs and an occasional bone.

And look at me over here, y'all. It took about seven crises, all at one time for old Hard Head here to figure it out. I needed to learn to ASK for things to meet MY needs. He was waiting. That belly-crawling humbleness isn't what queens and princess girls do.

We put on our red high heels and march in and say to our Father, "I need your help. You're powerful, and YOU own the cattle on a thousand hills, so here's my list." Now I'm going to go over here and adjust my crown while you work on that.

I'm actually kidding about adjusting my crown, but this part is my heart. God knows me better than anyone. He knows I will outwork five people. I don't have to tell Him that anymore. HE gets it. But the victory of the Kathy of 2017 is clearly different than the Kathy of 2010. And the difference is simply this: I learned to ask in specifics.

As I wind down and finish this chapter, I realize this little visit with you is nearly finished. I ask myself, what is the common thread that binds these 96,000 words together. What is the commonality of each word my heart insisted that I write? Persistence. Always persistence. The shenanigans of this three-year period in this unusual season of my life are full of God stories that are truly on my miracle list. The persistence of these women who knew how to pray is unmatched by all of the demons in hell. When women pray, the candidate with an 11 percent chance to win becomes the president. When we believe and pray corporately, a mom with two weeks to live SUDDENLY receives a double lung transplant. When women decide that enough is enough, the world stands at attention!

I am one of those women. I do more wrong than right. But I know Him. And He instructed me to write this book. I did exactly what HE told me to do. This is more than the journal of an old Tennessee Granny. It's a full-blown testament to His power. It's also a slight glimpse at the marvelous way He can use the broken things to prove who HE is. I am one of those broken things, proudly. When you look at me, you will see broken and messy. But let me tell you a little secret. God loves messy. God loves broken. It's all good.

I pray you've laughed, cried, and decided to get naked before God. I pray you seek truth more than money and popularity—it will serve you better. I pray you understand that God's not looking for perfect. He's looking for willing. And finally, I pray you learn to ASK for what you need. BE persistent. Keep asking. We have not because we ask not.

We're all learning, girls, we're all learning. As for me?

I asked Him to give me years. I wanted to make up for the ones that have been stolen. I asked Him to make a financial way when there was no way, for ME, Kathy. See, I had prayed that for my family a million times, and He had always come through. But now I was flying solo in these struggles. I asked Him simply to bless me. I kind of said, "God, I ain't settling. I want a long, blessed, large life. I will forever praise You with my words, my finances, my influence, and anything else you choose to bless me with."

And friends, you can take that to the bank. I will praise Him if I have to praise Him alone. I will serve Him if I'm serving alone. I will stand if I must stand alone. A promise is a promise. And I promised.

So don't mind me. I will just be over here having an occasional cupcake and living large. And when you see me, I hope you tell yourself this: "If God can use her, He can use anybody. Where do I sign up?"

And always remember, nothing in the world can take the place of persistence. Finish well.